Joseph Michael Flynn

The Story of a Parish 1847-1892.

The First Catholic Church In Morristown, N. J...

Joseph Michael Flynn

The Story of a Parish 1847-1892.
The First Catholic Church In Morristown, N. J...

ISBN/EAN: 9783337259211

Printed in Europe, USA, Canada, Australia, Japan

Cover: Foto ©ninafisch / pixelio.de

More available books at **www.hansebooks.com**

THE CHURCH OF THE ASSUMPTION, MORRISTOWN, N. J.

THE
STORY OF A PARISH

1847

THE First Catholic Church in Morristown, N. J.

Its Foundation and Development

1892

By the

Very Rev. Joseph M. Flynn, R.D.

Morristown, N. J.
1892

THE COLUMBUS PRESS, 120-122 WEST SIXTIETH STREET, NEW YORK.

TO
Our Predecessors in the Faith,
BOTH CLERGY AND LAITY,

WHO

SOWED IN TEARS

THAT WE

MIGHT REAP IN JOY:

TO

The Noble, Generous Flock
WHOSE PRAYERS, WHOSE GOOD WORKS,

WHOSE GENEROSITY

HAVE

SUSTAINED AND CONSOLED HIM

DURING THE

DECADE OF HIS MINISTRY,

THIS LITTLE WORK

IS LOVINGLY DEDICATED BY

Their Pastor.

CONTENTS.

CHAPTER I.

The Sowing of the Seed.—Early Trials. 1

CHAPTER II.

The Jesuit Fathers Schneider and Farmer.—Don de Miralles.—Washington and the Irish Contingent.—Pioneer Catholics. 8

CHAPTER III.

The Mother Church, Madison.—Fathers Senez and McQuaid.—Building of the first Church.—The first Bishop of Newark. 31

CHAPTER IV.

A Resident Pastor.—The Parish School.—Father D'Arcy. . 52

CHAPTER V.

Rev. J. Sheeran.—A new Church.—Archbishop Bayley.—Right Rev. M. A. Corrigan. 67

CHAPTER VI.

Changes and Improvements. — Death of Archbishop Bayley. 88

CHAPTER VII.

A promising Life ended.—The aged Pastor's last Illness and Death.—His eventful Life.—Bishop Corrigan transferred. 104

CHAPTER VIII.

The Rev. Joseph M. Flynn.—Right Rev. Winand M. Wigger, Bishop.—A new Bell.—The Morris Plains Mission. 116

CHAPTER IX.

The Sisters of Charity.—The Young Men's Association.—St. Virgilius.—Morris Plains. 133

CHAPTER X.

Temperance Work.—Church Bonds.—A Pastor's Reminiscences.—Catholic Benevolent Legion. . . . 146

CHAPTER XI.

The new Organ.—The Condit Property.—A Child of the Parish ordained.—St. Margaret's Chapel. . . 156

CHAPTER XII.

The Jubilee Retreat.—A remarkable Cure.—Corner-stone of new School.—Bishop McQuaid's Address. . 173

CHAPTER XIII.

Blessing of the School.—The Young Men's permanent Home. 190

CHAPTER XIV.

Paulist Mission.—St. Margaret's School.—Relic of St. Virgil.—A miraculous Healing.—The first American Catholic Congress. 211

CHAPTER XV.

St. Patrick's Day 1780 and 1890.—A new Rectory.—St. Margaret's enlarged.—The Burnham-Flynn Correspondence. 229

CHAPTER XVI.

Re-dedication of St. Margaret's.—Friendly Sons of St. Patrick.—The Strike.—All Souls' Hospital. . . . 248

CHAPTER XVII.

Parish War Record.—Gen. Joseph W. Revere.—Children of the Parish in the Confederacy. 270

CHAPTER XVIII.

Memorials.—Children of the Parish in the Service of the Church.—Men's Societies.—A Catholic Mayor. . . 278

APPENDIX. 288

PREFACE.

I AM not disposed to claim any merit for the labors of this narrative of events which have marked the origin and development of the Catholic Church in Morristown, New Jersey. I have written for my parishioners, and only when I was able to snatch a few leisure moments from other duties. Sometimes at long intervals; sometimes my pen had to be laid aside and the thread of my "Story" broken. I am aware that mine has been a difficult task. I have endeavored to put the facts truthfully and accurately, with no desire to hurt the feelings of anybody, or to reopen wounds long since healed.

My flock, I am sure, will extend even to this work that same forbearance which in the ten years of his labor among them they have so graciously shown to their Pastor. If, perchance, these pages go beyond our parish limits I pray my critics to believe that the sole motive which prompted this effort was to give expression to my gratitude to a generous, self-sacrificing flock — "to gather up the fragments, lest they perish," for the future chronicler.

THE AUTHOR.

Morristown, N. J., January 7, 1892.

THE STORY OF A PARISH.

CHAPTER I.

THE study of a Parish is somewhat akin to the contemplation of a structure erected according to the strictest rules of architecture, embodying the genius of the designer, startling and pleasing all by the harmony of its parts and its adaptability for the purposes which called it into being. Symmetry, grace, and loveliness are blended in a serene repose, soothing the eye and elevating the soul, and around it play the sunbeams, the varying hues of Spring-tide and Autumn, the golden splendor of Summer, and the melancholy sadness of Winter with its high lights and shadows. How little, however, is thought of him whose fertile brain evoked the masterpiece of art, whose lofty conceptions are crystallized in the everlasting granite or spotless marble! We know that Raphael, Bramante, and Michelangelo threw into St. Peter's the very heart and soul of their inspiration, to erect to the living God such a temple as the eye of man had never gazed upon.

But there are other monuments which thrill no less the beholder, and the names of their creators sleep in an impenetrable obscurity. The cross-crowned fane, lifting to the highest heaven the sign of man's redemption, may tell us neither of him whose genius conceived nor of the toilers whose strong arm and cunning eye, in the burning heats of Summer, or in the chilling blasts of Winter, unfolded to the wondering crowds who daily watched their labors, step by step, inch by inch, the beauties whose finished product Time has preserved to us in many a shire of Britain; by the glistening lake and verdant vales of Erin; in sunny Italy, in fair France, and in the hallowed soil bathed by our own Potomac. To the humble laborer who dug the trenches, to the artist whose chisel carved foliage on cusp and capital, a share in our grateful memory is due.

Thus we, in a later generation, survey complacently the stately Church; the spacious School, perfect in its appointments with Hall and meeting-rooms; the graceful Rectory; the well-kept walks of the peaceful God's-acre; but little thought we give to yonder moss-grown graves where repose the valiant Confessors who, in days gone by, kept alive and aloft the torch of faith, and, by unswerving fidelity and unflinching clinging to the Church of their fathers, made our present prosperity possible. They laid the foundations deep and secure.

Theirs it was to battle with poverty, and to wrestle with bitter prejudice. Theirs it was to share the contumely of Christ, to stand forth in defence of religion and fatherland, even, at times, at the cost of blood and at the sacrifice of fortune.

Theirs it was to bear the brunt of sneer and jibe, and to hear the ribald jest hurled at what they held most holy and sacred. Theirs it was to provide for the wants of the flock of little ones, who clamored for bread and raiment; to remember the poor old father and mother, left behind at *Home* in distress and desolation; and, at the same time, build the humble chapel, devoid of art and naked of ornament, save the Altar; and support the Soggarth who cheerfully shared their poverty and the contempt which bigotry and ignorance heaped upon them both. Hat in hand, with faltering step and hesitating speech, our fathers asked for work. Their broad brogue, their quaint and odd attire, gave unlimited fun and amusement, until checked by some sharp, keen retort, which while it wounded, soothed by its spontaneity and brightness.

Not rarely, indeed, was their going to meeting, and their attendance at evening prayer, made a condition of their engagement. Starve they might and would; but by any overt or implicit act deny their faith, never. With them, when it was question of faith, the motto was: Death before dishonor.

The week's toil over, came the preparation for the long and weary tramp to the nearest Church. The women donned their best gowns and put on their brightest ribbons; the men brought out their best suits, and wore the well-polished tile; and so, off to the common meeting-place, whence with others, bent on the same duty as themselves, they wended their way to Mass. Then the news was gone over: their trials, their loneliness for the Chapel, the goings on at *Home*, the bitter and, at times, almost intolerable persecution on the part of their masters and neighbors; and thus, with gossip and mutual sympathy, they plodded on until the goal was at hand, the Church was reached. The little bell rang from the sacristy window; all cut their stories short and hurried within. Perhaps they understood little of what the good Father said in his broken English. What mattered it?—he was a priest; he heard their confessions, baptized their children; offered for them the unbloody Sacrifice.

They were fortunate who had friends in the town, for comfort and food were assured, and they would not go home hungry. By no means should it be inferred that the Catholics, in those days, were lacking in hospitality; but the instinct of the Celtic heart to avoid giving trouble, forbade him to step beyond the limits he had set for himself. If his foresight had not prompted him to bring along the meagre lunch, he turned his steps homeward, and waited until his good wife had prepared the frugal meal for his very much sharpened appetite.

This is but a faint picture of what our forefathers and predecessors in the faith did so willingly for many years.

The little Church at Bottle Hill was the shrine to which the Catholics of Morristown, Mendham, New Vernon, Basking Ridge, and Boonton went for many years. Hither they brought their children to be baptized ; and at the foot of the Altar they pledged—the stout young Irish lad and the rosy-cheeked girl—their mutual love, and thence started on life's uncertain journey together. They have almost all passed to their reward ; but some few remain ; and the children of those departed remember the spot consecrated by their footsteps, where they awaited the gathering of the faithful few from the neighborhood, in sunshine and rain, in Summer as well as in Winter, at Sneeden's Crossing.

In these twilight days of Catholicity none presumed to the dignity and convenience of a carriage. But all afoot, men and women, young and old, walked down the now unused road, which runs parallel with the railroad track, to Madison.

In times still more distant, the nearest Church was St. Peter's in Barclay Street, New York; and more than one child was brought by slow stage or wagon to this venerable sanctuary for baptism. Old Thomas Burns, who came here about the year 1827, often told how he and William Collins walked all the way to St. John's, Newark, to make their Easter duty; and on their arrival met the congregation coming home from Mass. In their simplicity they feared to give the venerable Patriarch, good Father Moran, the trouble of hearing their confession ; and so they started for home, just as they had left, fasting; and, no doubt, they would have fainted by the wayside had they not met a kind-hearted

Samaritan near the Summit, who gave them a lift as far as Madison.

Tom never told without laughing heartily of his first situation in Morris Plains, and as part of the agreement was that he should attend school in Winter, the schoolmaster never allowed a day to go by that he had not something to say against the Papists or Popery, and would glaringly fix his eyes on him, while the children shrank from him as though he were pest-stricken.

We may wonder at all this in our present enlightenment, and may not realize the extent or depth of the hatred which prevailed against the Church and against all those who professed her doctrines; but this bigotry was to a large extent pardonable. They and their fathers were very near to the days of the great apostasy from the Church, which in the sixteenth century robbed from her bosom thousands of her children, and poured out on the scaffold the blood of priests and laymen who would not conform with their erroneous teaching. In the light of history, which we fortunately now possess, and which increases daily, we see the extent of the lying, calumny, and cunning her enemies had recourse to in the accomplishment of their ends to plunder and rob, and utterly annihilate, the Catholic Church, which stood as an impenetrable barrier to the lustful Henry VIII. To the vice of marital infidelity must be added extravagance and greed, and these could be gratified only by plundering and robbing churches and monasteries, on the pretext of the wickedness and excesses of the clergy.

It is easy to fabricate a lie, which loses nothing by its age, but seems to wax stronger and acquire a more piquant flavor by lengthening out its days. "Lie, lie!" said one of the most bitter enemies of the Church, "always lie; something will stick."

CHAPTER II.

IT is not easy to assign the date of the arrival of the first Catholic in this favored region of New Jersey. We know that the Irish were sent to the Colonies by shiploads to be sold as slaves. This was during and after the invasion of Ireland by Cromwell, whose memory recalls deeds of blood, cruelty, and rapine.

As the first settlers in Morris County came from Connecticut, it is not unlikely that they brought with them some unfortunate son or daughter of Erin, exiled and enslaved on account of attachment to faith.

Father Schneider, S.J., was the pioneer priest in New Jersey, and probably crossed Morris County frequently. The road in those days crossed Schooley's Mountain; and through lonely forests and rugged by-paths the priest sought out the Catholic, and gave to the little household the consoling ministration of our holy religion.

Years before the Revolutionary War a Jesuit, Father Farmer, visited this section of New Jersey, on his way to Macopin, now called Echo Lake, where there was quite a colony of Dutch Catholics engaged at the furnaces, which afterwards turned out the solid shot the Americans used so effectively against the British.

The early settlers of East Jersey had no desire to

harbor Catholics, and the freedom of conscience they were ready to extend to all believers in Christ, no matter how they might differ from themselves in religion, was not to include us: "No person or persons that profess faith in God by Jesus Christ, his only Son, shall at any time be molested, punished, disturbed, or be called in question for difference in religious opinion, etc., etc.; provided this shall not extend to any of the Romish religion the right to exercise their manner of worship contrary to the laws and statutes of England" (*Laws of East Jersey,* 1698). Instructions to Lord Cornbury, on his appointment as Governor in 1701, directed him to permit liberty of conscience to all persons except Papists.

The following, written on a slip, pasted on the fly-leaf of Father Farmer's Register: *You are to permit a Liberty of Conscience to all persons (except Papists),** was a constant admonition to the zealous priest of the dangers he was running. Hence his dress failed to indicate his clerical character, and his manner befitted the physician rather than the priest. Thus he safely passed through the Jerseys, ministering to the faithful wherever found without molestation. To throw off all suspicion, he wrote out the Missal with his own hand, and this he carried with him on his journeys.

Father Ferdinand Steinmayer, or Farmer, as he chose to be called, was born in Suabia, Germany,

---

* Instructions to Gov. Francis Bernard, of New Jersey, 1758.

October 13, 1729. He became a Jesuit in 1743, and arrived in this country in 1758. His field was the entire State of New Jersey, and it is evident that he visited Morris County regularly in the Spring and Autumn from 1768 to the time of his death. He died August 17, 1786.

He is described as "of slender form and having a countenance mild, gentle, and bearing an expression almost seraphic."

During the Leisler usurpation, 1688-89, a price was set upon the head of Major Anthony Brockholes and others who were denounced as Papists. Major Brockholes was a native of Lancashire, England, a Catholic, and very wealthy. To escape persecution he came, in company with Arent Schuyler, to New Jersey, and was enabled by his large means to buy extensive tracts of land in the central part of the State as well as at Pompton. Surely so wealthy and influential a man must have had a following, and in his service there must have been other Catholics.

The recondite historian, John Gilmary Shea, who more than any other knows the spots hallowed by the Missionaries of other days, in a letter to the writer says: "Father Farmer notes a baptism at the Wall-kill, which the Philadelphia wiseacres translated Wall Street. The Rev. Francis Beeston was at Mount Hope and Hibernia in October, 1787; at Charlottenburg October 21, 1788, and at Mount Hope May 3, 1789. The Rev. C. Vincent Keating paid a visit to Mount Hope April 30, 1792. The Rev. L. Graessl was at Charlottenburg on April 25, 1793; and on September 19, of the same year, he married, at the same place, John Philip Seeholster to Julia Vinyard. Father Graessl, elected coadjutor to Bishop Carroll, died before he was consecrated while attending the yellow-fever patients in Philadelphia."

Three days after the battle of Princeton, January 7, 1777, Washington with his troops arrived in Morristown, and took up his headquarters at the old Arnold Tavern, now the site of the Arnold building, on the west side of the Park.* With him as aide was General Stephen Moylan, brother of the Catholic Bishop of Cork.

Other Catholics among Washington's Generals who resided here at times between 1777 and 1779 were, La Fayette, Du Coudray, M. A. Roche de Fermoy, Kosciusko, De la Neuville, Armand, and Duportail.

In the army was a large contingent of Catholic Irishmen, raised by Captain Thomas Fitzsimmons of Philadelphia, and enrolled in the Pennsylvania Line. Beyond the Hills, on the Wicke farm, reposes the dust of many a poor fellow carried off by the smallpox, which raged fiercely for a time among the almost starved and ill-clad patriots.

On April 19, 1779, Don Juan de Miralles, a Spanish agent, arrived in camp, accompanied by the Che-

---

* Now standing in the Collis tract, Mt. Kemble Avenue, and known as the Colonial building, and purchased by the Catholics for a hospital.

valier de la Luzerne, Minister of France, and was almost immediately stricken down with pulmonary trouble, which ended fatally on the 28th. The Chaplain of the French Ambassador, the Rev. Seraphin Bandol, hurried on from Philadelphia and administered the last Sacraments to the dying Spaniard in the Ford house, now Washington's Headquarters.

An inaccurate and misleading account of the obsequies appeared in the Morristown *Banner*, 1889, to which the Very Rev. Dean Flynn made reply. As the statement contains a brief historical review of all the facts, it has been thought well to embody it.

Count de Miralles.

Eds. Banner:

I have just read Mr. Pumpelly's pen-picture of Don Juan de Miralles' brief stay, death, and funeral in Morristown. Such sketches are sure to excite interest and are, at the same time, calculated to invest with a new charm our pretty city, rich in natural beauty and in historic memory.

A few inaccuracies, however, mar Mr. Pumpelly's communication. Don Juan de Miralles was not an envoy, but "an unofficial agent of the Spanish Government, and was introduced in this way, that he might obtain a knowledge of the affairs of the United States, and communicate it to the Ministers of the Spanish Court. Spain was not yet ready to take an open and decided part; nor, indeed, was she ever ready to regard the American people as an independent nation till circumstances made it an imperious necessity." (*Am. Cath. Hist. Researches*, vol. vi. No. 2, p. 62; *Washington's Writings*, vol. vi. p. 187.)

Luzerne, moreover, wrote to Vergennes that Miralles confessed to him that he had no instructions from the Spanish Court; that his correspondence was with the Governor of Havana; that the Spanish Ministry had signified their general approbation of his conduct down to the end of August last; that he had received word from M. Galvez that he would be appointed Minister to the United States when the King should think proper to send one. (MS. Letter from Luzerne to Vergennes, March 13, 1780.)

The review of the troops with all its pomp and splendor, the fireworks in the evening, were all, according to *Thatcher's Journal*, in honor of the Chevalier de la Luzerne: "On the 25th the whole army was paraded under arms to afford M. de la Luzerne another opportunity of reviewing the troops; after which he was escorted a part of the way to Philadelphia. The Spanish gentleman remained dangerously sick of a pulmonic fever, and on the 28th he expired." (*Thatcher's Journal*, p. 151.)

In his letter to Don Diego José de Navarro, Governor of Cuba, Washington writes that De Miralles honored him with a visit, and " was seized on the day of his arrival with a violent bilious complaint, which, after nine days' continuance, put a period to his life, notwithstanding all the efforts of the most skilful physicians we were able to procure." (*Washington's Writings*, vol. vii. p. 27.)

"When Baron Steuben, on the 24th of April, had arranged the grand review of his battalions, to the delight of Washington, De la Luzerne and others, and that night, while the fire-works were flashing their beautiful eccentricities in the darkness, and the sounds of music and dancing were heard at O'Hara's, Don Juan de Miralles was tossing with a deadly fever. He died April 29, 1780."

Thatcher says: "A Spanish priest performed service at the grave in the Roman Catholic form. This priest, the Rev. Seraphin Bandol, Chaplain of the French Minister, came to Morristown to minister to the sick man, and "Miralles received the last Sacraments with great piety and contrition." (Shea, ii. p. 178.) As the priest was Chaplain to the French Minister it is more than likely that he was French, and not Spanish.

I fail to see "the seeming incongruity of such a funeral—such show in the very midst of such grim want and suffering among our brave troops." Don de Miralles was not an American. He had no personal interest in the result of the war. He came hither as a Spanish gentleman, lived here as such, and the "corpse was dressed in a rich state and exposed to public view as is customary in Europe." (*Thatcher's Journal*, p. 193.) The jewelry, diamonds, etc., had been his personal property; and his estate was large enough to pay the doctor's fees and the expenses of "all the profusion of pomp and grandeur." The administrators of his estate acted then as such officials do in our day—gave him a funeral suitable to his condition and means, and in accordance with the customs of his country.

Don de Miralles did not forget in his will those in whom he was interested. To each servant he gave a new coat. His Scotch boy Angus, held for a term of years, was to be liberated. His negro Raphael, wife and children, were to be given their freedom at the Havanna and two cavallaries of land.

The trend of the editors of *Rivington's Royal Gazette* and its patrons, not indeed towards the goal whither Washington and his brave army were striving, but rather towards the tyranny which precipitated the revolt, will account in a great measure "for the rage of Congress at finding no corpse under the cloth, the body having been several days before interred at Morristown." The bugaboo of Popery was evoked then, as now, to frighten and terrify the ignorant. France had just concluded an alliance with the struggling colonies, an alliance which meant men, money, arms, and ammunition at the critical period when Congress was listless, the colonists powerless and discouraged, and Washington himself on the point of giving up the struggle. The royalists and their supporters saw that the turning point had come. Hence their rage, and the bitterness of their invective. A hundred years ago what horrors Papist and Popery conjured up! It was this irresistible fear that by the French alliance Popery was going to triumph here which disturbed Arnold's conscience, and which led him to the step which has branded him with eternal infamy.

Not only Congress, but all those invited, knew that it was not the funeral of Don de Miralles but a service for the repose of his soul, in the Catholic Church (St. Mary's), they were called upon to attend. The invitation to Dr. Benjamin Rush reads thus: "The French Minister has the honor to inform Dr. Rush that there will be in the Catholic Church a divine service for the rest of the soul of Don Juan de Miralles at 9 o'clock in the morning." It bears the endorsement by Dr. Rush: "Received May 6, 1780, but declined attending as not compatible with the principles of a Protestant." All honor to the candor and sincerity of this consistent Christian!

Ebenezer Hazard, writing to Rev. Jeremy Belknap, of Boston, June 27, 1780, says: "Soon after the Minister of France returned to Philadelphia he sent cards to a number of gentlemen, informing them that on such a day 'there would be a Divine Service at the Romish Church for the rest of the soul of Don Juan de Miralles.' I determined to attend, and upon going into the church I found there not only Papists, but Presbyterians, Episcopalians, Quakers, etc. The two Chaplains of Congress (one a Presbyterian and the other a Churchman) were among the rest. I confess I was pleased to find the minds of people so unfettered with the shackles of bigotry. The behavior of the Papists in time of worship was very decent and solemn." (*Belknap Papers*, pp. 61, 62, Mass. Hist. Soc. Coll.)

In thus attending a Catholic service Congress was, no doubt, actuated by a desire to honor the memory of the Spanish gentleman, but likewise out of regard to the Minister of France, the ally of the United States; and in some measure to conciliate the French Canadians, who had been made the antagonists and enemies of the struggling republic by the bigotry of John Jay.

At a memorial service in the Catholic Church there is erected a catafalque, having the appearance of a coffin. Nobody is deceived, as none was deceived years ago when the mock funerals, casket, hearse, pall-bearers, etc., traversed the streets of the principal cities of the Union, to the booming of minute guns and tolling of bells at the same moment that his fellow-citizens in Springfield were bearing the remains of the martyr-patriot Lincoln to their last resting-place.

JOSEPH M. FLYNN.

P. S.—It may be of interest to know that two hundred years ago this coming Autumn John Tatham, a Roman Catholic, was elected to the highest position in the gift of the Proprietors, that of Governor of East and West Jersey. J. M. F.

The Journal of Dr. James Thatcher, Surgeon to the Revolutionary Army, contains a very graphic account of this the first public Catholic funeral in Morristown:

"29th April, 1780.—I accompanied Doctor Schuyler to headquarters to attend the funeral of M. de Miralles. The deceased was a gentleman of high rank in Spain, and had been about one year resident with our Congress from the Spanish Court. The corpse was dressed in a rich state and exposed to public view, as is customary in Europe. The coffin was most splendid and stately, lined throughout with fine cambric, and covered on the outside with rich black velvet and ornamented in a superb manner. The top of the coffin was removed to display the pomp and grandeur with which the body was decorated. It was in a splendid full dress, consisting of a scarlet suit, embroidered with rich gold lace, a three-cornered gold-laced hat, and a genteel cued wig, white silk stockings, large diamond shoe and knee buckles, a profusion of diamond rings decorated the fingers, and from a superb gold watch, set with diamonds, several rich seals were suspended. His Excellency, General Washington, with several other general officers and members of Congress, attended the funeral solemnities and walked as chief mourners. The other officers of the army, and numerous respectable citizens, formed a splendid procession, extending about a mile. The pall-bearers were six field officers, and the coffin was borne on the shoulders of four officers of artillery in full uniform. Minute guns were fired during the procession, which greatly increased the solemnity of the occasion. A Spanish priest performed service at the grave in the Roman Catholic form. The coffin was enclosed in a box of plank, and all the profusion of pomp and grandeur were deposited in the silent grave in the common burying-ground, near the Church at Morristown. A guard is placed at the grave lest our soldiers should be tempted to dig for hidden treasure. It is understood that the corpse is to be removed to Philadelphia. This gentleman is said to have been possessed of an immense fortune, and has left to his three daughters one hundred thousand pounds sterling each. Here we behold the end of all earthly riches, pomp and dignity. The ashes of Don de Miralles mingle with the remains of those who are clothed in humble shrouds, and whose career in life was marked with sordid poverty and wretchedness (p. 193)."

The body of this distinguished nobleman was exhumed and sent to Spain, but in what year the most careful investigation has failed to ascertain.

Mr. John Gilmary Shea wrote to the keeper of the archives at Madrid, who furnished him much valuable information, but could not find any document relating to Señor de Miralles.

On the farm now occupied by the Hubbard family, about one-half mile from Whippany, on the

Troy road, very near the old homestead, which is perhaps older than Washington's Headquarters, are the graves of Captain Michael Kearney and his sister Isabella.

It is said that at one time the doughty Captain owned nine hundred and ninety-nine acres; and this tract was called the *Irish Lott*. Here the courtesy and urbanity of the Captain attracted friends from far and near. His hospitality and good cheer made him hosts of friends, who crowded his stately mansion; for such, indeed, it was in those days. The present occupant of the farm states that the hands from time to time come across the wells which were located near the dwellings of the Captain's servants and slaves. It is said that the King gave him as much land as he could traverse in one day on horseback. The grave-yard which contains his remains, the spot selected by himself, on a charming knoll with pleasant views of hill and woodland on every side, is now in a sadly dilapidated condition. On the huge stone which covers his remains is the following inscription:

SACRED
To the Memory of
CAPTAIN MICHALE KEARNY
of His
Brittanic Majesty's Navy.
He departed this Life at
The IRISH LOTT
The Seat of his Residence in Hanover
On the 5 day of April A.D. 1797
Aged 78 years 6 months and 28 days.
In the Naval Service he was a brave
And Intrepid Officer which secured to
Him several marks of distinguished
RESPECT and CONFIDENCE.
In private Life he exercised the Virtues
Of Benevolence, Hospitaety and
Genteel Urbanity.

Adjoining this grave is that of his sister, and on her tombstone is the following:

J. K.   J. K.

SACRED
To the Memory
of
ISABELLA KEARNEY, daughter of
Michael Kearney and Sarah Kearney,
late Sarah Morris, of Morrisania,
who died on the 14th of February 1806
at the seat of the late Captain
Michael Kearny in the County of
Morris in the 90th year of her age.

It does not appear that these Kearneys were Catholics. The descendants of Captain Kearney moved to Amboy, and one of them achieved fame in the United States Navy. It is claimed that Philip Kearney, the hero of Chantilly, was descended from Captain Michael Kearny; so, likewise, the present General J. Watts Kearney, himself a Catholic and all his family, has sprung from this illustrious Celtic stock.

It was when Washington's Army was encamped in Morristown that the Father of his Country inaugurated the first national celebration of St. Patrick's Day. These facts are taken from the Order Book, one of the many treasures to be seen in the Washington Headquarters, Morristown, N. J.

General Orders issued to the Troops encamped at Morristown, N. J., by Washington, March 16th, 1780.

HEADQUARTERS, MORRISTOWN, N. J.
March 16th, 1780.

Officers for duty To-morrow:
Brigadier-General Clinton,
Major Edwards,
Brigade Major Brice.

The General congratulates the Army on the very interesting proceedings of the Parliament of Ireland, and of the inhabitants of that Country— which have been communicated, not only as they appear calculated to remove those heavy and Tyrrannical oppressions on their trade; but to restore to a brave and generous people their ancient Rights and Freedom, and by their operation to promote the cause of America. Desirous of impressing on the minds of the Army transactions so important in their nature, the General directs that all Fatigue and working parties cease To-morrow the seventeenth, a day held in Particular regard by the people of that Nation. At the same time that he orders this as a mark of pleasure he feels on the Occasion, he persuades himself that the celebration of the day will not be attended with the slightest rioting or disorder. The Officers to be at their Quarters in Camp and the Troops of each State are to keep within their own encampment.

PENNSYLVANIA LINE,
  DIVISION ORDERS,
    March 17th, 1780.

The Commanding Officer desirous that the celebration of this day should not pass by without having a little Rum issued to the Troops, has thought proper to direct Commissary Night to send for a hogshead which the Colonel has prepared for this express purpose in the vicinity of Camp. While the Troops are celebrating the anniversary of ST. PATRICK in innocent mirth and pastime he hopes they will not forget our worthy friends in the Kingdom of IRELAND who with the greatest unanimity have step'd forth in opposition to the Tyranny of Great Britain, and who like *us* are determined to be *free*. The Colonel expects the Troops Will conduct themselves with the greatest sobriety and good order.

  Signed: FRANCIS JOHNSTON
    Col. Com'd't 2d Penna. Brigade.

It will be seen by the above that in the Pennsylvania Line were many *Irish*, both officers and soldiers; and in the *Official Register of the Officers and Men of New Jersey in the Revolutionary War*, compiled under the administration of Governor Theodore F. Randolph by Adjutant-General Stryker, a cursory glance shows that many of the New Jersey Regiments contained a liberal number of Irishmen, over four hundred officers and soldiers with unmistakably Irish names being credited to the Southern Counties.

It is quite certain, then, that during the winters of 1779 and 1780 the number of Catholics in and around Morristown far exceeded the number of Catholics at present in our Parish, made up of the Irish Catholics in the Pennsylvania, New York, and New Jersey regiments, and the French and Polish officers attached to the line.

The condition of the faithful at this period was most pitiable. Owing to the suppression of the Society of Jesus, induced by the Bismarck of Portugal, Pombal, the tireless missionaries who had labored with so much zeal and fruit were powerless to continue their great work.

The Bishop saw and recognized the urgent necessity of faithful, God-fearing laborers for the Lord's vineyard; but where were they to be found? The French Revolution had sent the flower of the priesthood to England and some few to the United States, among them the illustrious Bruté, Cheverus,

Maréchal, Dubois, and Flaget. But what were these few in the harvest-field? Our Catholic predecessors were scattered far and wide in almost every county of the State. Shipwrecked on the Jersey coast, the Irish emigrants settled on a spot known then, as now, as Irish Mills; thence they wandered into Salem, Camden, Hunterdon, and Morris Counties.

Without Priest or Mass, except on very rare visits from Father Farmer, they were married by the Squire or Magistrate; and their children, if they themselves did not, attended the Protestant Church for the reason that it was the only one in the neighborhood. Their companions and associates were of an alien faith.

It is not surprising, then, that the Celtic names which prevailed in Morristown in the first quarter of the present century are not found on our Church Records.

With their faith the children lost likewise the distinctive character of their family names. McGee becomes in its filtered state Magee; McCarthy becomes Mecarty; Kearney becomes Kerny or Kearny; Callahan becomes Callinan; Raferty becomes Raverty. All these names still prevail in our midst and are the indices of both the country and religion of their progenitors.

A list of letters, uncalled for in the Post-Office October 1, 1807, contains the following names: Andrew Darsey, Michael Flaherty, John Kelly. Who were they, whence came they, or whither did they go, none knows.

It is just possible that they may have been soldiers whose hearts, perhaps, were smitten by some fair maiden in Morris; for, as we know, the Celt's heart is very susceptible to Cupid's charms, and once in the meshes he falls a willing victim.

In a Morristown paper appeared the following amusing card, which points but too clearly to the nationality of the writer:

A COWARD.

Whereas, a certain little sharp-faced son of Vulcan has frequently challenged the subscriber to a single combat, saying "the Hibernian he could whip." And whereas, I have week after week waited upon said bragadocia, and have always found that he had drawn in his horns: Now I do hereby pronounce him a coward and a mushroon, and shall in future think him beneath my notice.

HENRY BYRNE.

Morris Town, October 14, 1812.

Two years later appeared an advertisement:

FOR SALE.—That valuable Tavern Stand, most pleasantly located, situated on the West side of Morris Green.

ELIZABETH O'HARA.

January 13, 1814.

It is generally believed that the O'Haras kept this hotel during the Revolution.

In a conversation, which the writer had in February, 1881, with a bright, motherly old lady, who with her husband came to this country from a little town in the County Cavan in 1816, the following interesting facts were gleaned:

"I shall begin my story with my arrival in New York. In those days two sail-boats served as a ferry to convey passengers from the City to Paulus Hook, now Jersey City.

"We crossed over to Paulus Hook, and hiring a wagon we started on our journey to Caldwell. There was only one street in Jersey City, called the Rope Walk. After an all day's ride we arrived in the evening at Caldwell. There was not a single Catholic in the neighborhood.

"You may imagine how we felt, and you will not be surprised that in a few months we moved to Macopin, where we heard there was quite a gathering of Catholics. A year or two before our arrival Charley O'Brien died in Newfoundland, some miles distant from Macopin. He went there to teach school, saved his money, bought land, built factories, and soon was the wealthiest man in that section. He owned as far as he could see, and was the first to build bark factories and an iron mill. Charley was taken sick, and sent to New York for a priest. The priest came all the way on horseback, and the close-fisted sick man gave him five dollars for his trouble. He left him, however, fifty dollars in his will; but his heirs never executed the wish of their father, and the priest never saw a penny of his legacy. But his possessions melted away, and eventually his only son died in the poorhouse."

Thus ends the story of dear old Mrs. Littell, long since passed to her reward; always staunch in the faith, her hospitable roof sheltered more than one missionary, bent on his search after the lost and strayed sheep; generous and lavish in prosperity, patient and cheerful in adversity, she was a type of the pioneer Catholic.

To Bottle Hill, now Madison, driven from their homes and land by the fury of the French Revolution, came goodly numbers of French aristocrats known as *émigrés*, and to these were added other French families who were obliged to flee from the island of Guadeloupe when the slaves rose up in rebellion against their masters. Many of their descendants still with us were the seed of Catholicity in this county.

Van Schalkwick Beauplands, the Boisaubins,* Basmont, Roche-Fermoy, Cornet de St. Cyr, Blanchets, Lavaal Duberceau, and Thébauds are names illustrious not only by their birth, but likewise for their robust faith. Amidst the prejudices which prevailed a hundred years ago they clung to the old Church, to its practices and its creed. Visits were occasionally made to them by the Rev. Anthony

---

* Vincent Boisaubin Beaupland, who is buried in Morristown, was an officer of the body-guard of Louis XVI.

Kohlman, S.J., and the Rev. John Power, pastor of St. Peter's Church, Barclay Street, New York.

It is said that one O'Hara taught a classical School in Morristown in the first decade of this century, which was the germ of the subsequent McCullogh School.

In 1825 Charles Berault, a Catholic and a native of San Domingo, lived in the Revere House on DeHart Street. He married a Mlle. Des Abbeyes, also of a wealthy San Domingo family. Another daughter was Madame Chegarray, who taught a fashionable Young Ladies' Academy, afterwards purchased by Bishop Bayley, and the cradle of Seton Hall. This is now the property of the Sisters of Charity on the old Convent road to Madison.

A certain Benjamin Douglas kept a Diary, now in the possession of the Brookfield family, his descendants, which contains the following entries:

"The first Roman Catholic service performed in the Township of Chatham was in the house of Lavaal Duberceau, at Bottle Hill, Sunday July 30th, 1825, by Rev. O'Donahue. Text, fifth chapter of Galatians."

Father O'Donahue visited Madison once a month from Paterson and said Mass in the upper part of the Academy. His Sunday evening instructions were attended by large numbers of non-Catholics. His light-hearted gaiety drew to him the hearts of all, especially the children.

Once when on his way to Macopin with Father Bulger, a furious down-pour of rain drenched them both to the skin. When they arrived at Mr. Littell's the good host's wardrobe was rummaged and soon the priests were arrayed in picturesque costumes more or less entire. Father Bulger was the more fortunate in finding a complete outfit; and, while he sat near the big log fire reading his breviary by the canny light, Father O'Donahue in shirt-sleeves and very roomy trousers amused the youngsters with his feats of ventriloquism.

The early part of this century is for Catholics the period of the Dark Ages. The records, if kept, have been lost or destroyed; or, perhaps, hidden away in some musty chest. Almost all the grenadiers who planted the faith hereabouts, amid tears and bitter trials, have passed to their reward; and the traditions have either utterly died out or become woefully entangled. At the Cathedral in New York there are no archives.

Paterson is the mother church of Northern New Jersey, and from this centre the priests made their round of duty through Passaic, Morris, Sussex, and Warren Counties. The best-known of these pioneer priests is Father Bulger, who was at Paterson in 1822. His remains are interred in front of the old St. Patrick's Church, New York City.

Rev. L. D. Senez.

CHAPTER III.

IN 1834 the Catholics of Madison had the blessing of a resident priest, the Rev. Father Herard. The parish is reported vacant in 1839. On January 1, 1840, the Rev. Richard Newell opened the baptismal and marriage registers of St. Vincent's Church, Madison; and his last entry bears the date October 16, 1842.

Dr. Newell enjoyed the confidence and esteem of his congregation. When he bade his flock farewell the touching scene was one not to be forgotten. His voice trembled with emotion, and his words were scarcely audible amidst the sobbing and sighs of the congregation; even now the old folks cannot recall the memorable day without emotion. He died quite recently. His successor was the learned Ambrose Manahan, afterwards pastor of St. Joseph's, New York, but resident in Madison until after April, 1844.

February 6, 1843, Amedée Boisaubin, the founder of the Church in Madison and its most generous benefactor, went to his reward. The religious service, both at the Church in Madison and at the grave in the Cemetery of the First Presbyterian Church, Morristown, was conducted by Father McCloskey, who was subsequently raised to the dignity of Bishop of Albany, Archbishop of New York, and Cardinal of Holy Church.

From August, 1844, to January, 1845, the Madison Mission was in charge of the Rev. Patrick Kenny, who died in the South. For five months a Rev. Father Joseph attended the spiritual wants of the parish, until the advent of the Rev. Dominic Senez.

Father Senez presents to his fellow-priests a well-rounded, laborious, and fruitful career. From the golden summit which he reached in 1890, when in obedience to his Bishop he yielded to a strictly local celebration of the fiftieth anniversary of his ordination, what a vista—from the Seminary of St. Sulpice to the sanctuary of St. Mary's, Jersey City—stretches out before him!

Cardinal Piè, the converted Jew Ratisbon, and hosts of other classmates who in every clime have added to the conquests of Mother Church, lustre to the venerable name of Jean-Jacques Olier, and other names to the roll of Martyrs, have fought the good fight and long since passed to their reward. Almost alone he remains, a living witness of the piety and zeal which, in Matignon, Cheverus, Bruté, Dubois, pierced the bigotry and anti-Catholic hatred of Puritans and attracted their respect and sympathy.

If Father Senez would consent to narrate the experience begun in the missions of Morris, Sussex, and Warren Counties, there would be no brighter pages in Christian annals. To pass to his reward without leaving to us this inheritance of his efforts to keep the little flock within the fold of the Church, and to bring the light of truth to those who sat in darkness, would indeed be an irreparable loss.

With almost no knowledge of the language of those entrusted to his care, without any other treasure than that garnered in the sacred precincts of the Seminary, he came among us in the Autumn of 1845.

This was for him the morning of an unclouded life. Late and early he bore the heat and burden of the day. He went to every gathering of the country folk—*vendues*, as the auction-sales in those days were called—and there searched for the priceless jewels of men's souls.

"The first time I saw Father Senez," said old Tom Degan, "was at a *vendue* near Madison."

"If I am not mistaken," said the good priest, accosting Tom and his wife in broken English flavored with a strong French accent, "you are an Irishman and a Catholic."

"And if I am not mistaken," replied Tom, "you are a Catholic priest."

This was their mutual introduction. There was no road throughout the three counties he did not traverse.

Sometimes while making inquiries about Catholics, or the road, he unexpectedly found one of the faithful. It was just this way when, arrived near the banks of the Delaware River, he discovered a

Catholic family living near Montague, and baptized the little ones. The oldest son is an honored and distinguished priest in New Jersey. Generally by carriage he made his visitation, owing to the fact that no railroad facilities existed. In his carriage, too, he slept; for the hostelries at that time, while maintaining a reputation for good cheer, put forth no claim for the virtue which ranks next to godliness.

Once, it is said, he sat down to a smoking-hot dinner of chicken pot-pie and all the accessories which tickle an appetite already over-sharpened by a long drive and a long fast, and was on the point of beginning the attack, when the Irish Catholic waitress whispered in his ear:

"Father, it is Friday."

"Well, now," laughed the priest good-humoredly, "why did you not wait to tell me after I had finished my dinner?"

At another time, near Mount Hope, he treated the faithful to the solemnity of a High Mass. The church was the shelter of the forest, whose stately trunks rose up on every side, whose interlaced branches formed the roof. Two of the men held up a sheet on the weather side of the altar, to shield the priest from the wind. The choir was the priest's serving-man, who sang the entire service unassisted by instrumental or vocal accompaniment.

In addition to this field, Newark, Paterson, and Jersey City have been hallowed by his apostolic zeal; and in these congregations still lingers the aroma of his spirit.

When he first visited this desolate and disheartening field there was but the one Church, that at Madison, erected by the generosity of a devout child of France. But Madison has been the fruitful mother of many children. No fewer than twenty-three Catholic Churches lift to heaven the Cross in the three counties which were the limits of Father Senez's first parish.

New Jersey now has two sees, Newark and Trenton; two hundred and eighty-eight priests; and a Catholic population of two hundred and forty-five thousand.

Of the half-dozen fellow-harvesters all—the patriarch Moran, the saintly Kelly, the tireless, jovial Rodgers, the impetuous O'Reilly, the venerable Father Balleis—all are gone save Father Senez, whose days may God lengthen to be for us a reminder of His mercies to past generations, as a model to us of the present!

More could be said—more, indeed, should; but humility bars the way. His is it to unlock those treasures whose silence makes it now impossible to divulge that which might dim the lustre of a crown won by labors for Christ, and partaking of the contumely of the Master.

The only fitting encomium to sum up his life and labor is that of the Gospel: Well done, good and faithful servant!

In the Springtime of 1844-45 good Father Howell was tempted to sample the pastures and pure air of Morris County, and, combining business with pleasure, he baptized quite a number of children in Morristown, Dover, and Mount 'Hope. A Catholic woman married to a Protestant was denied the convenience of a carriage by her husband, and walked with her child all the way to Elizabeth to have it baptized, as it happened there was no priest then at Madison.

There is considerable dispute relative to the house where the Holy Sacrifice of the Mass was first offered in Morristown. By some it is maintained that it was in a house formerly on the property of Dr. Dodge, Morris Street; by others, in a house on McCullogh Avenue; again, by some, in the Thébaud house, which long ago stood on Mr. John G. Foote's farm; and finally, by not a few, that it was in the Johnson house on South Street, on the way to the race-track, which was called by a subsequent Catholic owner Bellevue. Wherever it was, it is generally admitted that the priest sought and received the hospitality of Mr. John Rogers. John Rogers was among the earliest settlers, and his home was looked upon as a headquarters for the clergy whenever they made a visitation.

In 1847, however, steps were taken to secure a lot to build the Church. The site on which the new Rectory now stands was bought from John

Rt. Rev. B. J. McQuaid, D.D.

Kennedy, of Philadelphia, for $400. At the outbreak of the French Revolution, Father Senez resigned the pastorate to return to his native land. Previous to his departure a "bee" was held to dig the foundations of the new church. Father Senez opposed the building of a basement, but finally yielded to the entreaty of Father McQuaid, and this feature was embodied in the plans. The honor of turning the first sod belongs to Patrick Cavanagh. Mr. Egsall built the masonry, and Mr. Muchmore did the carpenter work.

Before the walls were built, Father Senez left, and the work devolved solely on Father McQuaid. To Father McQuaid alone belongs the entire credit of building the first Catholic Church in Morristown; and of paying, not only for the structure itself but for the land on which it was erected. Three different times has this honor been wrested from him and unjustly given to another. This may seem to some a matter of indifference; but for the Catholics here it is all-important to know to whom they are indebted for the Church which cost more sacrifices, more anxiety and care from both priests and people, than would, to-day, the erection of a cathedral. Father McQuaid appointed William Nevins treasurer, and all the moneys passed through his hands. On the 15th of August the modest Church was entirely roofed, and Father McQuaid gave the Church the title of the Assumption in honor of the Blessed Mother of God, whose great feast saw the culmination of the hopes and desires of the little handful of Catholics.

On Christmas Day, 1848, Mass was said for the first time in the new Church by Father McQuaid. Simplicity and poverty were everywhere apparent. The altar consisted of some planks laid on barrels. The little congregation of from forty to seventy made themselves as comfortable as possible without pews or kneeling benches. A fair number of Protestants was present, among them Mr. Bonsall.

"Now," said Father McQuaid, "we depended on the goodness of God and the intercession of the Blessed Virgin, and we are all right. Through frost and cold we have collected by five and ten-cent offerings the funds necessary to build and enclose the Church, and now we have everything except the pews."

There was little decoration and very little comfort in the new Church, but there was great fervor. The poor exiles were full of gratitude to God that they had now a sanctuary in their midst where they might assist at the Holy Sacrifice of the Mass; reconcile themselves to Him in the tribunal of Penance; and bring their children to be baptized and instructed in their holy faith. Father Senez had borrowed the money to pay for the lot, but the people set themselves to work and rested not until they had paid back every penny of the loan.

Fortunate, indeed, it was for the Catholics of Morristown that Father McQuaid came among them. As a student he was always in delicate health. It was long feared that the young Levite would fall a victim to consumption; and only a short time before his ordination Bishop Bayley, then President of Fordham College, saved his life, when seized with a severe hemorrhage from the lungs, by a timely application of one of his father's old-fashioned remedies.

Previous to the ordination of Father McQuaid, Bishop Bayley was appointed the Secretary of Bishop Hughes. One morning the stern Bishop, who would brook no interference with his plans if he were a little out of sorts told his Secretary to order Father McQuaid to report to St. Mary's Church, Grand Street, New York. With his knowledge of the delicate health of the young priest and the arduous labors which confronted him in the city parish, Father Bayley hesitated to notify Father McQuaid. One day, finding his Bishop in good humor, the Secretary told him he had not written to Father McQuaid. "Why not, why not?" said Bishop Hughes abruptly. "Because," said Father Bayley, "the mission of St. Mary's will kill him." "Well," said the Bishop, "what will I do with him?" "Send him to Morris County, where the air is pure, and where he will have plenty of out-door exercise."

Thus came the young priest, delicate, indeed, in health, but with a strong will, a clear conviction of duty, the zeal of an apostle, and a courage that nothing could daunt. He was ever at work. Behind his trusty mare he jogged along the road, the reins in one hand, his breviary in the other. Day after day he journeyed from Madison to the most distant part of his extensive parish. Wherever he heard of a Catholic his zeal sought him out.

One day he travelled as far as Franklin Furnace, where he heard a Catholic was working, and asked him for a subscription. With eloquent fervor he told his hearer the poverty of the Morristown mission, but in vain. The tepid child of the Church was untouched by the pastor's story.

Father McQuaid was on the point of leaving empty-handed as he came, when two Orangemen who were in the crowd put their hands in their pockets and gave him a dollar. Tired and hungry, he turned his horse's head homeward, and many hours after awoke in his carriage at Madison. During the journey he had fallen asleep, and the faithful beast had carried him in the darkness and over the rough country road safely to his own home. He made his first start to collect funds for the Church in February, 1848, and did not rest until he had paid every cent of indebtedness.

His position was no sinecure, for his parish stretched from Milburn and Springfield through Morristown, Dover, Stanhope, Waterloo, and Newton to the brick tavern opposite Milford, Pennsylvania, and back again by Deckertown, Franklin Furnace, Boonton, Hanover, and Whippany to

Madison. Although separated by some miles from the little flock resident here, he never relaxed his vigilance over it. One Winter's night a party of the boys and girls was assembled in a building situated where the Lyceum now stands, and all were enjoying themselves with music and dancing, and, perhaps, other amusements of which the pastor did not approve.

Quite suddenly and very unexpectedly a stranger covered with snow stood in their midst. As he unwrapped his muffler and removed his fur cap, Father McQuaid appeared before them. Without hesitation or waiting for a word from him whom they feared as well as loved, one and all disappeared through doors and windows.

It seemed the more he had to do the more he accomplished. Recognizing the importance of Christian education, he opened a Catholic school in Madison, and taught it himself for a whole year. Hardly had he set things aright when he started a Catholic school in the basement of the Morristown Church. The beginnings were humble, it is true, but the principle was established that the school was not of less importance than the church.

While abroad Father Senez purchased a set of candlesticks and a crucifix for the main altar. Father McQuaid, meanwhile, had not been idle. On his return to Madison Father Senez saw many changes. A larger field awaited this indefatigable missionary, and his Bishop assigned him to complete the present St.

Patrick's Cathedral, Newark. But what was to be done with the candlesticks? The poverty of the good father would not allow him to donate them to the Church, and of church funds there was not a farthing. Mrs. William Collins and Mrs. John Rogers pleaded to be allowed to raise sufficient to pay the cost of these articles. Together they journeyed from house to house, from Morristown to Madison, to Whippany. Finally their persistent zeal was rewarded. They raised the sixty dollars, and the church ornaments remained in the Morristown Parish. The crucifix still surmounts the tabernacle on the high altar, and the candlesticks are used for Requiem Masses.

Strenuous efforts were made to complete the Church, put in the pews, and finish the sanctuary.

On Sunday, March 5, 1849, Bishop Hughes dedicated the Church. An interesting account appeared in the leading New York Catholic newspaper:

A NEW CHURCH.

MORRISTOWN, N. J., March 10th, 1849.

To the Editor of the Freeman's Journal:

DEAR SIR: Last Sunday was a happy day for the Catholics of Morristown. On that day the Church which, by hard struggling, they have been enabled to erect, was dedicated to the service of Almighty God. Now at length, within sight of their own homes, they have an altar around which they may gather in humble adoration of their

1. THE OLD SCHOOL—THE FIRST CHURCH.
2. INTERIOR VIEWS BEFORE REMOVAL TO NEW SCHOOL.

Maker. Now, at their own doors, they have a temple within which they may hear the same truth their Saviour taught, and soon in the basement of that Church they will have a school for their children. For this great favor they do not fail to thank most heartily the good God who has been pleased to grant it. And not a little of their success in its erection they ascribe to His Holy Mother, under whose invocation it is placed, with the title of the "Assumption of the Blessed Virgin Mary." The Church is a plain frame building, with the basement under its whole extent. It is 58 by 38 feet, and will seat about 300 persons. The sanctuary is sufficiently large and spacious; on one side of it is the vestry, and on the other the confessional. On the steps back of the altar were six large silver-plated candlesticks and six more of a smaller size; on columns at each side were statues, one of the Virgin holding the Infant, and the other of the Angel Guardian leading a boy. Though the interior of the Church was not quite finished, yet its whole appearance on the day of dedication was neat and chaste, and I am sure that before long the Catholics of the town will complete in good taste what they have so well begun. At half-past ten Right Rev. Bishop Hughes began the dedication, assisted by the Pastor of the Church, the Rev. Mr. McQuaid. Mass was then celebrated. After the Gospel the Bishop preached for about an hour. The Church, and principally its distinguishing feature of Unity, formed the matter of his discourse. It was in his usual clear and forcible style, and whilst plain to the humblest mind in that large audience, the most intelligent and best educated must have felt as they heard coming from the preacher's lips, not the mere figures and flowers of rhetoric, but the solid arguments of reason, that they were in the presence of their Master. The pews and aisles were fairly crammed, while many had to remain round the doors and windows and hear as best they might. I need not say that all were pleased—the Protestants to hear so eloquent a divine and the Catholics to see their Bishop, who had so kindly come to bless them and the Church. The Bishop preached again in the afternoon. Much the greater part of his hearers were persons not belonging to the Catholic Church. They heard explained how Catholics maintained what was so absolutely necessary for their corporate existence, the Spirit of Unity, and how Protestants managed to split and resplit into a thousand and one different and opposite sects. Morristown belongs to the mission of Madison, one of the most interesting of the diocese. Mass had been celebrated here before there was a Bishop in New York, and when St. Peter's was its only Church.

The first Catholics settled near Madison—then and until a late date known by the name of Bottle Hill—towards the close of the last century. They had been obliged to fly from the French West India Islands, at the breaking out of the Revolution in France.

Vincent Boisaubin was the first settler, around whom several families soon located themselves. In one of their houses, in the year 1809, the holy Sacrifice of the Mass was offered up by l'Abbé Vienet, who came out here from New York. The congregation consisted of about twenty-five persons. Previous to this time, the Catholics had been in the habit of going to New York to attend to their religious duties. The settlement was afterwards visited by Father Malou. Somewhat later, Rev. Mr.

The Madison Church and its Offspring. 45

O'Donahoe officiated here regularly every month. After him, the Rev. Father Power attended it. At first, Mass was celebrated in a private house; then the upper part of the Academy was hired and fitted up with an altar, etc. In 1833 Rev. Mr. Herard became the resident pastor. A house was purchased which served the two purposes of a chapel and dwelling. In 1839, at a time when bigotry was rank and prevalent in these parts, and when the scandalous tales of Maria Monk and other abandoned characters were devoured most greedily; when the ladies amused themselves at their tea-parties by piously narrating the horrid doings of the benighted Papists; when the ministers ranted and the newspapers were filled with scurrilous abuse of what their editors were ignorant of, the Catholics of Madison and neighborhood thought it not a bad season for erecting in the midst of all this bigotry a church in honor of God, and as a proof of the strength and vitality of that body of men which almost everybody was so busy calumniating.

They cheerfully gave as far as their means would allow them, but had it not been for the extreme generosity of two sons of the first settler, they would never have had the really beautiful Church which now adorns the village of Madison. It is considered by all as one of the best-finished country churches in the diocese.

All this section of the State was attended from Madison. In 1847 a Church was built at Dover, by Rev. Mr. Senez, and another at Boonton Falls; in 1848, one at Morristown. And now, within the one county of Morris, we have four churches. Is there not here an increase, and has not God blessed this mission?

Should you judge this sketch at all useful, it is at your disposal. Yours most respectfully,

A. C. P.

According to Father McQuaid's estimate in 1849, the Catholics belonging to the Morristown mission, stretching out for miles into the country in every direction except towards Madison, numbered, including babies in arms, about one hundred and twenty souls. The first efforts of the priest were necessarily directed to the salvation of those already within the fold of the Church; but even at this early period conversions were not unfrequent.

In 1843, William Fulton was received into the Church by the Rev. Dr. Ambrose Manahan; and the first convert baptized by Father McQuaid was Mrs. Laurence Johnson.

In 1850 the first festival, or tea-party, as it was called, was held by a few of the ladies of the congregation in what is now Farmer's Hotel in Market Street, then owned by Nathan B. Luse, and used by Isaac S. Runyon for a private school, another floor by the Odd Fellows and Freemasons, and the upper story as a hall.

The brass band of the town furnished the music. There was no dancing. About one hundred and fifty dollars, clear of all expenses, were realized, and Father McQuaid was overjoyed with the result, because it enabled him to pay each of three creditors the fifty dollars he owed.

The first sexton was Mr. William O'Toole, whose

weekly salary was fifty cents. In September, 1850, Father McQuaid opened the first Catholic school in Morristown, with Mr. Tracey, from New York, as teacher. He was one of the old school of hard taskmasters whose theory and practice ran on the line of Solomon's injunction: "Spare the rod and spoil the child."

One Antoine, a Frenchman, brutally murdered his master and his wife, for which he suffered the death penalty. This incident provoked an intense hostility to all foreigners, and, as a matter of course, the Irish were the first victims.

Two poor laborers were driven by threats from their homes and compelled to seek refuge in Mr. Ford's woods, there to linger until the passion of the rowdy element had cooled down.

The Irishmen who worked in Mr. Vail's Speedwell Works were attacked, and more than one scrimmage took place; but the Irish succeeded in defending themselves. This condition of things continued until Mr. Vail took sides with his Irish employees, and gave their shopmates to understand that he would tolerate the question of nationality no longer, and that the persecution must be stopped.

Mr. Vail was not only a thorough mechanic but an upright man, who aided the worthy and defended the weak. Hence it is not surprising to find an endorsement of his policy by those employed in the works conducted by Messrs. Whelpley and Canfield. The following card appears in the *Morristown Banner* of current date:

"THE TEN-HOUR LAW.

"To Ed. W. Whelpley, Esq., and B. O. Canfield, Esq.:

"The undersigned, some of whom have worked for the above twenty years, desire to express their satisfaction with the number of hours they work and wages received.

J. A. Berry, Foreman,	Patrick Doyle, Foreman,
James Murphy,	Lawrence Welsh,
Bernard Welsh,	Bernard Timothy,
John Doyle,	Dennis Foley,
Michael Kinsella,	B. W. Berry.

"MORRISTOWN, N. J., October 31, 1850."

The fire of charity may grow dull but rarely dies out, unless by an overt apostasy. The habit of faith revives when the Spirit of God again broods over it and awakens it into activity. The priests found many who, through no fault of theirs, had not approached the Sacraments for years; and how touching was their joy when the coming of a priest enabled them to rid their conscience of guilt by confession, and to receive into their heart their Lord and God! Such an one was old John McGowan, who for forty years had not knelt to a priest. Father McQuaid shrived the good old man, and the fervor with which he received Holy Communion edified every one.

MOST REV. JAMES ROOSEVELT BAYLEY, D.D.

THE BEGINNINGS OF SETON HALL COLLEGE. 49

In 1853, New Jersey, separated from New York, was raised by the Holy See to the dignity of a diocese, and the Rev. James Roosevelt Bayley was appointed Bishop. This was an important event, not only in the history of the diocese, but in the history of our Parish. Very soon after taking possession of his See, Bishop Bayley purchased the Chegarray School and opened Seton Hall College, with the Rev. Bernard J. McQuaid as its first president. This promotion to a field for which his executive ability admirably fitted him necessitated the severing of the ties which held Father McQuaid to parish work, that he might concentrate his time and talent on the creation of a home where Catholic youth would be thoroughly grounded in knowledge and religion, and where a clergy for the growing needs of the Diocese might be trained under the eye of the Bishop.

Father McQuaid was succeeded by Rev. Father Madden. The wide field of the Madison mission still remained unchanged, and tested to the utmost the physical endurance and zeal of the priest. Father Madden was equal to the rigorous demands of both. It is safe to say that in the three years of his administration the faithful were not neglected, the spiritual wants of the flock were well attended to, while the temporalities were carefully and prudently watched over.

Good Father Madden was forced, as his predecessor, and alas! his successors, to the unpleasant necessity of holding picnics for the purpose of supporting his mission. One of the veterans tells us: "We had a picnic for the children, suggested and conducted by Father Madden. The lunches were all prepared at Mrs. Rogers's, as there was no priest's house here then. The children all met at the old Church and marched in a body down the Mountain road to Mr. Collins's woods, now Mr. Foote's. There were all kinds of games for the boys and girls, and all had an enjoyable time at these picnics." Father Madden, who loved athletic sports, engaged with zest in the amusements, and always carried off the palm in the jumping contests.

From the Baptismal Record it appears the care of the Parish was entrusted at times to the Rev. L. Hoey; and occasional entries indicate that the Rev. Alfred Young, now of the Paulist Fathers, together with the Very Rev. Dean McNulty, and, now and then, the Rev. D. J. Fisher came from Seton Hall College—now the old St. Elizabeth's Convent—to say Mass, catechize the children, and administer to the wants of the congregation. The Morristown Catholics held Father Young in high esteem. His genial manners made him friends everywhere. The young flocked around him. At the sick bed his charm of manner never failed to cheer, and his tender message of patience plucked out the thorn of suffering and substituted the holy calm of Christian resignation.

Father McNulty displayed then as now the burning zeal which no obstacle could stay or hinder. The heat and cold were alike a matter of indifference when it was a question of duty. Were a carriage convenient to help him in his round of duty, well and good. If not, like Chaucer's worthy Pastor,

> "On foot, and in his hand a stave,
> This noble example to his flock he gave:
> That first he wrought, and then he taught;
> Out of the Gospel he that lesson caught."

CHAPTER IV.

THE Rev. L. Hoey, who was appointed to the new Mission of Morristown, cut off from Madison in 1860, was the first Priest to reside permanently here. He stopped at Mrs. Rogers's eleven months, during which time he labored hard and zealously for the erection of the priest's house. His ability as a mathematician attracted the attention of his superiors, and secured for him a professorship in the new college.

The first picnic organized by the newly-appointed Pastor is best described by one who was there:

"On July 4th, 1857, Father Hoey held the first grand picnic in the woods. Bright and early that morning Mr. Collins, Mr. Patrick Dempsey, and Mr. Degan were ready to carry the things to the picnic grounds, where the willing ladies had gone ahead to prepare the tables. Mass was celebrated at nine o'clock, at which all the Sunday-school were present and as many of the congregation as could be. After Mass, headed by Father Hoey, the children, followed by the adults, marched to the grounds. The music was supplied by a fiddler and an Irish piper, and the most prominent features were the breakdowns by the old folks. The enjoyable fun was not to last long, for about four o'clock dark clouds began to gather, and as fast as the provisions could be packed in the wagon they were taken to Mr. Collins's barn, a short distance from the woods. The teams had barely reached shelter when down

REV. L. HOEY.

came the rain. All hastened to the tent which had been erected on the grounds, and under its protection dancing was again resumed. The fun was under good headway when down came the tent on the picnickers' heads; and the white dresses of the ladies were marked with the labelled stamp of the tent-maker. When the storm ceased, the men hung their coats on the limbs of the trees and danced till they were dry. At this picnic chances were given out for the first time. Mrs. J. Doyle had given a cake beautifully iced, which the ladies did not know how to dispose of till Father Hoey came up and started it at ten cents a chance, and in a short time thirty-seven dollars were realized. At the breaking up that evening, all volunteered to return the next night to Mr. Collins's barn and finish the refreshments and dance. The piper was brought in, the cows turned out to the lots, but the horses were left in their stalls to share the fun, and the motto was, 'Drink, dance, and be merry.' And so everybody did. This ended our first picnic."

His efforts to build a priest's house were successful. A lot was purchased from Mr. Hull, editor of the *Jerseyman*, for the sum of one hundred and fifty dollars, and in 1861 operations for the building began. The masonry was done by Cyrus Pruden, and the carpentry by Muchmore & Lounsbury.

About this time the old graveyard was bought from William Collins for five hundred dollars.

The parish school started by Father McQuaid was not allowed to remain stagnant. The school had not, it is true, all the appointments now considered necessary; the rooms were dark, very warm in Summer and correspondingly cold in Winter. A great stove stood in the middle of the room, and a pipe was placed through one of the windows, but not too far out of the reach of the tricky boys. When the tasks became irksome, or the tempting chestnuts strewed the ground, or the ice was in prime condition for skating, a sod conveniently thrust down the stove-pipe checked the draught, filled the room with smoke and gas, and necessitated the dismissal of the school.

When Mr. Tracey severed his connection with the school he was succeeded by Mr. Donlin. Miss Slater, of Massachusetts, and a Mr. Faulkner, whose knowledge of the English language was too limited to make him a successful teacher, were engaged and taught for a short time. These teachers taught previous to 1860.

That the school might be kept together until a competent person was found to take charge of it, Father Hoey himself taught during the vacancy which occurred about the time of his appointment. A Miss McDonald, with sufficient confidence in her ability to teach and rule the masons, painters, plumbers, and carpenters of the present day, presented herself for the arduous position; but a short experience convinced her of the serious mistake she had made.

Mr. O'Neil was then secured; and, although gifted with considerable talent, was forced to resign on account of ill health. To him succeeded Mr. Meehan, who is remembered as "teaching the A, B, C's with the children on his knee, and both teacher and pupil enveloped in the smoke of his pipe." Then appears Mr. Fennessy "in a white shirt, ruffled upon either side of the bosom; this, together with his personal appearance, evoked such a volley of cheers from the scholars that he was mortally offended, and decided to punish severely the unruly children by teaching them only for the short space of a half a day."

The absurd and hateful anti-Catholic and anti-Irish spirit, fed by the ignorance and scheming of preachers and newspaper editors, nourished by others whose intelligence should have served them better, made its sting felt in Morristown, as in almost every village, hamlet, and city of our country. There is a vague tradition of an attempt to destroy the little Church first erected here by the lusty young bigots of that day, possessed of more brawn than brain. But a fanatic is usually a braggart; and the tidings that the miners from Dover were ready to march down to protect the Catholics and avenge any insult offered to them, cooled the courage of the bullies and dissipated their plans. But, from time to time, the old hatred cropped out, especially on St. Patrick's day.

Washington, whom every citizen, and especially those from Fatherland, must venerate, with the instinct of a true patriot recognized the aid he received from the Irish exiles dwelling in the colonies, both in men and money, freely and generously given; and so, first of all, with graceful propriety ordered, in this very spot, the first public recognition in the new Republic of the Saint held in special reverence by the Irish race.

But the old folks who remembered the Teagues and Paddies for their prowess in battle and their gallantry in the camp had passed away. Their ignoble sons forgot the debt they owed to the brave and persecuted race; and not content to let them dwell in peace in a land watered with their blood, they chose rather to insult them whenever opportunity offered.

It were well to strive to forget these indignities; but it is proper to make mention of them, the better to accentuate the forbearance, the Christian charity of our forefathers. It was not unusual to see strung up on a flag-pole or suspended from a tree a stuffed figure to represent St. Patrick, with a string of potatoes about his neck, a whiskey bottle in one pocket and a codfish in the other. It was such a sight that aroused the lion in Patrick Smith as he saw the effigy of his patron swaying in the wind from the flag-staff in the Park. The assuring words and wise counsel alone of Colonel Vail prevented him from cutting down the flag-pole. On a like occasion another Smith, a namesake of Patrick but no relative, saw a similar figure pendent from a tree. His good wife brought him an axe, and down

THE END OF ANTI-CATHOLIC FEELING. 57

came both tree and effigy. The last appearance of this vulgar exhibition was in Market Street, a few doors down from South.

The war, the new generation of the native-born sons of these old exiles, full of the courage of their fathers and excelling them in intelligence, ranking with those who differ from them in creed, and on an equal footing in point of education and social standing, have put a last touch to such puerile ebullitions of bigotry.

An earnest search for reminiscences among the early settlers and the newspapers of the day fails to discover anything worthy of special mention. The outbreak of the war called many of the children of the parish to the front, where they upheld the reputation of their forefathers for loyalty to the flag, bravery in battle, and patience in imprisonment.

Even as late as the War period Catholics were so lightly esteemed that on Thanksgiving, 1861, in a historical sermon, preached by the Rev. David Irving, D.D., in the first Presbyterian Church, Morristown, in an allusion to the religious statistics of this County, he does not even mention the Catholics, who had not only a Church and resident pastor, but likewise a parish school in active operation.

In 1864 the Church was incorporated, the Board consisting of Rt. Rev. James Roosevelt Bayley, the Very Rev. Patrick Moran, the Rev. Lawrence Hoey, Messrs. Henry James and Patrick Rowe.

On the death of Mr. James, December 22, 1864, Mr. William Dwyer was appointed to fill the vacancy.

In 1865 the school was found inadequate for the accommodation of the children, and was enlarged at an expense of eight hundred dollars.

> Times go by turns, and chances change by course,
> From foul to fair, from better hap to worse.

Discord, when it springs from those alien to our faith, is deplorable. There is nothing exceeds in bitterness fraternal strife. So, when dissension divides a parish the whole body seems paralyzed, and only after years of patient endurance does the healthy reaction set in, and the members again resume their functions.

The chastening rod scourged our little flock. The peaceful serenity of the young parish was disturbed; and it is only now, after the lapse of more than a quarter of a century, that the sad memory has passed away. It is not desirable to recall it.

The Rev. James D'Arcy was appointed pastor July, 1867.

Father D'Arcy's magnetism, his winsomeness, were irresistible. Gifted with more than ordinary ability, by careful study he enriched his mind. Of an ardent, generous nature he was strong in his attachments, and while he loved the land of the Stars and Stripes, he could not forget the land of his birth—the Emerald Gem of the Sea.

Rev. P. McGovern. Rev. James D'Arcy. Rev. M. A. Madden.

His eloquence, always of a high order, touched the zenith when telling the struggles, the sufferings, the sad, sad story of Ireland. The last oratorical effort of his too-brief career was his ever-memorable panegyric of St. Patrick in the Cathedral, Newark, on March 17.

Keenly alive to the ennobling traits of his countrymen, he was not insensible of their failings. He realized that to intemperance was, in a large measure, to be attributed their poverty, their misfortunes, and their crimes. Hence he strove mightily against the demon of drink, and succeeded in organizing almost all the men of the parish in a Temperance Society, which for many years made its influence felt, and saved not a few from this dangerous pitfall. To-day there are still with us those who took and never broke Father D'Arcy's pledge.

He was indefatigable in his efforts to spread the Christian virtue of temperance. January 2, 1868, he delivered a lecture in Washington Hall, which was largely attended not only by Catholics but by those not of our faith.

On Saturday, May 21, 1868, "good" Father Madden was prostrated by an apoplectic fit in Newark, and his soul passed away to God on Sunday morning. Father Madden was only forty-three years of age when he died. But in the short span of his ministry he had accomplished much for God. His sympathetic nature endeared him not only to those to whom he was allied by ties of country and religion but who differed from him in belief.

But this great loss was felt in Morristown more than elsewhere. The people here had learned to love, to idolize Father D'Arcy. And now they were to lose him.

On the 2d day of June, in obedience to his Bishop, he left us to assume the pastoral charge of Madison. The grief was wide-spread and the regrets were mutual on the part of priest and people.

At a meeting of the parishioners of the Church of the Assumption of the Blessed Virgin Mary, held at the Church in Morristown, on Tuesday evening, June 2, 1868, Thomas Burke in the chair, the following preamble and resolutions, as submitted by the committee, were unanimously adopted:

Whereas, Our beloved Pastor is about to be removed from us, and feeling it is our duty to express our thanks to him for his earnest labors in our behalf since his arrival in this place, and our sorrow for his departure from our midst; therefore be it

Resolved, That in Rev. James A. D'Arcy we had a zealous and pious priest, a "priest after God's own calling," whose sole anxiety and care was the good of the people.

Resolved, That wherever he goes his memory shall be revered by each one of us, and we shall look back with pleasure to the short but happy time he spent among us.

Resolved, That we shall always obey his holy teachings and imitate his many virtues.

Resolved, That a copy of these resolutions be engrossed and presented to him.

Resolved, That these resolutions be printed in the *True Democratic Banner,* the *Jerseyman,* and *Newark Journal.*

REV. AND DEAR SIR:

We the undersigned, in behalf of your many sorrowing friends and admirers of this parish, and the Temperance Societies here established and so tenderly fostered by you, do hereby beg leave to tender you this address in slight token of our heartfelt gratitude for your most faithful and successful labors in our behalf, during, alas! your brief sojourn in our midst; while at the same time we would thus bear public testimony to our heartfelt and inexpressible regret at the action of our Rt. Rev. Bishop in removing you at this time from the parish. We would not in any event fail deeply to mourn over the great loss sustained in the early death of Father Madden—and alas! how fast has brother followed brother

"From the sunlight to the sinless land";

but now when we remember that his death is the direct cause of our inexpressible bereavement in being compelled to submit to the removal of you, our beloved Pastor, to fill the vacancy thereby created, we can but acknowledge the weakness of all language adequately to express our sorrow at the melancholy event; and while unable to anticipate a period when your removal could be made without filling our hearts with sadness, your departure from among us at the present time seems doubly to be deplored. We cannot but feel that we now, more than ever, require your services and spiritual guidance in order to the preservation of that unity, brotherly love, and harmony of action so essential for the accomplishment of the greatest good, in the different Temperance Societies and religious sodalities formed and nursed by you in this city and vicinity with a parent's tenderest care and solicitude; and, while acknowledging the debts of gratitude due from us to your predecessors in the holy ministration of this parish, we feel compelled from a sense of justice to state that we recall the name of no one of them whose labors have accomplished so much for the advancement of our holy religion in so short a period as during your brief mission of eleven months, during which time we have learned to love and honor you as our Pastor. Fresh in memory will ever remain the recollections of that parental care and tenderness exhibited by you in providing for and watching the growth of our infant T. A. B. Society, until it numbers in its ranks one hundred and thirty members; also, your earnest labors in establishing a branch society, now composed of nearly one hundred members, together with the "Cadet Society" of all the boys in the parish between the ages of ten and eighteen. Upon this, the eve of our separation, with eyes and hearts filled to weeping, with what force do we recall the touching language contained in your farewell address, when alluding to the "inadequacy of words to express the sentiments of the heart"; thus it seems to us now at the thought of being so soon deprived of the ministry and guidance of one who in and out of season has so zealously and unremittingly labored for the highest good. Well we know you looked for an approval higher than that of men, and yet we would not forget that it is "sweet to be remembered" by friends, and that it often happens in this world that too little of love and gratitude are shown in return for kind offices and true devotion to duty in promoting the cause of truth and religion here on earth. Hence we would offer you these expressions of our gratitude, feeble and imperfect as they are, in return for the solicitude so long and often manifested by you for us and those dear to us, for your earnest and untiring exertions in our behalf, and for your anxiety shown that all should know and practise the precepts of our holy Religion. You are now about to reap the reward of our labors in witnessing the grateful sight of your Church filled to overflowing—the evening devotions numerously attended and the children of the congregation trained in virtue and morality to be a blessing to society, their parents, and their Church.

You came among us a stranger, as you truly said, with no recommendation whatever but the dignity of your priestly character. But your faithful labors and self-sacrificing devotion continued to inspire confidence and love among your people until the name and memory of Father D'Arcy are written indelibly upon our hearts. And now, Rev. Sir, in behalf of this parish, we bid you a reluctant but most affectionate farewell.

THOS. W. BURKE, *Chairman*,
CHAS. MEEHAN, *Secretary*.

Michael L. Keefe,   Cornelius Holly,
William Dwyer,   Martin Murphy,
D. A. Roberson,   B. W. Dempsey,
Jeremiah Mulhall,
Committee.

GENTLEMEN: I thank you very much for this your kind and affectionate address. These parting words of yours I will long and reverently cherish. Indeed, if words could give expression to the feelings of my heart, you would have to listen to words expressive of deep and sincere regret; but words, however well selected, and eloquence, however chaste, are at best but cold and lifeless things compared to the ideas they are used to express; and any words of mine on this occasion would fall far short of the emotions which swell up within my breast.

It would indeed be strange if, looking back on the eleven months passed amongst you, I could not find many ties which bind me to this place; ties to sever which makes the sorrow of our parting all the more poignant. Eleven months ago I came to you a stranger, with nothing to recommend me to your favor save the dignity of the priestly character which I bore, and I now freely and gladly admit that since my advent amongst you I have found nothing but kind, manly, honest hearts. When appointed your Pastor, it was a time when such an event was on my part unlooked-for and undesired; my duty, however, was clear, and I accepted the position so kindly tendered; I felt the full force of the compliment it conferred and the deep obligation it created, and if action during these past months always corresponded with intentions and feelings, I would not fail, now at their close, to be altogether unworthy of your affectionate esteem. All I then promised I hope I have fulfilled. I then told you, the first time I addressed you, that all I had to offer was an earnest desire for your well-being and happiness, and a great willingness to labor to help you to attain them; and your presence here this evening more than compensates me for my efforts in your behalf, for I look upon it as a testimony coming from you that the confidence you reposed in me has not been betrayed. Your allusion to my efforts in the cause of temperance recall many things to my mind which I would like to dwell upon. Some of my happiest hours have been spent in laboring for the cause of temperance; in trying to lift up the fallen, encourage the weak, elevate the aspirations of the poor, broken-hearted victims of intemperance. Your kind co-operation always sustained me and my labors were spent on a not unfruitful soil. The work remains—may its influence long be felt!

Gentlemen, a few days more and we are parted; you may sometimes recall my name, and, as your address expresses it, you wish that I will not forget you. I promise it. Other scenes 'tis true await me, and other kind friends will, I hope, bid me welcome; but no length of time, no familiar faces, no loving hearts can break or weaken the solid chain of kindly friendship whose golden links we have been forging for the past few months together.

This your address I thankfully receive as a "souvenir" to be preserved for your sakes. To the efforts I have made in promoting your well-being I ascribe no vain importance; nor do I claim for these efforts any high reward; but it so happens that you have spoken of them in words so kind that I cannot but value highly the parchment which contains them. Long after many of you have passed away—long after even the ink in which these words are penned may have faded, the memory of the words herein written may help to console, animate, and encourage me; and if I should ever have to turn over a dark page in the history of my life may they come to shed the golden radiance of happier days upon it; for, as the poet says:

> "Let Fate do her worst, there are relics of joy,
> Bright dreams of the past, which she cannot destroy.
> They come in the night-time of sorrow and care,
> And bring back the features that joy used to wear.
> Long, long be my heart with such memories filled ;
> Like the vase in which roses have once been distilled :
> You may break, you may shatter the vase, if you will,
> But the scent of the roses will hang round it still."

May your words be such relics of joy—bright dreams of a happy past! May their perfumed breathings ever remain! May they be whispered balm and sunshine spoken! May these—"Benign, blessed sounds"—never die in my heart, but with rising accents may they ever remind me of my duty to ask for you from above long life, prosperity, and happiness.

JAMES A. D'ARCY.

Rev. James Sheeran.

CHAPTER V.

THE insane rage of those who threw off the authority of the Church in the sixteenth and succeeding centuries against everything that the faithful, from the days of the Apostles down to our own time, held most sacred, is and must remain an enigma. In their fury priceless literary treasures were destroyed. Stained windows of exquisite coloring and design, altars, statues, rood-screens, chantries, the testimony of the faith and piety of preceding generations, were beaten into dust or profaned by vile and unholy uses. There was a motive for plundering the beautiful shrines, dazzling with gems and glittering with polished gold and silver. But why attack the Cross? why tear the sign of man's redemption from its rightful place twixt earth and heaven, lifting up the heart from the dross of this world and pointing to the better things of our true home?

The human mind, like a pendulum, sways alternately from one extreme to another. The soul is naturally Christian, and the Church attracts men because they find in her what their hearts crave. Every decade of this century witnesses a closer approach to Catholic dogma and practice. The Cross, a generation ago the distinctive emblem of the Catholic Church, now tops the temples of every sect and denomination.

But this and like changes were not effected without misgivings. People stared and wagged their heads. The journals deemed the subject worthy of grave editorial comment. In a certain newspaper of the county issued November 26, 1868, appears the following:

"It looks curious to see a Cross erected on a Methodist Church. A fine large one of stone shows conspicuously from the new Methodist Episcopal Church. Methodism is a live religion and is making rapid progress. Its clergy are among the most eminent in the land; and as its members have become wealthy they have built churches which are grand in their external appearance, and elegant and comfortable in their interior arrangement. We hope, notwithstanding, that the Methodist Episcopal Church will always have an abundance of seats for the people.

"But the Cross—we hardly know what to say about it. It is there. It looks well. It is in perfect harmony with the rest of the building; and perhaps will be unobjectionable, if no other emblems are indulged in."

The Rev. P. McGovern took charge of the parish on the departure of the Rev. James A. D'Arcy, about October, 1865. Messrs. Patrick Rowe and William Dwyer were reappointed trustees. Father McGovern busied himself with the spiritual interests of the flock entrusted to him. His gentle nature, when aroused by the misdoings of his children, plainly evidenced that he knew how to be severe where leniency failed.

He alone seemed to distrust his own ability; and he was content to see the members of the Church increase, so that crowds filled every nook and corner of the little edifice, and the overflow lingered on the steps, the sidewalk, the street. His ringing voice was heard to good purpose on Decoration Day, 1869, when in the old Cemetery, over the dust of the departed heroes of the Civil War, he told his flock of the duties they owed their Country, and of the reciprocal claim they had to enjoy to the fullest the liberties guaranteed by the Constitution, and to stand on an equal footing with every creed and shade of belief in the land.

His close reasoning and fervid delivery excited wide-spread comment, and made a deep impression on his auditors.

As to building a new church, he was satisfied that it could not be accomplished. "Why," said one of the parishioners—"why, Father McGovern, do you not build a new church, to cost, say, about twelve thousand dollars?"

"A new church! Twelve thousand dollars! Morristown? Nonsense!!" replied the good priest, as he indignantly left the house, accompanied by his dogs.

Yet the new church had to come because it was absolutely needed. The only question was, who should undertake the task?

The very thought of building, of incurring a debt, appalled the pastor and flock. The pastor resigned in the Autumn of 1871, and withdrew from a charge never entirely congenial. The most perfect harmony, however, existed between him and his people; and when he left he was sincerely and deeply regretted.

The Rev. James Sheeran succeeded to the pastorate, October, 1871. Father Sheeran was a born leader of men, an ideal nineteenth century priest. His life was varied by almost every incident that may happen to layman or priest.

Courtly and well-mannered as the aristocracy of the South he loved so ardently; gentle as a woman; brave as a lion; firm and unyielding when conscious of his rights, he scored with biting sarcasm the element, present in every parish, which contributes words instead of money, and thwarts by cavilling the efforts of the pastor whom they are unwilling to aid either by example or encouragement. He certainly was no respecter of men. No obstacle, however great, could turn him aside from his purpose. Fear was an unknown element in his nature. Of this he gave ample proof during the War, when, attached as Chaplain to the corps of General "Stonewall" Jackson, he was never absent from an engagement, was always in the thick of the fight, and ready to impart advice to this greatest fighting general of the Confederacy.

"General," said he one day, during the progress of a bitter fight in the Shenandoah Valley, "why don't you do thus and so?"—detailing a movement which he thought would be effective against the enemy.

"Father Sheeran," replied Stonewall Jackson quietly, "who will be responsible for this battle, Father Sheeran or General Jackson?"

Again, when the yellow fever broke out in New Orleans, and all the Fathers in the house were prostrated, he alone remained to attend the sick-calls; and for weeks never slept in his bed, but napped on a lounge whenever a brief respite permitted.

In attending the sick in tenement-houses he frequently found two or three in the same bed victims of the dread disease. He would lie down between them, and, placing his ear close to their pestilent breath, hear their confessions. Not only did he minister to them spiritually, but prepared the corpses for burial and helped to carry the coffined remains to the dead-wagon.

In the gloom of a deserted, pest-stricken city, an eye-witness of scenes terrible beyond description, without the sympathy or cheering words of a single *confrère*, he never lost heart, but bent his every energy to encourage his brethren, to sustain the afflicted, to provide for the orphan, and bring solace to those whom death and disease had deprived of kindred and friends.

Father Sheeran was one of the most efficient of the Redemptorist missionaries. Possessed of a voice of unusual silvery *timbre*, which he managed with rare skill; witty and forcible in his side-hits and argumentations, he soon became the most popular of the band.

When the war broke out he was South, and, together with Father Smulders of the same Congregation, was assigned by his Superior to attend to the spiritual wants of the Confederates. There was nothing of the gold lace or gilt edge connected with his position. The soldiers' meagre fare was his; their hardships in camp and bivouac he shared. Realizing the importance of the events which were daily happening, he kept an accurate diary, for which at the close of the conflict he was offered a large sum of money by a Southern firm of publishers; this he refused.

After the battle of Winchester, while attending some Union soldiers, he was made prisoner by General Sheridan and confined in Fort McHenry, near Baltimore. Through the influence of Archbishop Spalding he was released, and was again enabled to enjoy the sweet calm of community life. But he never forgave General Sheridan. The fact is that they were alike in temperament, and when the clash came neither would yield. As the General had behind him plenary military power, Father Sheeran was conquered but not subdued.

A brief term of rest, and he was commissioned by his superiors to go to New York and collect funds for the Mission Church about to be erected in South Fifth Avenue, near Canal Street. Owing to a disagreement with his Rector he asked to be allowed to withdraw from the Congregation. His petition was granted, and he was adopted for the Diocese of Newark by Bishop Bayley. Pending a permanent appointment, he assisted in the parish of Hackensack. Such, in brief, is his history to whom the Catholics here are so much indebted.

In October, 1871, Bishop Bayley made him Rector of the Morristown parish. Already far advanced beyond the meridian of life, his naturally strong constitution was weakened by hardships in the field and on the mission. Although providentially preserved from contagion in the yellow-fever epidemic through which he had passed, the awful strain dealt a blow to his health from which he never recovered.

In the month previous to his coming Jeremiah Mulhall was appointed trustee to fill the vacancy occasioned by the death of Mr. Patrick Rowe, September 28, 1867. The economy and prudent administration of Father McGovern had freed the parish entirely of debt; so that the way was clear to proceed with the construction of the new Church.

This task demanded the entire attention of the Pastor. Hence he sought and obtained help from the Passionist Monastery at Hoboken, to attend to the little flock at Baskingridge and Mendham.

Fortunately a suitable site, secured by the wisdom and forethought of Bishop McQuaid, remained on which to erect the house of God, which was to excel all other church buildings in Morristown in size, in beauty and solidity, and to lead the way for the adornment of the temples of worship, and the abolition of the barn-like structures called churches which disfigured our city. Mr. L. J. O'Connor was selected to draw up the plans and design of the new building. In the Spring of 1872 everything was in readiness. The bids were in, the weather was propitious, the congregation in expectation. On May 7 the bids were opened in presence of Father Sheeran and the Trustees. It was found that M. M. Parsons offered to build the Church and furnish all the material for the same for the sum of thirty-seven thousand dollars, exclusive of the Sanctuary windows and altars. As this was thirteen hundred dollars lower than the other bids, the contract, by resolution, was awarded him.

The dead buried in that portion of the site covered by the new Church were reverently removed. A busy throng of laborers dug the foundation, and by June the masonry had progressed sufficiently to permit the laying of the corner-stone. Bishop Bayley administered Confirmation on Sunday, June 30, 1872; and in the afternoon the ceremony, which had been awaited with much anxiety, took place. The weather was all that could be desired. A cloudless sky, the trees and grass garbed in the bewitching splendor of Springtime, the air echoing with the melody of birds and filled with the fragrance of cherry and apple blossoms, the societies, the acolytes, priests, and Bishop arrayed in their

THE CHURCH OF THE ASSUMPTION.—INTERIOR.

vestments, all made an effective and impressive scene. Mr. Lundy, of the Morristown *Republican*, gave a vivid pen-picture of the ceremonies, which is reproduced in its entirety:

"In spite of the intense heat of Sunday last, Morristown was all alive in the afternoon with persons wending their way to the corner of Maple Avenue and Madison Street, where the ceremony of laying the corner-stone of the new Roman Catholic Church was to be performed by Bishop Bayley with imposing ceremonies. A special train over the Delaware, Lackawanna and Western Railroad, from New York, and which arrived at Morristown about noon, brought about one hundred persons, among whom were priests from the Monastery of the Passionist Fathers at Hoboken, the clergy of Seton Hall College and the St. Elizabeth Convent, together with a number of invited guests.

"Bishop Bayley arrived the evening previous, and was a guest at the pastoral residence. On Sunday morning he confirmed over two hundred children belonging to this city, Baskingridge and Mendham. About 2 P.M. the grounds in the neighborhood of the church began to present a wonderful scene of hundreds of people gathered together, a sight somewhat unusual of a Sunday in Morristown. Wagons, in which were crowded all who could obtain room, arrived from Dover, Mendham, Rockaway, Whippany, Baskingridge, Madison, and other places, and took up position around the foundation of the new building.

"Every inch of shaded room was quickly appropriated, and men and boys climbed by scores into the trees that line the grounds. One English elm of extraordinary size contained by actual count fifty-seven of these acrobats. The citizens of Morristown were out in force, and by the time the services commenced fully three thousand persons were about the grounds, all eager to have a good view of the ceremonies. These began at half-past three P.M., the procession, consisting of the Bishop, clergy, and alcolytes, at that hour entering within the limits of the foundations. As soon as the entering prayers were said, the procession took its way to the corner-stone, where is to be reared the tower.

"In front came a priest bearing a large crucifix, and followed by alcolytes dressed in red robes with white surplices. The Bishop was in his full robes, with the mitre upon his head and the golden crook in his hand. He was supported by Rev. Dr. Seton, and behind him came the other priests. Prayers were said by the Bishop and priests, and the former then assisted in placing the corner-stone in position, and, tapping it with his crook, declared it duly laid. The stone is about four feet in length by three wide and ten inches thick. On the side facing Maple Avenue is the inscription, in old English text:

> CHURCH OF
> THE ASSUMPTION,
> JUNE 30TH, 1872.

In the centre of the stone was a receptacle of about ten inches long by six inches wide and deep, and into this a tin box was deposited. In this box was the following manuscript statement:

"'Laying of corner-stone of the New Roman Catholic Church at Morristown, New Jersey.

"Dedicated to Almighty God under the invocation of the Assumption of Our Lady, the Blessed

Virgin Mary, the laying of the corner-stone of this new, spacious, and beautiful edifice was performed on Sunday, June 30, in presence of an immense concourse of people of different denominations, by the Bishop of the Diocese in which it is situated—Right Rev. Dr. Bayley, Diocese of Newark, N. J.

"At the date of this ceremony, June 30, 1872—

"The Holy Pontiff Pius IX. rules the Church;

"The Most Rev. John McCloskey, D.D., is Archbishop of the Province of New York;

"The Right Rev. James Roosevelt Bayley, D.D., Bishop of Newark;

"Rev. James Sheeran, Pastor of the Church;

"Ulysses S. Grant, President of the United States;

"Hon. Joel Parker, Governor of the State of New Jersey;

"Hon. J. W. Ballentine, Mayor of Morristown.

"Architect of the new Church, L. J. O'Connor, of New York City;

"Contractor, Mahlon Parsons; Masons, Shawger & Merrit.

"Ecclesiastics present at ceremony as follows:

"Rev. Monsignor Seton, D.D., of Convent St. Elizabeth Station; Rev. Dr. Wigger, of Madison, N. J.; Rev. Father McCarthy, of Dover, N. J.; Rev. F. Aloysius Blakely, Passionist, West Hoboken, N. J., and others.

"After laying and blessing the corner-stone the Bishop addressed the people for over an hour.

"He said that long since he had made a resolution that he would bless no more corner-stones during the heated term, but, notwithstanding his resolution, he had blessed one a week ago, one on that day, and was engaged for the same service two weeks hence; therefore he thought he should make no more resolutions, or at least should say nothing about them if he did. He said there was no duty connected with his office as Bishop that he performed with more pleasure than blessing the cornerstone of a new church, and he congratulated the Catholics of Morristown that they were to have a new, large, and commodious building erected and dedicated to God, and in which to worship Him; and not the Catholics only, but the Protestants too, he congratulated, as the new Church would be another influence for good in their midst, another altar erected to the Most High, whence faith and justice and purity should emanate to bless the place, and where Protestants could, if so disposed, drop in and hear a lecture or sermon, and become somewhat familiar with the doctrines and teachings of the Catholic Church, in regard to which there was the most profound ignorance even among the most learned and intelligent non-Catholics.

"The Bishop then, in a somewhat humorous way, proceeded to dispose of several illusions under which Protestants were laboring in regard to the Church; as the finding of a Bible by Martin Luther, which led to his conversion, 'when,' said the Bishop, 'at that time no less than forty editions of the Bible had been printed, and no less than nine of them in the German language, and it was impossible that Luther should not have had familiar access to them.'

"And in reference to Confession, he observed that it was probably the belief of every Protestant in Morristown that the priest was paid for his services at confession, 'when,' said he, 'every one of you knows that you not only pay him not a cent, but that he could not take it if offered him, and that if you had all the gold in California the laws of the Church forbid him to touch a cent of it.'

"He alluded to several mistaken ideas which were held as truths by non-Catholics, and hoped the new Church would tend to dispel them.

"In alluding to what he termed the persecutions of the Catholics in Germany, he said that, although no prophet or son of a prophet, he predicted that the Pope would remain in the Vatican, and the Jesuit fathers in Germany, long after Bismarck and the German government were laid in the dust; that the Catholic religion would continue to increase and prosper; that the world could not do without them yet, for to them it looked, as it had always looked, for the maintenance of law, order, the rights of property and stability of government. It was the great conservative party, he said, which was to save the world, and every civilized nation on earth had been converted to Christianity by the Catholics, and in most cases by apostles sent directly from Rome.

"He paid a compliment to the late President Lincoln, with whom he had been acquainted and of whom he had formed a favorable impression, denouncing his murder as a most wicked and foolish act, and he thought the country would have been much better off if Mr. Lincoln had lived.

"Paying his respects to Henry Ward Beecher, who was a schoolmate of his, he accused him of easily floating down the river with the tide without making any effort to stem the current, and patting every one on the back as they floated along.

"The strike for eight hours he alluded to as a delusion and a snare, advising his hearers to have nothing whatever to do with it; to continue to work their old, honest ten hours; 'for,' said he, 'the two hours, if obtained, will be spent in great part in the grogshops, and the manufacturer will be obliged to tax all the articles which you buy at a higher rate in order to continue his business, and eventually it will come out of you after all. He was not used to talking politics, however, and allowances must be made for his remarks in reference to them, as the only politician whom he ever cared much about was Andrew Jackson, and he had been dead twenty years.

"Now, said he, you have commenced to build a new and beautiful church. It is one thing to commence and another thing to finish. The latter could only be accomplished by unity of purpose and action. All must work together. Each one, however poor, could contribute something. Better lay up your treasures in the stones of the new Church than leave it to erect a costly tomb for yourself; for in the latter case, in a few years even, your name would be forgotten, but when dedicated to God in the new Church He would never forget it. It was an act of faith, a treasure laid up in Heaven. He impressed on the minds of his hearers the duty of building as fine and grand a church as possible; that it was the duty of Catholics everywhere to rear edifices consecrated to the ever-living God as grand, as costly and imposing as possible, following the example of the old Christians, who, although poor and needy, had reared those fine old cathedrals in Europe which were to this day the wonder and admiration of the world.

"The Bishop is a well-educated and refined scholar, a man of fine appearance and address, and speaks fluently, pleasantly, and to the point. His remarks were principally of a practical nature throughout, showing a thorough knowledge of subjects treated and also of human nature.

"He held the vast audience in the broiling hot

sun for an hour and a quarter, and dismissed them with his blessing.

"In conversation afterwards with Bishop Bayley we learned that he went to school for some time with Mr. Ezra Fairchild, at Mendham, about thirty-five years ago. Of the older residents of Mendham the Bishop spoke freely, remembering most of them very well, and asking after several of the old families. He declared that to his mind Morristown and Mendham were the prettiest places he had ever seen in his travels."

In closing his remarks Bishop Bayley appealed to the people to aid their pastor in his efforts to raise up a house worthy of the living God by contributing of their worldly goods, and to stimulate the flow of the living spring of charity by their generosity. Three hundred and one dollars were raised. No time was lost. Material, bricks and lumber littered the ground. Higher and higher rose the walls during the Summer; and the copious offerings of the Catholics proved their anxiety to have and build a suitable church.

The time had now come to cut off Baskingridge and Mendham, and relieve Father Sheeran from the care of these congregations. The two offshoots had attained a sturdy and healthy growth, and were able to support a pastor. The Rev. L. Danielou was appointed to take charge of the new mission.

In August of this year, Bishop Bayley, who had labored with so much fruit and zeal, and had accomplished great things for religion since his elevation to the great responsibility of Bishop, was transferred by the Holy See to the Archdiocese of Baltimore. He would gladly have renounced the honor of Primate and successor of Carroll, Kenrick, and Spalding in the illustrious Mother Church of the United States, and abided with his first love; but his protests were in vain. His separation from the field where the best years and efforts of his life had been spent almost snapped his heart-strings. It may, indeed, be questioned if he ever recovered from it. For from that day his health began to decline. He was, as he himself said, "too old a tree to be transplanted." His bluff, honest character would not permit him to conceal his dislike of his new charge. He lost no occasion to laud everything he had left behind at the expense of everything that surrounded him. Comparisons never conciliate; and so, while commanding the respect of clergy and people by his ability, zeal, and family prestige, Archbishop Bayley never won their love. His loss was keenly felt by his old flock. When he was invested with the pallium the priests of his dear Diocese of Newark were present almost to a man. The Archbishop never ceased to love the priests and flock of Newark with the ardent affection of a father. He was always ready to receive them, to stop all other business to entertain them, to give them precedence and attention over even great dignitaries.

In 1874 two young priests, who had lately been ordained in Seton Hall Seminary, one of whom had served the Bishop's Mass in the Newark Cathedral as a boy, and, later on, was to hear the last Confession of the Archbishop, on their way to visit St. Charles's College, stopped at the archiepiscopal residence to pay their respects to their former Bishop, who had just returned from St. Louis.

The present Cardinal, his successor, then Bishop of Richmond, was awaiting him in the parlor. No sooner had the visitors from Newark been announced than the Archbishop hastened from his study to welcome them, and with an arm around each ushered them into his room. Here, much to their embarrassment, feeling that they were instrumental in detaining the distinguished visitor, Archbishop Bayley entertained the young priests and parted with them regretfully after a long and delightful chat.

To his death he maintained these friendly relations, and he was never so happy as when, in the old Bishop's home, he recalled old events, surrounded by the faces of those who had shared his toil and merit in the trying hours of his episcopate.

The unexpected oncoming of the cold weather necessitated a halt in the building of the new Church. A nipping frost came so unexpectedly that there was no opportunity to protect the walls. All the rigors and unpleasantness of an exceptional Winter prevailed. Successive frosts and thaws impaired what, under other conditions, would have been an unexcelled piece of work; and when, in the early Spring of 1873, labor was resumed, much had to be rebuilt. To the credit of the contractor be it said that he spared no effort to put up a structure which would at the same time attest his skill and give satisfaction to those who employed him.

In February, 1873, the news flashed across the water that the Administrator, the Very Rev. M. A. Corrigan, was named Bishop of Newark by the Holy See. To Bishop McQuaid, then on a visit to Seton Hall, Doctor Corrigan turned, after reading the despatch sent him by Mr. McMaster, of the New York *Freeman's Journal:*

"Is there no escape?" said he.

"None," replied the Bishop; "you must accept the burden."

Archbishop Bayley's keen and unerring estimate of men secured for the important Diocese of Newark a worthy successor. Trained under his own eye, and drilled into the methods which shaped his own administration, and won for the Diocese the stately position it now holds in the Church of the United States, Michael Augustine Corrigan brought natural executive ability, ripe scholarship, and solid piety to the exalted dignity which was forced upon him. Dr. Corrigan's preparatory studies were made under the venerable Father O'Reilly at St. Mary's College, Wilmington, Delaware; and completed in the nursery of Bishops, Mt. St. Mary's, Emmittsburg, Mary-

Most Rev. Michael Augustine Corrigan, D.D.

land, from which he was graduated in 1859. He was chosen one of the little band sent by the Bishops to form the nucleus of the American College, which they hoped to establish in the centre of Catholic unity. His gentle manner, his application and singular purity of life, attracted the attention and won for him the respect and confidence of his classmates and superiors. On one occasion, when the little band of American students was in the presence of Pius IX., his Holiness singled out young Corrigan, whom he called "the American St. Aloysius."

He was ordained priest September 19, 1863, in the Cathedral Basilica of St. John Lateran, by Cardinal Patrizzi.

On his return to his native land, August, 1864, he was made professor of dogmatic theology and Holy Scripture in the Seminary of the Immaculate Conception, South Orange, N. J.

When the See of Columbus, Ohio, became vacant, the prelates looked to him as one worthy in every way to fill the difficult position, and on their recommendation he was preconized by Pius IX. The great dignity, the responsibilities, overwhelmed the young priest. He pleaded everything, his youth, his inexperience, with his own Bishop, with Archbishop McCloskey, and finally, yielding to his entreaties, the Holy Father acceded to his wishes. For a little while he was safe.

To his work in the Seminary he was entirely

devoted. The transfer of Father McQuaid to the Diocese of Rochester, as its first Bishop, enlarged his opportunities and entailed new responsibilities on Doctor Corrigan. He was made president and bent every effort, every talent, to bring the College up to the high standard to which its founders aspired. On the elevation of Archbishop Bayley he was made Administrator, as he had exercised for some time the duties of Vicar-General. In May he was consecrated Bishop, in St. Patrick's pro-Cathedral, Newark, by Cardinal McCloskey. The Sanctuary, the aisles were crowded with representatives of the hierarchy, and the clergy of his own and other dioceses. The Rt. Rev. Bernard J. McQuaid preached an eloquent sermon. And thus the young Bishop was launched on his new work; and bravely did he face the troubles and anxieties which the financial straits of St. John's Church, Orange, caused him at the very outset of his administration.

The fragrance of the chrismatic unction had not been spent when he came to Morristown to exercise for the first time one of his episcopal functions. The mechanics had responded to the urgent appeals of Father Sheeran; the last touch of the brush had been given, the last blow of the hammer heard, the new Church was, at length, ready for dedication.

On Ascension Thursday, May 22, 1873, a leaden dulness overspread the sky. The rain fell in torrents. Without, everything was dismal and sombre, but within the walls of the church what joy filled the hearts of pastor and flock! Bishop Corrigan solemnly blessed the new Church, and the ceremony was followed by solemn Pontifical Mass. After the Gospel the Rev. Dr. Edward McGlynn preached from the text: "Thou art a priest for ever according to the order of Melchisedech" (Psalm cix.) There was a large attendance of priests and people. The music rendered during the Mass was by a choir selected from the different churches in Newark. Thus, twenty-five years from the erection of the first humble sanctuary, the pioneers who survived saw their first efforts eclipsed, the tender shoot developed into a mighty tree, and a dwelling-place enshrining the Holy of Holies which far exceeded their hopes and expectations. The Lord had, indeed, builded the house, and their labors had not been in vain.

CHAPTER VI.

AMPLE room was afforded in the new Church for the accommodation of all.

In point of fact, the congregation seemed to be lost in it; and not a few were heard to say that Father Sheeran had made a mistake in building it of such large dimensions. In style it borders on the Gothic, and taken altogether is well proportioned and adapted for its scope. It is built of brick, made in the vicinity, trimmed with Ohio sandstone. Its dimensions are one hundred and twenty-two feet in length by fifty-two in breadth. The spire, disfigured at the angles of the base by meaningless pinnacles, is almost graceful.

In apportioning the pews Father Sheeran had regard to the priority and long service of the pew-holders. The veterans had the first choice regardless of their poverty or slender incomes, the priest judging rightly that their claim was superior to all others.

The old frame structure had served its purpose well; it was now altered for the accommodation of the school children.

Miss Maggie O'Brien was employed as teacher when Father Sheeran assumed charge of the parish, and by the engagement of Miss Robbins suitable provision was made for the increased number of children. She enjoys the reputation of being one of the best teachers the parish school ever had. In October, 1873, Thomas W. Burke was appointed Trustee.

Miss Robbins was succeeded by Miss Susan Coxe. The school work was progressing favorably, as the pastor, freed from the cares and anxieties of building, was enabled to throw into it his old experience; and he soon convinced the children that he expected them to respond to the efforts he was making for their advancement. The teaching staff was at this time Mr. Coyle for the boys, and the Misses Coxe and O'Brien for the girls.

As the expenses of the new building had exceeded the amount of contributions it was necessary in July, 1874, to raise a loan of fifteen thousand dollars. Mr. Thomas Degan was appointed Trustee October, 1874. Scarcely a breath of discord disturbed the harmony of this period. A great effort is followed by the lull of repose.

The machine-works at Speedwell, which had given employment to a goodly number and a thorough training to the youth whose talents were towards mechanics, were removed. The bell was silent. The historic building that recalled the birth of the locomotive—the mighty civilizer of the world—the telegraph, the submarine cable, to which are for ever linked the names of Vail and Morse, were abandoned. Nature was to drape their crumbling walls and decaying timbers with creeping vines and wild flowers; and the waters rushing through the unused flume sobbed a passing requiem. A great blow was struck to the only industry in the community, from which it has not since recovered. Many were compelled to leave the parish, and sever ties begotten of a common kinship and common trials.

The building of the Asylum at Morris Plains made an opening, and gave employment to many.

The obscure town hidden among the hills of Morris County, blessed with a ceaseless flow of purest water, sheltered from the rude blasts of Winter, began to attract the attention of physicians and health-seekers.

The salubrious air brought back the glow of health to the sick, and invigorated the strong. It was found soothing to weak lungs; and many who had sought, in vain, relief from their infirmities abroad, or in the debilitating regions of our Southern climate, regained steadily their robustness, and from transient visitors became rooted to the soil. The great natural beauty of Morristown; its gently sloping hills, crested with oak, elm, and maple; its well-laid-out and well-kept streets, invited the attention of the capitalist and induced the wealthy of the great Metropolis to make it their home. The tide of good fortune was setting in. Villa sites were bought, and architect and landscape gardener combined to adorn our City and its surroundings. The fascination of the locality is complete. Its children find elsewhere no attraction; and the stranger abides here with content.

The harvester Death had been busy, and young and old had paid the last penalty. The little graveyard was filled. The people clustered beneath the shadow of the Church; and even as a sanitary measure it became necessary to look around for another burying-place.

In the Spring of 1875, a beautiful spot, about a mile distant from the city, and containing about fifteen acres, was selected. The rolling character of its surface, the dense forest and thick undergrowth, required considerable toil and outlay of money. A portion was surveyed and laid out for immediate use. It lies between the angle formed by the Whippany and the Columbia roads. From its highest elevation the City may be seen stretching east and west; and to its tranquil boundaries are borne the subdued tones of the Angelus bell.

The failing strength of Father Sheeran incapacitated him from attending to his work; and when he applied to Bishop Corrigan for an assistant, the Rev. Joseph Vassallo was appointed.

An attempt was made to rid the parish of the debt by assessing it *pro rata* upon all the adults of the congregation. Many responded generously, and direct donations to the amount of two thousand six hundred and ninety-one dollars were received; but the Pastor's efforts did not avail. The amount donated was but a drop in the bucket; so the burden remained.

An unfortunate incident happened to disturb the

harmony then reigning. An Italian who, in a fit of jealous rage, had murdered a compatriot was found guilty of murder and sentenced to death. Father Vassallo attended him in his last moments, and Father Sheeran sought to prevent an autopsy after the execution. This, it was claimed, was a legal necessity. But Father Sheeran did not concur with this view, and refused to receive the body and give it Christian burial. As is customary in such controversies, there resulted not a little friction and bad feeling.

An important step for the welfare of the children was now made. Vocations began to abound, and the Novitiate of the Sisters of Charity at Madison was fitting the candidates for their responsible duties as Christian teachers.

From every side came petitions to Mother Xavier for teachers. The influence of the children of St. Vincent had already made itself felt in the parish schools and orphanages of the Newark diocese.

Father Sheeran's claim was recognized, and arrangements were made in September, 1875, to send two of the Sisters from the mother-house every day. A little room was added to the school, and fitted up with a stove and cupboard. Here, after the noon dismissal, the Sisters prepared their lunch in light-hearted gaiety and contentment. Their hallowing influence over both boys and girls was at once apparent. The success of the school was assured.

In November the Rev. Joseph M. Flynn, whose

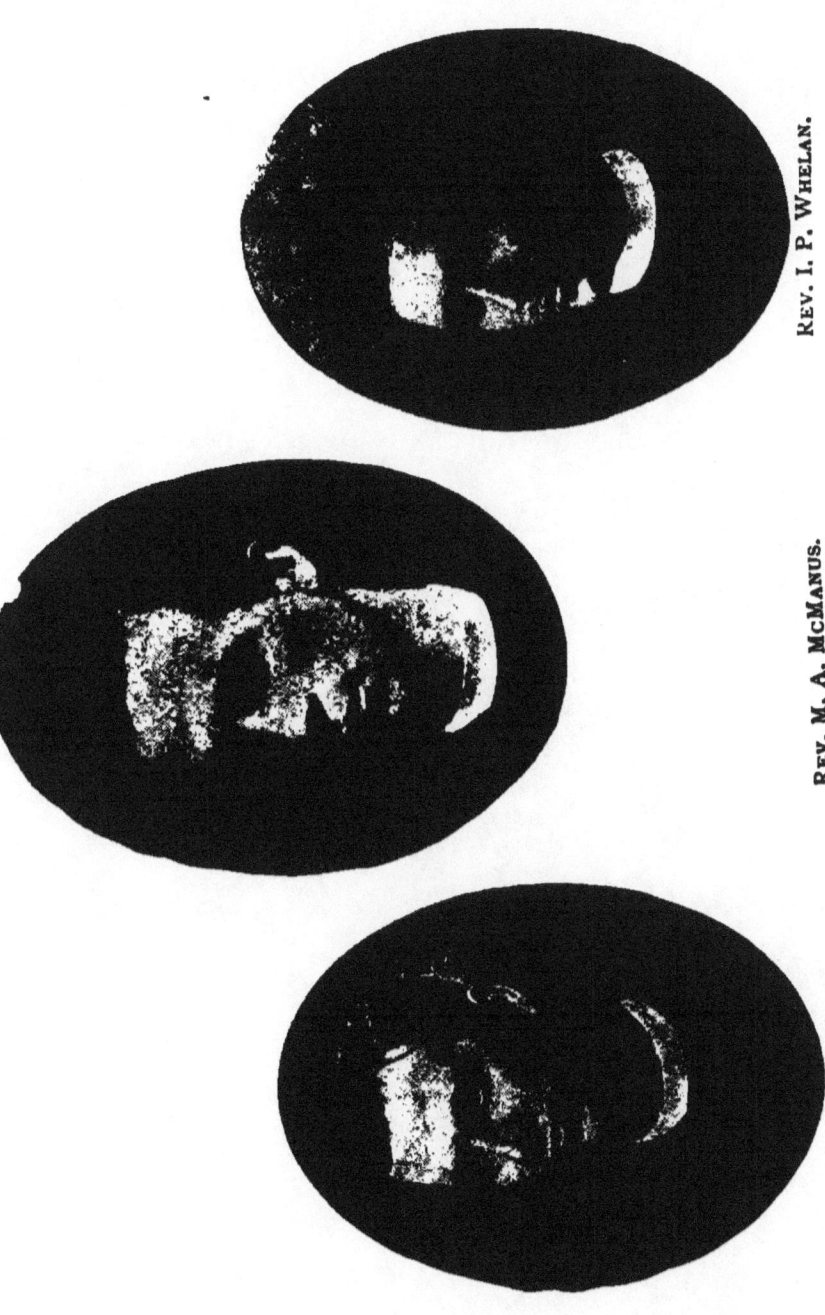

shattered health had brought him almost to the verge of the grave, was sent to Father Sheeran as assistant in place of Father Vassallo. The pure air, the solicitude and attention of Father Sheeran, had their effect, and so rapidly that himself and friends were filled with astonishment. Under the advisement of the pastor Father Flynn organized a Temperance Society among the young men of the parish. His stay, however, was too brief to accomplish much in this direction; for, in February, 1876, he was transferred to St. Peter's Church, New Brunswick. The Rev. Samuel Walsh filled a brief appointment. He was succeeded by the Rev. Michael A. McManus.

The time was now favorable for Father Sheeran to take a well-earned rest. He longed to visit again the land of his birth, and to see once more the scenes and companions of his childhood. The parishioners made up a comfortable purse, and he started on his voyage with the prayers and good wishes of his flock. While abroad he visited Paris and purchased the beautiful vestments still preserved. The demon of discord set to work on his return, and a passing unpleasantness marred the pleasure he experienced at being once more with his people.

The good old man, while possessing unusual shrewdness and perspicacity, was easily imposed upon, especially by so-called friends. Honest and sincere himself, he never dreamt of questioning the sincerity of the motives of those by whom he was surrounded, and in whom he reposed the fullest confidence. He had never learned, nor, having learned, could he ever apply, Talleyrand's maxim: "Treat your friend as though he may one day be your enemy; and your enemy as though he may one day be your friend. He paid the penalty, and saw his mistake when it was too late.

The Rev. J. M. Giraud succeeded Father McManus. The Rev. J. J. Schandel filled a temporary appointment about September, 1877. He was superseded in November by the Rev. J. Poels.

In the early fall Archbishop Bayley returned to seek in New Jersey some relief for his ailments. His disease puzzled the doctors. There did not seem to be any organic trouble; and still it was evident that he was very ill.

He was welcomed by the Bishop and priests of the Cathedral, and all the care that love and veneration could prompt were lavished upon him. But in vain. Medical skill availed naught. He languished, lingered from day to day, and died October 4, 1877.

James Roosevelt Bayley, born outside the threshold of the faith, was descended from the oldest Knickerbocker families, whose ancestors came over with Hendrik Hudson and settled on Manhattan Island. Brought up in the Episcopal Church, his soul, naturally Catholic, was earnest in the search after truth. With his natural leaning to piety, he determined to consecrate himself to the service of

God in the ministry. His early education was received in the once-celebrated school at Mendham, N. J. Thence he proceeded to Amherst College, Massachusetts, and later on we find him entered at Trinity College, Hartford, to prepare himself for the ministry of the Episcopal Church. His studies, however, were completed under Dr. Jarvis, at Middletown, Conn. In due course of time he was ordained and elected by the vestry Rector of St. Peter's Church, Harlem. Here his dignity of character, warm heart, and kindly manners won for him hosts of friends. While devoting himself with all the ardor of his nature to his duties, he still found time to gratify his taste for reading. History, biography, and patristic literature gave him especial pleasure. Visiting one day at Fordham the home of a poor Irish laborer, on a mission of charity, he met a Catholic priest, with whom he formed a friendship which lasted during life. The two had many a theological bout and tilt, and the result was that between the friendship of the good priest and the works of the Fathers—more than all by God's grace—we find him resigning his charge in the fall of 1841 and resolved on going to Rome in search of the truth. He was not long in the Eternal City before he was convinced that there was no truth outside the Catholic Church, and that he had hitherto been following a will-o'-the-wisp. He asked to make a retreat. He was baptized conditionally and received into the Church by the

Jesuit, Father Esmond, and confirmed the same day, April 28, 1842, by Cardinal Franzoni, in the chapel formerly the rooms of St. Ignatius. We next find him in the grand Seminary of St. Sulpice, Paris, where he made his theological studies. Returning to New York after a narrow escape from shipwreck, he was ordained priest March 2, 1844, by Bishop Hughes. In 1845 he was made the Bishop's Secretary, for which his habits of exactness and his eye for detail had admirably fitted him. During this interval it was, we believe, that he acted as President and Vice-President of Fordham College, and for a time exercised his priestly duties in Staten Island. There was then a steady flow of emigration setting towards the United States. The ships were crammed with living freight; the food was bad, the air below decks foul, and the voyage long. Little wonder, then, as the vessel entered the port of New York, many a poor fever-stricken emigrant lifted his languid eyes but to gaze on the stony walls of quarantine and the restless waters of New York Bay.

Here Father Bayley worked with indefatigable zeal. For the faithful he had the comforts of the Sacraments; for all a kind smile, an encouraging word.

He gave to the press about this period *The Life and Letters of Bishop Bruté* and *A Sketch of Catholicity in New York*. Both works were honored with a second edition. In 1853, the new diocese of Newark was formed, and Father Bayley was appointed its first Bishop. Together with Rev. John Loughlin, preconized to the new See of Brooklyn, and Rev. Louis de Goesbriand to the new See of Burlington, Vt., he was consecrated in St. Patrick's pro-Cathedral, New York, October 30 of the same year, by Archbishop Bedini, Papal Nuncio. His new diocese was a fallow field: his priests few, his churches encumbered with debts—many already in the hands of the sheriff—his people poor and despised. He brought to surmount these obstacles a vast experience, a willing heart, and a firm trust in God. While not gifted with extraordinary brilliancy, he possessed that most rare gift, common sense. His keen eye soon read the character of all those with whom he came in contact; his judgment was rarely at fault, and in his forecast of future happenings he seemed to have been gifted with prophetic certitude. Always vigilant in the discharge of his responsibilities, and realizing the necessity of discipline in aiding to build up with the rude material at hand the magnificent structure of a Catholic diocese, his heart tempered the dictates of his mind and led him to exercise leniency at times when severity would have been excusable. An omnivorous reader, he possessed the rare faculty of treasuring up the gems he met with in the classics; and, as he had travelled extensively, his portrayal of men and things was most vivid and realistic. The anecdotes handed down from father to son touching the quaint manners and customs of the old Patroons were ever on his tongue, and told very frequently, in truth, but always with that quiet humor and pleasing twinkle in the eye which secured for him the attention and laughter of his audience. He easily adapted himself to his surroundings. It mattered not where he found himself: in the back-country town, standing on the platform waiting for the train, he was as much at home with the folks lounging around the depot and differing from him in religion as he was with his brothers in the hierarchy. Any one might approach him. The timidity of childhood was dissipated by his attractiveness; and when he visited the schools, as he did frequently when at home, the shyness of the boys and girls melted away before the pleasant sunshine of his smile. Rich and poor alike, the righteous and the unrighteous, the learned and the ignorant, the Catholic and unbeliever, were one and all cordially received by him, and left his presence soothed and comforted by his kind and cheerful words. If not demonstrative, he was strong in his attachments. He loved the old friends, the old places, the old-fashioned ways of doing things. Although a convert, his faith was simple as a child's, and as strong and robust as an early Christian's.

Foreseeing the necessity of Christian education, he set to work to establish parochial schools. To his mind the school should be first, the church after; for, as he was wont to say, a parish without a school is not worthy of the name. That God blessed his labors is evident from the fact that twenty-five years later, of all the dioceses of the United States, Newark ranked third, if not second, in having the largest number of pupils attending parochial schools. The little grain of mustard-seed—the community of the Sisters of Charity established at Madison—had grown and spread until at the time of his death there were about three hundred and seventy-five Sisters in the Diocese. His vigilance and activity were everywhere felt. He would stroll into Sunday-school on a Sunday afternoon and chat with the children—showing them his ring or telling a story; the next Sunday he would be perhaps a hundred miles away.

From the Seminary at Seton Hall—the object dearest to his heart—have gone forth a band of young, active, well-trained priests, animated with his zeal, and stimulated by his works and by his example—to be spent for Christ's sake in saving the souls of men. He lifted up his flock from their obscurity and won for his religion, despite deeply-rooted and bitter prejudice, a place of honor and esteem. All might not succumb to the convincing force of his sermons, but all readily yielded to him that respect and reverence which superior minds command without seeking. His presence—so full of majesty and dignity—attracted the admiration of all; yet he was as simple and as approachable as a child. You might see him standing on Washington

Street, returning from his visitation, or from a walk, in conversation with an old colored servant, his face lit up with that kindly smile so peculiarly his own; and often, after celebrating Pontifical Mass, did he come to the rescue of some poor old creature struggling with the considerate clergyman or sexton, and send her off in joy with a "God bless you, my child."

Convening a synod of the clergy in Baltimore, he enacted many salutary regulations, particularly respecting the clerical dress and mixed marriages. Though not a musician himself, he, first of all his predecessors, and, it might be added, alone of all his brothers in the Episcopate, carried out the recommendations so many times expressed in the councils of Baltimore: installed in his Cathedral a male choir, and had the majestic liturgy of the Church sung in her own grand and devotional melodies.

Illness obliged him to go abroad for relief; and, after seeking in vain the restoration of his health in Vichy and Homburg, he returned to his old home to take up temporary quarters in his old rooms in Newark, August, 1877. His ailment baffled the skill of the physicians, who waited on him with tender devotion. Despite the pain from which he was never free, he was always so cheerful, so full of anecdote, that it was difficult to believe him ill. Finally, October 4, 1877, fortified by the Sacraments of the Church he loved so well, in his old room, in his old bed, in his dearly loved Newark, surrounded by Bishop McQuaid, Archbishop Corrigan, Rt. Rev. G. H. Doane, Fathers Toomey, Flynn, and Sheppard, his pure soul was loosed from its prison of clay, and was in the presence of its judge. Full of faith and good works, James Roosevelt Bayley went to receive his reward.

The grief and sorrow of the Catholics were shared by those not of our faith. All joined in testifying their respect for his sterling worth. An obituary which appeared in one of the leading Newark newspapers gave a very true estimate of his character:

"Those who knew personally Bishop Bayley knew a disciple of Christ full of benignity, humility, and loveliness; with a quiet dignity that always commanded respect for him, and yet a measure of sympathy and tenderness that attracted all towards him as to a friend. They knew a prelate endowed with wisdom, learning, high administrative ability and zeal for the propagation of the form of Christianity in which he believed, combined with all consistent toleration of the faith of others; a gentleman of culture with manners simple, refined, and agreeable. It is not often that one meets a man who measures up closer to the common ideal of a wellrounded, perfect character. For instance, he was bold and aggressive like St. Paul; with convictions that manifested themselves in unceasing toil, despite obstacles and discouragements. The number of churches which sprang up under his rule in the Diocese, Seton Hall College, the Convent School at Madison, the asylum for children, the hospital, the schools in every parish, testify that he was 'in labors most abundant.' At the same time he was loving, like St. John. He had a most charitable spirit. While a firm believer in the Catholic Church, he desired peace and friendliness with all Christians, disliked controversies and demonstrations likely to stir up bitter contentions. In all things was he conciliatory when conciliation was not compromise. When he first came to Newark and began his work of establishing here the Catholic religion, no little opposition was excited among people who regarded the Roman Church as a foreign institution and a foe to liberty and enlightenment. He alluded to this in his address in the Cathedral on the day of the consecration of the edifice two or three years ago, and gladly testified that this bitter feeling against him in time had passed away, and that for many years had he found among Protestants many warm friends. It passed away because instead of meeting the outside opposition with polemical sermons or pamphlets, or showing in any way a belligerent spirit, he quietly went on with his official duties. He chose, by founding Seton Hall College for the higher education of Catholic youths, St. Elizabeth's Academy at Madison, and other educational institutions, to make his answer to the charges raised against the cause which he represented. As a preacher Archbishop Bayley was effective and pleasing. His imposing presence would have fixed upon him the attention of a congregation though his address had been less engaging. Of full height, with a well-rounded but not heavy figure; a massive, handsome head; a forehead broad and high, from which the hair was brushed back; a face fine in every feature, and pleasing in its expression of mild dignity, goodness of heart, and intellectual strength, the Archbishop was commanding in person, whether in plain broadcloth or wearing his rich canonicals, with the mitre upon his head and the golden crosier in his hand. In direct and often plain language he gave vigorous expression to his thoughts. His discourses might be beautiful in diction; they were sure to be forcible and instructive. In delivery he was intensely earnest, and yet calm and easy, for culture ever tempers and moderates.

"The body of the dead prelate was clothed in pontifical vestments and placed in state before the high altar of St. Patrick's Cathedral. On Friday morning Bishop Corrigan sang the Requiem Mass, and immediately thereafter the body was taken to Baltimore, whence, after a solemn Requiem Mass in the Cathedral, the remains were conveyed to Emmittsburg, Md., and placed beside his aunt, Mother Seton."

CHAPTER VII.

IN May, 1878, Father Poels was assigned to the pastoral charge of Mendham and Baskingridge. Morristown had now to depend on St. Michael's Monastery, Hoboken, and various Fathers came thence to minister spiritually to this charge, as Father Sheeran grew more enfeebled.

The spirit was willing, but the body was worn out. It is a pitiable sight to witness the struggle of a brave man, who has been a leader among men and has always been first in the race—it is pitiable to see him strive to keep up. In vain does he spur on the once-willing steed. The race for him is spent, and the day of triumph over. The work was still here, his heart was in it, but nature had been tested to the extreme limit. If he failed the fault was not his.

In August, 1880, the Rev. Arthur Henry, a young priest in the very bloom of his ministry, but in the grasp of death, was sent to try the benefits of our mountain air.

In his brief career he had labored hard, and presaged a life rich in results for the Master of the vineyard.

The Rectory built by Father Hoey had long inconvenienced both pastor and curate. In fact, the only room the assistant had was of such narrow and limited dimensions that, when furnished with a bed,

THE SISTERS' HOUSE.

the priestly belongings and a chair, there was just about room to turn around. When desirous of studying or writing a sermon the parlor was at his disposal; and, more than once, the unhappy curate had to retire—breaking off an eloquent passage in the sermon he was working out for the following Sunday—or scattering to the winds the few sentences he had laboriously acquired, to permit a visitor to transact his business with the Pastor.

It was determined to extend the Rectory at a cost of three thousand dollars. Meanwhile the insidious disease which had fastened on Father Henry prostrated him. It seemed as if his purgatory had to be passed here; for added to his lung trouble came an attack of the measles. And as he lay in bed tossing with fever, worn out with want of sleep, his ears were assailed by the piercing ring of the trowel and the heavy blow and thud of the hammer.

He passed away September 6, 1880, leaving behind the precious memory of rare virtue, disinterested zeal, and of a character rich in manly qualities. His funeral was largely attended by the priests of the Diocese, and by the young men of Elizabeth, to whom he was specially endeared because of his efforts in their welfare.

The priest's house, now more roomy, was more comfortable. But while those improvements made his abode more pleasant, and contributed to his contentment, they availed naught in restoring Father

Sheeran's health. In March, 1881, he received as a helper the Rev. Ronald B. MacDonald, large of frame and large of heart. It is not possible to exaggerate the kindness of Father MacDonald to his venerable superior. He tried in every way to relieve him of all anxiety and worry; and his zeal and activity awakened new life in the parish. Every want of the old priest was anticipated, every yearning of his heart gratified. But the end was at hand. The poet Whittier has written of

> "The weariness of unshared power,
> The loneliness of greatness,"—

and how well the lines apply to the priest! The incessant, unremitting discharge of the gravest of obligations, the saving of immortal souls; the isolation of his position, looked up to for counsel and advice, and with few around him to whom he may go in trials and perplexities; he, who must be all to all in difficulties and doubtings, is left to cut the meshes, for his individual ability is regarded as superior to that of all combined. In affliction he is without sympathy, for he is thought to have steeled his heart against the loving impulses which the ordinary mortal is weak enough to betray and not strong enough to overcome; in sickness and death he is without prayer, for his long familiarity with grace-giving fountains seems to exempt him from the help others stand in need of. Like St. John, he pillows his head on the breast of Jesus;

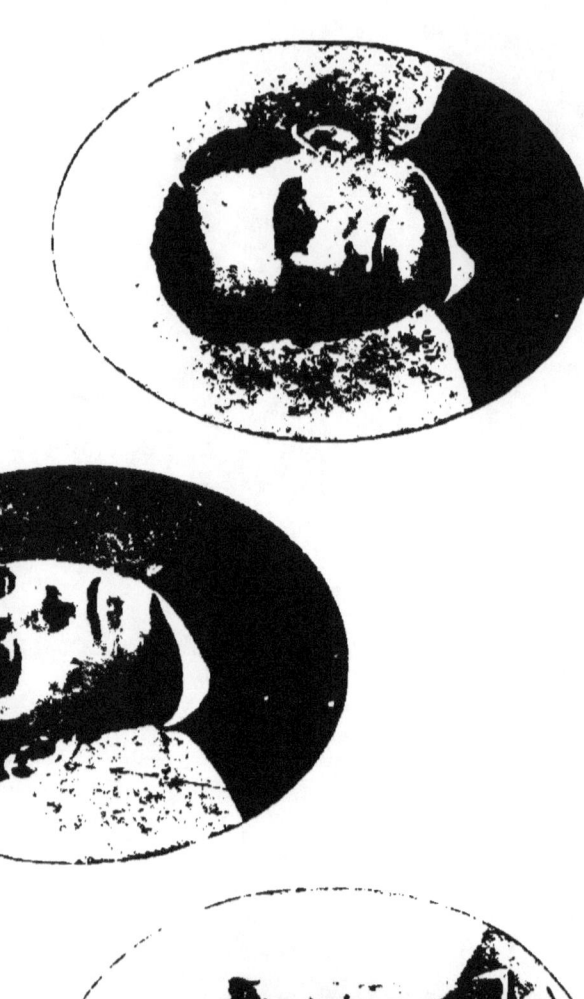

but, unlike the beloved disciple, he is still peccable and needs the succor of prayer this side and beyond the tomb.

On Sunday, April 3, the trials of Father Sheeran terminated; and the good priest, full of merit, comforted by the holy Sacraments, went to his reward. At the Masses Father MacDonald astonished the congregation by announcing the approaching death of their Pastor and asking their prayers in his behalf.

While the body became weaker and weaker his mind was still clear, as he frequently inquired about the affairs of the parish. In the afternoon it was evident that he had not many hours to live; again at Benediction he was recommended to the faithful; and, when Father MacDonald returned to the rectory, the aged Pastor was in his death agony. About four o'clock, peaceful as a child, without pain or struggle, his soul passed into the hands of his Judge. Father Sheeran was dead.

The joys of the approaching Easter were overshadowed in gloom. The sadness of Holy Week was intensified by the personal grief of the members of the parish. The one theme was his virtue, his kindness of heart, his labors for their good.

The men of the parish organized and appointed watches to guard the remains of the good priest until he was consigned to Mother Earth. Preparations were made for the funeral, which, on account of the solemnities of the week, was fixed for Wednesday. The immediate cause of his death was apoplexy.

Born in Temple Mehill, County Longford, Ireland, 1813, he was therefore in the sixty-eighth year of his age at the time of his death. At the age of twelve he left his home and friends in Ireland and went to Canada, and from this time he shaped his career, began the battle of life and pushed his way upward by his own exertions.

After spending two years in Quebec he took up his residence in New York, where he soon found employment.

Despite his daily cares and application to business, he found time to engage in good works. He attached himself to the Sunday-school of St. Mary's Church, Grand Street, and conscientiously discharged for a long time the duties of teacher. As the tide of emigration was setting westward, he was borne along, in the hope of bettering his condition, to the country beyond the Ohio, then considered the far West.

For many years he taught school for the Redemptorist Fathers in Monroe, Michigan, and in this work he was eminently successful. Educated in the stern school of adversity and cast upon his own resources at an early age, he was in full sympathy with his scholars, whom he desired to spare the trials he had experienced in his own life. In addition to the onerous work of teacher he added the responsibility of editor; and he was for a long time a frequent correspondent of the *Freeman's Journal*. His views reflected his own sturdy character and boldness, and gained for him a wide reputation. It is not to be wondered at that one with his strong personality and decided views should enter the arena of politics.

Whilst he never would consent to accept office, he was ever ready to do battle for his party, and on one occasion was a delegate to a National Convention.

When, however, he entered the priesthood, although never relinquishing his political views, he abstained entirely from mingling in politics.

In 1853 he entered the novitiate of the Redemptorists, in whose service he had for so long a time been engaged, and was regarded by them in consequence as a lay member of their order.

In 1857, now forty-four years of age, he was ordained priest. He was assigned to labor in New Orleans. His restless activity quickly manifested itself. He saw the necessity for better accommodation in the school and proposed to the Father Rector the project of erecting a new building. When asked of the probable cost of what he considered a suitable school he astonished his superior by telling him that fifteen thousand dollars would be required. The proposal was scouted immediately, as the impoverished condition of the parish would not permit such an extravagant outlay. But Father

Sheeran was not a man to submit quietly to the repression of a favored project when convinced of its absolute necessity.

Time and again he broached the matter, and was so persistent that his superior finally yielded; but gave Father Sheeran distinctly to understand that he would have to raise the money himself and be solely responsible.

Imagine the astonishment of the fathers and the congregation when, instead of an expense of fifteen thousand dollars, the building erected cost almost ten times that amount.

Owing to the nature of the soil it was found necessary to expend a large sum of money in driving piles to make the foundation secure.

At the outbreak of the civil war he was appointed Chaplain of the Thirteenth Louisiana Regiment, and served with unselfish devotion those under his charge throughout the long struggle from the first Bull Run to Richmond. Not only did the dying and dead command his care; but in field and in camp his fearless denunciation of vice common to a soldier's life achieved good results, and won for him the esteem and admiration of both officers and men.

The confines of the camp were no limit to his zeal in the discharge of his duties. Frequently he violated the stringent army regulations by going beyond the lines to attend sick-calls, or to bring the consolations of religion to those he found in the neighborhood. This brought him in conflict with General Stonewall Jackson.

Going to his tent one day, General Jackson sternly rebuked the priest for disobeying his orders, and reproached him with doing what he would not tolerate in any officer of his command.

"Father Sheeran," said the General, "you ask more favors and take more privileges than any officer in the army."

"General Jackson," replied Father Sheeran, looking the soldier straight in the eye, "I want you to understand that as a priest of God I outrank every officer in your command—I outrank even you; and when it is a question of duty I shall go wherever called."

The General looked with undisguised astonishment on the bold priest, and, without replying a word, left his tent.

At the close of the war he returned to New Orleans, but, owing to ill health, he went to Detroit and finally to New York; and by his personal efforts raised most of the money for the construction of the Redemptorist Mission Church in South Fifth Avenue.

When he left the Congregation he visited Bishop Bayley in Newark, and tendered his services. Bishop Bayley rather bluntly told him that there was no vacancy in the diocese. As, however, he was on the point of leaving the room the Bishop called him back and said that the Morristown parish was without a pastor, and, as nobody seemed to want it, he might take it, if he chose.

Father Sheeran replied that he would go up and see it, and on his return give the Bishop a decided answer.

When he went back to Newark, after surveying the field in Morristown, he said to the Bishop that it was a nice country parish, and consented to take it. Thus was he appointed Rector of this mission. He at once entered upon a long course of labor, which terminated with his death.

By his influence and exertions, and in his undertaking cheerfully aided by his parishioners, the Church of the Assumption was built, which ranks among the finest churches in the State.

He devoted great attention to the school, caused a new and large cemetery to be purchased and laid out, and enlarged the pastoral residence, so as to meet the wants of the parish. In addition to all this he attended unaided to the wants of the parishioners until age and infirmity compelled him to seek for assistance. In his death the Church lost a zealous and active worker, and the Catholics of this parish a priest whose best monument will be the great work he has left behind him, which will long perpetuate his memory.

The funeral services took place on Thursday morning, April 7, at the Church, at 9:30. After the singing of the office for the dead a high Mass of Requiem was said by the Rev. P. Smith, of Jersey City, assisted by some thirty priests, among them Fathers McNulty, Vassallo, Corrigan, and others well known here. The sermon was preached by Monsignor Doane, of Newark, and the ceremony of blessing the body was performed by Most Rev. Archbishop Corrigan, of New York.

He was buried in the plot, close to the gate, selected by himself years before.

Mr. McMaster, an old friend, in the editorial column of the *Freeman's Journal* noticed his death, and among other things said of him:

"At an early age he came to New York. He was engaged here, for many years, in business. Out of a desire to do good he went to Monroe, Michigan, to teach a parochial school, under the pastoral care of Father Smulders, of the Redemptorists. Mr. Sheeran married and had two children — a daughter who died in the Benedictine Convent, in Westmoreland County, Pa., and a son who died in the novitiate of the Redemptorists. The death of the latter inspired Mr. Sheeran with a desire, gallant and noble in its sentiments, to take the place of his deceased boy in the Redemptorist novitiate. He entered, and notwithstanding the difficulties of age somewhat too much advanced, and habits of personal independence settled, finished his novitiate and his scholastic course, and was ordained. His disregard of danger in face of the yellow fever has been spoken of in some of the daily papers. That is the rule for Catholic Priests as Soldiers of the Cross."

The diocese was now without a Bishop. The Rt.

Rev. M. A. Corrigan, D.D., was appointed coadjutor Archbishop of New York, with the right of succession, and assigned to the titular See of Petra, October 1, 1880.

The Vicar-General, the Rt. Rev. Monsignor George H. Doane, was deputed by the Holy See to administer the affairs of the diocese until the appointment of the Bishop. Monsignor Doane requested Father MacDonald to discharge the duties of rector pending the appointment of a pastor.

Father MacDonald accomplished a great deal during his brief stay and made many friends outside of the congregation. So strong a hold had he on the affection of the parishioners that strenuous efforts were made to install him rector. Had he been regularly affiliated to the diocese, and had his term of service been of sufficient duration, his chances for a permanent appointment would have been excellent; but the Rt. Rev. Administrator, in view of these circumstances, could not accede to the wishes of the petitioners.

On Sunday, June 12, 1881, the acting Pastor announced to the congregation that his connection with the church was about to be severed, and that the Rev. Joseph M. Flynn was appointed Pastor by Monsignor Doane, and would arrive the latter part of the week and begin his work among them. Father MacDonald bespoke for the new Pastor the same kind treatment he himself had experienced, and took occasion to thank them for the many acts of kindness shown to him during his appointment. The congregation was visibly affected, and it was with sorrow that they parted with the priest whom they had learned to love.

On Saturday, June 18, the new Pastor, Father Flynn, arrived, and Father MacDonald took his departure for other fields.

CHAPTER VIII.

JOSEPH MICHAEL FLYNN was born January 7, 1848, in Springfield, Mass. The early years of his life were spent chiefly in New York. He attended school, taught by the Christian Brothers, in St. Vincent's Academy until 1859, when, on the removal of his family to Newark, N. J., he was sent to the parochial school attached to St. Patrick's Cathedral, then located on High Street, now occupied by the Women's Hospital connected with St. Michael's.

In 1861 he left school and entered a printing-office. In May, 1864, he enlisted in Company B, Thirty-seventh New Jersey Volunteers, and was mustered into the United States service June 22.

This regiment, organized in response to a call issued by Governor Parker for one hundred days' service, was made up chiefly of youths ranging from sixteen to eighteen years of age; and when Colonel (now General) E. Burd Grubb, the commander, was taunted with bringing down to the front a lot of chickens, he reto. ced: "Yes, but they are all game chickens." And so it turned out.

Although their term of service was short, this regiment did great work in the intrenchments before Richmond and in front of Petersburg.

Foster, in his *New Jersey and the Rebellion*, thus writes of the Thirty-seventh New Jersey Volunteers:

VERY REV. JOSEPH M. FLYNN, V.F.

"This regiment remained in the rear of the Hare House Battery until their term of service had nearly expired, doing duty in the trenches in 'the front,' and contributing their quota to the fatigue parties working on the fortifications in that vicinity. On the 25th of September the Tenth Corps retired from the front, being relieved by the Second Corps, and moved towards Deep Bottom, to take part in the movement upon Chapin's Bluff, which took place a short time afterwards. The same day the following highly flattering general order was promulgated:

"'HEADQUARTERS TENTH ARMY CORPS, ARMY OF THE JAMES, BEFORE PETERSBURG, VA.

"'*General Order No. 34:* September 25, 1864.

"'The Thirty-seventh New Jersey Volunteers, on the 26th instant, will leave for Trenton, N. J., reporting to the Superintendent of Recruiting Service of the State, to be mustered out of service at the expiration of its enlistment.

"'The Major-General commanding cannot part with this regiment of one hundred days' men without expressing his gratification and satisfaction with their conduct. They have endured fatigue, encountered the rebel foe like good soldiers, and have gained the esteem of the veterans of this corps.

"'He is confident that when they return to New Jersey, a State that has furnished such soldiers as Kearney, Mott, and Torbert, they will continue to sustain the veterans they have left at the front, doing what Sherman advised: "Fighting this out like men."

"'The Major-General commanding will be pleased to assist the commanding officer of this regiment in organizing it to aid in the finale of the rebellion in conjunction with this corps.

"'The Quartermaster's Department will furnish transportation.   By command of

"'Major-General D. B. BIRNEY.

"'EDWARD W. SMITH, Assistant Adjutant-General.'

"It was an unusual occurrence for the commandant of a corps to issue a general order so complimentary in its tone upon the muster out of a single regiment which had done nothing more than this one had to distinguish itself. But, remembering that this was a perfectly raw regiment, composed of men of all ages and degrees of imperfection, and in no small degree of mere boys; that it arrived in three days after leaving its camp at Trenton within the range of rebel cannon, and there remained until its return home, the men going into the 'glory holes' in the immediate front at Petersburg, and there doing their duty like veterans, with very few opportunities for drill or improvement, it is not remarkable that the Major-General commanding the corps should deem them worthy of the compliment which he bestowed upon them. The regiment was engaged in no battles, but in the dangerous duty of the trenches and rifle-pits five were killed and twenty-nine wounded. In addition, there were thirteen other deaths, mostly from typhoid fever. The regiment was mustered out on the 1st of October, 1864."

Private Flynn was promoted Seventh Corporal, before Richmond, July 3, 1864.

On his return he resumed work at the printing-case and press, and enlisted in the Second Regiment of the State Militia.

The desire of his childhood to enter the sacred ministry was reawakened at this period, and in September, 1865, he entered St. Charles's College, near Ellicott City, Md. His health, never vigorous, weakened by the exposure and incidents of a soldier's life, broke down in the first year of his college course.

His physicians ordered him to abandon his studies, giving as a reason his delicate constitution, which was unequal to the strain a long course of studies would impose upon it. For four years, however, through many ups and downs, now almost at death's door and again apparently in renewed health, he persevered, and in March, 1869, was permitted by Bishop Bayley to enter Seton Hall College, South Orange, N. J.

The good Bishop thought it useless for the young Levite to pursue his studies further, and consented to his entering Seton Hall, as he expressed it, "simply to gratify the wishes of a dying man."

In 1870 he was graduated from the College, and in the fall of the same year entered the Seminary attached to the College. On the completion of the four years' course of theology he was ordained to holy priesthood May 30, 1874.

His class was one of the largest ever ordained in the Diocesan Seminary. On June 13, 1874, he was appointed assistant to Rev. Patrick Corrigan, pastor of St. Bridget's Church, Jersey City. The training received here shaped his career. To him was entrusted by the pastor the care of the schools, the training of the Sanctuary boys, both for serving the Altar and singing the Vesper services, and the sick-calls of a very unhealthy locality. The malarious character of the neighborhood so affected him that his physicians insisted upon his removal to a healthier region.

In November, 1875, Bishop Corrigan assigned him to assist Father Sheeran in Morristown. Hither he came completely shattered in health, and his rapid recovery led to his removal to other fields, where laborers were in greater need. So, after a brief and pleasant stay in Morristown, full of gratitude to the pastor for his kindness and to the people for their sympathy, he left February, 1876, for St. Peter's Church, New Brunswick.

For three months he discharged the duties of assistant priest to the Rev. Patrick Downes, then administrator of that parish.

On May 7, 1876, he was called by the Right Rev. M. A. Corrigan, D.D., to St. Patrick's Cathedral, Newark, and made the Bishop's private secretary.

He successively filled the offices of Diocesan Chancellor, Master of Ceremonies, Secretary of the Commission of Investigation, and for over a year, while Vicar-General Doane was abroad in search of health, administered the parish, until his return in 1879. On June 15, 1881, the Right Rev. Monsignor

Doane appointed Father Flynn rector of the *Church of the Assumption*, Morristown.

On Saturday, June 18, Father Flynn arrived at his new post and assumed the responsibility of Pastor. It did not take him long to realize how firm a hold Father MacDonald had upon the hearts of the congregation, how earnestly they desired to retain him, for their reception to the new priest was by no means enthusiastic or warm. A single visitor came to him on the night of his arrival to bid him welcome to his new field of labor; and, while candidly expressing his admiration for the outgoing administrator, declared his desire and intention to aid the new pastor in every way.

On Sunday morning Father Flynn introduced himself to his parishioners at both Masses. At the High Mass he preached on the Holy Eucharist, as the Sunday was within the octave of the Feast of Corpus Christi. At the close of the sermon he thus addressed his audience:

"My feelings this morning, dear brethren, are akin to those of the captain of a vessel sailing for a distant port. He knows that his vessel is staunch. He knows the location of the port to which he is bound. But what may happen from the time he leaves the harbor where his vessel has been moored until he arrives at his destination, he knows not. Fair weather and foul; the fierce buffeting of mighty waves; the wearisome annoyance of calms, must he expect.

"So I come before you to-day, conscious of my inability to rival those who have preceded me in the pastorate, and yet full of trust and confidence in you who have so generously seconded their efforts.

"It is impossible for you to overestimate the labors of your late pastor, Father Sheeran; and you would indeed be ungrateful were you to forget the kindness and zeal of Father MacDonald. The reverence in which you hold the memory of both is my great encouragement. Without any previous experience, I may say, in the administration of a parish, you must take me as I am. I can only promise to labor for you to the best of my ability, and to guard sacredly the trust committed to my charge. God works powerfully through secondary causes, and makes use of the meanest instruments to achieve the greatest results to His honor and glory. Let us assist one another by prayer. While ready and willing 'to spend myself and to be spent' in the great work of the salvation of your souls, I must look to you to second my efforts. From a financial stand-point it is smooth sailing; for, in view of the many undertakings which have been carried on to a successful issue within the past ten years, the debt is very insignificant. With regard to the spiritual condition of the parish I can say but little, as time alone will make me familiar with your needs and requirements in that direction. It cannot be gainsaid that the capital sin of the age is indifference in those things which pertain to God, and which are above the realm of this world. In the business of life man is apt to become so absorbed in making provision for the wants of the body as to lose sight of the interests of his soul.

"Some would measure the success of the pastor by the annual income of the church, by the magnificent buildings, by the splendor of the ritual, and the large attendance at the services; but not so. The kingdom of God is from within. That pastor is blessed and consoled who sees around the confessional throngs of penitents, who feeds the multitudes weekly, if not daily, with the Bread of Life. The benediction of God rests on that parish where virtue triumphs and vice is rendered powerless; where the old edify by their example of Christian virtue; and the young, by their loyalty to the Church, by their efforts to be a light shining in the midst of darkness, give hope of the future success of the Church. As, on the one hand, I may not fail to give to the temporalities that care and prudence which they may demand, I must, nevertheless, put forward my best efforts to labor for your spiritual and eternal interests. So let us on—I to toil and labor, you to respond to my efforts, that one day both pastor and people, happy in the precious possession of never-ending happiness, we shall reap our reward. So let us work that on the last great day I may regard you as my glory and my crown."

An active movement was set on foot to raise a monument to the memory of Father Sheeran. The congregation responded generously, and a massive granite monolith marks his last resting-place.

To promote devotion, to bring down the special blessing of God on the parish, a statue of the Sacred Heart was placed in a niche at the Gospel side of the altar.

Special attention was given to church societies. These societies, approved by many Popes and enriched with spiritual blessings, are the very life of a parish. They foster a spirit of prayer, and lead to the frequentation of the Sacraments. Their members are sanctified, and their very example is a standing reproach to the indifferent and the lukewarm. The sight of men and women approaching the holy table leads others to imitate their example.

A jubilee was proclaimed this year by our Holy Father Leo XIII. To prepare the faithful for its graces the Rev. James McCallan, of the Society of St. Sulpice, was invited to preach the retreat. The spiritual exercises were enriched by the eloquence of the reverend preacher. Large numbers approached the Sacraments.

The Young Ladies' Sodality, organized in 1877 through the efforts of the Rev. Father Giraud, was desirous of obtaining a suitable banner. The members quickly raised a sufficient sum to defray the necessary expenses. The work was entrusted to the

Rt. Rev. Winand Michael Wigger, D.D.

cloistered Dominican Nuns in Newark, N. J. They fully maintained their high reputation for artistic skill. The banner is of white silk, embroidered in blue, and in the centre is a beautiful copy in oil of Murillo's "Assumption."

In August news reached the expectant Catholics of the Diocese of Newark that the See made vacant by the promotion of Archbishop Corrigan was filled. The future Bishop was to be the gentle, saintly, and zealous Dr. Wigger, of Madison, N. J.

Winand Michael Wigger, born December 9, 1841, in New York City, received his classical education in St. Francis Xavier's College, New York, and his theological training at Seton Hall Seminary and at the College Brignole-Sale, Genoa. He was ordained priest in 1865, and sailed for America October 2 of the same year.

Cholera broke out on the steamer *Atalanta*, and the young priest was indefatigable in his attention to the sick. On the arrival of the vessel at quarantine, he asked and obtained permission to remain on the pest-stricken vessel until the last vestige of the dread disease had disappeared, and for two weeks he stood at the post of danger.

Bishop Bayley attached him to the staff of the Cathedral, and in this extensive parish for four years he edified all by his piety, zeal, and fidelity. The sick, the poor, the distressed, found in him a true friend, whose kind words encouraged them, and whose generous hand was ever ready to assist them.

In this field he won the esteem of his superiors, and the love and admiration of his flock, and in 1869 was promoted to the Madison parish, made vacant by the death of Father D'Arcy. While here he busied himself with the interests of his new parish, and purchased land and erected a church and school in Chatham.

In May, 1873, the financial disaster which had almost ruined St. John's Church, Orange, made it necessary for the Bishop to secure a pastor to overcome the many difficulties. Bishop Corrigan looked to Dr. Wigger as eminently fit to cope with the situation. Without a moment's hesitation, Dr. Wigger abandoned the ease and amenities of Madison to obey the voice of his superior, and to engage in the almost hopeless task. In less than six months he paid eleven thousand dollars of the indebtedness. In February, 1874, at his own request, he was relieved from St. John's and assigned to the pastoral charge of Summit.

In June, 1876, he was again transferred to Madison, and was welcomed by his old parishioners, who recognized the excellent traits of the good priest, and also by those outside of the church, who esteemed him for his sterling Christian qualities.

In vain did he try to evade the great dignity and responsibility of Bishop. Rome was inexorable. He was consecrated by Archbishop Corrigan, assisted by Bishop Loughlin and Bishop McQuaid, in the Cathedral, Newark, October 18, 1881. Not only the title but the mantle of his predecessors has fallen upon Bishop Wigger. The zeal of a Bayley, the gentleness of a Corrigan are his. Since his elevation he has not only perpetuated the spirit of his predecessors, maintained the discipline which characterized their administration, but he has advanced the spiritual and temporal interests of the flock over which he so worthily presides.

Up to this period the tower of the Catholic Church in Morristown had stood like a dumb monitor. The congregation had to trust to the uncertainty of the clock at home to reach the church in time for the services. The sweet message of the bell had not as yet reached their ears. The Pastor set out for Baltimore, and found in the establishment of McShane & Co. a splendid bell, which had been made by that firm for the Atlanta Exposition. On the morning of his arrival it had just been taken from the mould, and word was sent to the bell-founders that the managers of the Exposition desired them to send a chime instead of a single bell. Thus it happened that the bell, which had cost so much extra care and money, was thrown on the hands of the firm.

It was offered to Father Flynn for exactly the price of the metal; but it was stipulated that, in case of purchase, the bell should first be used in the Oriole celebration, which was being held at this time. The bell was bought for six hundred and fifty-four dollars and forty-eight cents. In the evening, as Father Flynn was on his way to take the train, he saw the glare of the torchlight procession winding through the streets of Baltimore, and heard, ever and anon, high above the noise of martial music and the shouts of the bystanders, the sweet tone of the bell which was soon to be hung in the spire of our Church in Morristown.

The first official act of the newly-consecrated Bishop was to bless this new bell. On Wednesday evening, October 19, 1881, the Right Rev. Winand Michael Wigger, D.D., assisted by the Rev. Michael A. McManus and the Rev. Joseph M. Flynn, in presence of a large congregation, solemnly blessed the bell, following every detail of the ritual for this beautiful ceremony, and named it in honor of Ireland's great Apostle, St. Patrick. Archbishop Corrigan preached at the close of the ceremony, and gave an interesting history of the origin and significance of bells in Catholic worship. Mr. Martin O'Brien and Miss Maud Clarke acted as sponsors. Messrs. John McAnerny and Martin O'Brien, Mrs. R. H. Clarke and Miss Maud Clarke, each contributed fifty dollars towards the purchase, and the balance was raised by the congregation. Morning, noon, and night the glad tidings, " THE WORD WAS MADE FLESH AND DWELT AMONG US," are wafted far and wide, lifting the heart from the cares and anxieties of this world to the hopeful contemplation of the peace beyond, tempering the miseries and afflictions of life with the thought that He walked the rugged path before us, and awaits at the end of our pilgrimage to crown and comfort us. Not by the Catholics alone, but even by those outside the true Fold, is the deep significance of this touching devotion to the Incarnate God felt and realized.

The Rev. E. C. L. Browne, a Protestant minister residing in Charleston, S. C., contributed the following poem to the *News and Courier* of that city. It is prefaced by the following:

"For a long time I lived in close proximity to St. Peter's Catholic Church and School, and the soft-toned bell that regulated the life of the worshippers came unconsciously to regulate mine. I grew to depend upon its constant and unobtrusive voice. Its morning, noon, and evening peal was as a 'note of soft recall,' speaking in something like the language I have inadequately ascribed to it here:

> "The Angelus is ringing!
> Rise, heart, to grateful prayer;
> Rise and salute the new day dawning.
> Remember Whose strong love,
> Descending from above,
> Has held thee in its tender care,
> And kept thee till the morning.
> Oh! rise and sing Whose constant thought
> And faithful might,
> In dark and light,
> Have life to conscious blessing brought,
> Thy tribute to His love.
> The Angelus is ringing!

"The Angelus is ringing!
As comes high noon with crowding care,
How press life's duties hard around thee!
How quick the world with wiles has bound thee!
But that clear voice from upper air
　Recalls thee from thy strife.
　　In fulness of the day,
　　Lift up thy heart and pray.
On higher, holier life
　The Angelus is ringing!

"The Angelus is ringing!
Welcome the night with hush and rest.
　Peace once more settles down
　Upon the turbulent town.
　Let this evangel floating o'er
　Recall it to thy heart once more,
And quiet to thy breast.
Come deeper thoughts with deepening ray;
　Day's sordid themes
　And all low dreams,
Be by this high suggestion swept away!
　The Angelus is ringing!

"Morn, noon, and night, O faithful bell!
Thy warnings to my conscience call,
Though on the ear unmarked they fall."

In the appointment of Father Flynn to the pastorate of Morristown by Right Rev. Monsignor Doane, the Administrator, there was question of the extent of his power in the premises. Hence, to supply any defect which may have existed in his title, the Right Rev. Bishop Wigger wrote to the incumbent:

"MADISON, October 28, 1881.

"DEAR FATHER FLYNN:

"As, to say the least, it is doubtful that your appointment by Monsignor Doane to the parish of

Morristown was valid—to remove all doubt, and to render your position secure, I hereby appoint you Rector of the Church of the Assumption, Morristown. I am sure that you will work successfully, and do much good in the parish. Indeed, you have already done much good during the few months that you have been there.

"Wishing you everything that is good, I remain your sincere friend,

✠ "W. M. WIGGER,
"*Bishop of Newark.*"

In the Autumn his parochial visitation brought Father Flynn in closer touch with the little band of Catholics in Morris Plains. The State Retreat for those afflicted with mental disorders contained a very considerable number of Catholic inmates, both patients and attendants.

To journey to Morristown to Mass was, in the case of one class, an impossibility; of the other, a matter of serious difficulty. Moreover, at Wilsonville, adjacent to the Retreat, lived a score of families who, only at long intervals and in fine weather, were able to walk to the mother Church. A census of the Catholics was taken, and the feasibility of starting a church laid before Bishop Wigger. In a letter dated November 21, 1881, his Lordship indicated his views: "Your kind letter, giving account of the number of Catholics in Morris Plains, has been duly received. From your report it is quite evident that a little church is needed at

Morris Plains, and I empower you to purchase a suitable plot of ground on which to build one."

Accordingly a site was secured; and, until the erection of the church, an effort was made to have Mass in one of the houses conveniently located and sufficiently roomy for the accommodation of those who might desire to attend.

This, and the increasing ministerial work in Morristown, and the important supervision of the school, made the services of an assistant priest a necessity. December 3 the Bishop wrote: "Father Whelan may be relieved at any time, and, if so, will be sent to you, as you desired."

The Rev. Isaac P. Whelan reported some time in the month of December, and the Right Rev. Bishop added to the other duties of the Morristown priests the care of the Whippany mission.

On Christmas day Holy Mass was said for the first time in Morris Plains in the house of Andrew Murphy. The room was crowded, and the scene recalled to many the stories told them by their fathers of Catholicity forty years ago.

Thereafter Mass was regularly celebrated every Sunday. Between attending to the two Masses in Morristown, one in Whippany, and another at Morris Plains, Sunday was a busy day for the priests, who, from early morn to high noon, knew not a moment's rest.

CHAPTER IX.

A SHORT time before his death Thomas Burns donated his house and lot to Father Flynn.

This valuable property, in front of the Church, was the object of much solicitude on the part of previous pastors. Although a personal gift, Father Flynn deeded it to the Church. The Sisters of Charity, engaged in school work, came from the Mother House daily and returned at the close of school. But, in the diocese of Newark, the Sisters of Charity, an offshoot of Mount St. Vincent, New York, introduced by Bishop Bayley and trained according to his spirit, are something more than teachers, for their work extends beyond the classroom to the Sanctuary, to the sick-bed, and to the homes where poverty prevails.

The assistance rendered by them to the Pastor, their efficiency in matters beyond his reach, the influence of their example, cannot be too highly estimated, or receive the due measure of praise.

The house was altered and furnished, and in January, 1882, Sister Gaudentia, as Sister Servant, with Sisters Cecilia Rose, Eugenia, and Teresita, took up their permanent residence among us.

The Young Men's Association, which had been formed in the previous Autumn, rented two rooms in the Bates building, and in order to furnish them and to adapt them to their needs, a bazaar was held on February 13, 14, and 15. A neat sum was realized, and thus the first encouragement was given to that body which was to effect so much good by elevating and refining our Catholic young men. Among other benefactors was Mrs. Revere, who donated a billiard-table. An antique bath-tub from the Rectory found place in a room partitioned off from the rear apartment. To these humble and meagrely furnished rooms came every evening the founders of our present Association. They were their own janitor. On entering the rooms the dignified directors would take off coat and hat, and would away, some to start the fire, others to sweep the rooms, others to wash the cuspidores. All found something to do, and were cheered in their work by a running fire of jest and gibe, and merry laugh and song. Many of the old members affirm that these were the brightest and happiest days they have ever known.

Mr. Charles H. Knight, at this time, volunteered to go among our townsmen and raise a sum sufficient to decorate the Church. His efforts were eminently successful. He handed over to the Pastor seven hundred and sixty-five dollars. Before, however, undertaking this work, it was thought advisable to improve the ventilation of the Church. This was effected by opening every other one of the clerestory windows, and the adoption of the Hitchings patent attachment secures an abundant supply of fresh air, making the Church sweet and wholesome at all times.

The decoration was entrusted to Herman Bodes, and the two paintings, one of St. Patrick preaching to the King at Tara, the other of the death-scene of St. Columba in the monastery chapel at Iona, are the work of Gustave Kinkeln. The first painting, on the Epistle side of the choir, recalls the story familiar to all; with the second, on the Gospel side, not many are acquainted. It will be best to embody the graphic account of the great pulpit orator, Father Tom Burke:

"Columba was now seventy years of age, and he prayed that he might die at Easter. God sent an angel to tell him that his prayer was granted. Now mark the Irish heart again. The moment that he heard that his prayer was granted he prayed to God to let him live for another month, for he said to the monks: 'My children, I pray that I might die to pass my Easter Sunday in Heaven. God said he would grant my prayer; but then I thought that you are after fasting a long Lent upon bread and water, and that you are all looking forward to Easter Sunday as a day of joy, and if I died on that day it would be a sad and sorrowful day, so I asked my God to put it off a month more.' The month passed; it was Saturday night, and Columba in the morning told his children the monks, 'This night I will die and take my rest.'

"The monks were accustomed to go into the church precisely at twelve o'clock. The bells rang and Columba was always in the church at prayer.

When he was not studying, he went before the others into the dark church—there was no light—and knelt at the foot of the altar. Dermot, his servant, his faithful man, followed the old man, and groping about in the church for him, at first not being able to see him, exclaimed, 'O father, dear father! where art thou?' A feeble moan soon was heard, and he came to where he lay. The other monks came in and brought torches in their hands, and found Columba stretched out, dying, grasping the foot of the altar; dying under the very eyes of that Lord and God whom he loved so well; dying with a heart long since broken with love for the Lord Jesus, and for the dear land that he left behind. They lifted him up, and with his dying lips he said, 'Come around me, that I may give you my last blessing.' He lifted his aged hand, and before the sign of the Cross was made the hand fell by his side, the light of human love departed from his eye, and one of the most glorious souls of apostles and martyrs that ever lived was borne aloft by the angels to join the illustrious band of Erin's Saints."

The Church was very much improved in appearance, the light colors employed on the walls and in the panels of the roof seemed to give greater breadth and height, and the subdued tones of salmon and light blue, the spotless purity of the altar in white and gold, standing out from the reredos of brown with emblems in olive green, impart to the edifice a devotional character which impresses every visitor. Sister Gaudentia went among the parishioners and, with the offerings she received, purchased the Wilton carpet for the Sanctuary and side chapels.

On Ascension Thursday, May 18, 1882, the Right Rev. Bishop Wigger, D.D., reopened the Church. At the Pontifical Mass the school children sang for the first time. The Sacrament of Confirmation was administered; and, in the evening, there was a reception of members and enrollment in the Young Ladies' Sodality and Children of Mary. At the same time those who had been confirmed renewed their baptismal vows.

Sunday, June 18, the beautiful Munich statue of St. Anthony of Padua, presented by Mrs. Patrick Welsh for her son John Vincent, was blessed and placed in a niche on the Epistle side of the altar.

The congregation had by this time outgrown the limits of the half-past eight and half-past ten o'clock Masses. The hours were inconvenient for many of the housekeepers and domestics, and the increased number of children was huddled wherever accommodation could be found in the side aisles and gallery. Fortunately the Bishop at this period detached Morris Plains and Whippany, made them a separate parish, and placed over them as pastor the Rev. James J. Brennan.

On July 13, 1882, the Rev. D. McCartie, the Bishop's Secretary, wrote to Father Flynn:

"The absence of several rectors and assistants,

who have obtained permission to travel for the restoration of health, has caused a deficiency of priests in some parishes of the Diocese. In order to supply the wants of the churches deprived of this ministration, the Bishop finds it necessary to distribute more equally the reverend assistants who are at present available.

"For this reason he is constrained to remove Father Whelan from Morristown, and transfer him to a parish where his services are more urgently required. As the duty of attending Morris Plains would be too onerous a task for you unaided, his Lordship has considered it advisable to annex that mission to the parish of Whippany, the revenues of which will be thus rendered more easily adequate to the support of a priest.

"You are requested to furnish Father Brennan with all requisite information regarding the condition and management of the mission, and to effect such arrangements as may enable him to assume full charge of it within one week from the present date."

The vacancy created by Father Whelan's removal was supplied by the Jesuit Fathers of St. Peter's Church, Jersey City.

Father Brennan entered with zeal upon his new duties. The fine weather tempted him to gather his little flock under the shelter of a tent, and thus the Catholics of Morris Plains worshipped their God as did the Israelites of old. On October 11, 1882, Bishop Wigger wrote to Father Flynn:

"I hereby formally delegate you, and ask you to

Rev. James J. Brennan.

be kind enough, to lay the corner-stone of the new Church to be built in Morris Plains."

When the erection of the Church was first contemplated Father Flynn desired and intended to place it under the patronage of St. Virgil, Archbishop of Saltzburg, one of the most illustrious of God's servants, but eminent for his learning, apostolic zeal, and ceaseless energy in preaching the faith and exterminating heresy. Feargal, or the modernized O'Farrell, was born in the South of Ireland of a princely family. He profited so well by the teaching in the schools for which Ireland was noted, that, on his arrival in France, about the year 743, he was most graciously received by Pepin, son of the great Charlemagne, and recommended by him to Otilo, Duke of Bavaria. It is interesting to know that this Irish monk was among the first, if not the very first, to teach the existence of antipodes and the sphericity of the earth. The fact is easily demonstrated and comprehended in our day, but in the time of St. Virgil it was a bold doctrine to broach and required unusual strength of character to stand by convictions so counter to all preconceived notions and to the erroneous views on cosmogony in full vigor at that period. He built a magnificent basilica in honor of his predecessor St. Rupert, in which he enshrined the relics of the Saint, and which he made his cathedral church. He was canonized in the Lateran Basilica July, 1233, by Pope Gregory IX. In life and after his soul was freed from its prison of clay God set the seal of His approval on the life and virtues of our Saint by the many miraculous cures effected not only at his tomb, but in St. Mary's, Morristown, which prides itself on the possession of a portion of his precious relics.

Father Brennan entered warmly into the views of his predecessor and decided to place the little Church under the protection of this great Confessor. For the first time in America did St. Virgil receive this honor. New interest was awakened in the history of his life and labors, and the descendants of his fellow-countrymen were quick to give him the love and reverence to which the servants of God are entitled, and which redound entirely to His greater honor and glory.

Although it goes beyond the present period of our narrative, the history of St. Virgil's is outlined from its inception to the end.

Soon after his appointment the Rev. Joseph M. Flynn sought to collect the few scattered Catholics north of Morristown. He wished also to afford the opportunity of hearing Mass to those employed in the State Asylum for the Insane at Morris Plains. Consequently, after due announcement, the Holy Sacrifice was offered on Christmas Day, 1881, in the parlor of Mr. Andrew Murphy, at Wilsonville, near the Asylum, three miles from Morristown and one from Morris Plains.

For over six months he continued the service, made collections and obtained subscriptions to the amount of $444.68, which he used to purchase an acre of ground, at a cost of $500, on Hanover Avenue.

On June 14, 1882, the Rev. James Joseph Brennan, recently of St. John's Church, Paterson, was appointed Pastor of Whippany and Northfield. On July 20, Morris Plains was substituted for Northfield, and on the 23d of the month, at 10:30 A.M., he celebrated Holy Mass at Wilsonville as successor to Father Flynn, the collection being $1.53.

In order to accommodate some who desired a more convenient location he borrowed from the Morristown Catholics a large tent, which he pitched near the new church lot. In that frail and temporary shelter, which might be likened to the stable of Bethlehem, he offered the Holy Sacrifice for the first time on the 6th of August.

At first, in this humble sanctuary there were no pews, but a few boards and chairs; no floor but the bare ground, no carpet but the stubble of new-mown wheat; the altar was a pine table with the bare requisites for the Holy Sacrifice and a few fresh flowers. The people went to confession in public view back of the altar-table, behind a few hemlock boards. There was no altar-rail, no communion cloth; and they received with the pall, without support, except from their faith.

On the approach of cold weather, September 24,

the hall of the public school was procured and used until near the close of the year.

Meanwhile, on September 28, Right Rev. W. M. Wigger granted permission to erect a church at Morris Plains at a probable cost of one thousand two hundred dollars. He afterwards allowed a debt of one thousand five hundred dollars to be incurred.

On October 15 the corner-stone of an edifice thirty feet by forty-five was laid in the presence of several hundred persons by Rev. Joseph M. Flynn, who also delivered an appropriate sermon on the glory and perpetuity of the Catholic Church.

Before the building was half completed the Holy Sacrifice was offered up in it, at 10:30 A.M., on Christmas, 1882, exactly one year from the celebration of the first Mass at Wilsonville.

Owing to slender resources it was nearly another year before it was completed and dedicated to the service of God by Bishop Wigger, December 16, 1883. Even then it took a few more years to provide the necessary and suitable means for the proper celebration of the various offices of religion.

On December 13, 1886, through the liberality of Mr. Cornelius Conklin and wife, a large and more eligible site was purchased for one thousand five hundred dollars with the expectation of some day having the church, the school, and the rectory in close proximity. In August, 1888, the church was moved to the new property, which comprises more than two acres at the junction of Mountain Way

St. Virgilius' Church, Morris Plains.

and Hanover and Speedwell Avenues, in the very heart of Morris Plains. At the same time the Church was enlarged and a belfry and a gallery built. Then the grounds were graded, laid out, planted with trees and enclosed. Many other improvements were also made from time to time, so that after a long and hard struggle the Church of St. Virgilius is comfortable and respectable, if not imposing.

On the evening of December 20, 1889, a new bell, weighing nine hundred and eighty-one pounds, was blessed by Bishop Wigger, assisted by Very Rev. Joseph M. Flynn, Rev. Maurice P. O'Connor, Rev. Joseph H. Hill, Rev. Joseph C. Dunn, and the Rev. Rector. The bell, called after the Apostle of Ireland, bears the following inscription :

"ST. PATRICK,
GIFT OF MR. AND MRS. C. S. CONKLIN
TO THE CHURCH OF ST. VIRGILIUS,
MORRIS PLAINS, N. J.
W. M. WIGGER, BISHOP.
JAMES JOSEPH BRENNAN, PASTOR.
1889."

After the blessing an appropriate sermon on the history of bells was delivered by Dean Flynn, who also concluded the services by giving the Benediction of the most Blessed Sacrament.

The average receipts of the Church are about two thousand dollars a year, and the value of its property, excluding debts, is over ten thousand dollars; the number of souls about one hundred and fifty. The lay trustees have been Mr. Michael Glennon, Mr. John Coleman, and Mr. Thomas Fahey. Among the benefactors may be named Mr. and Mrs. C. S. Conklin, Mrs. Elias S. Higgins, Mrs. John P. McHugh, Mr. Charles H. Raymond, Mr. P. Malone, Mr. Richard McCurdy, Mr. Andrew Murphy, Mr. D. M. Merchant, Mr. Charles Marsh, Mr. J. W. Roberts, Mrs. Stephen Whitney, Mrs. William McGuiness, Miss Sarah Daly, and Mrs. Mary McKee.

To resume the events which merit attention in the Morristown parish, it is but just to direct attention to its benefactors.

Kind friends are not wanting to make use of their means for the embellishment of the house of God. The leaders of the Rosary Society bands undertook to place a memorial window to perpetuate the life and labors of their late Pastor, Father Sheeran.

Mr. Patrick Farrelly and his wife requested the privilege of placing windows in the Lady Chapel in memory of their deceased children. From the house of Mayer & Co., Munich, came the exquisite specimens of that decorative art which adorns many churches in Europe, but which, up to this time, had found no patrons in the United States. The Father Sheeran memorial window contains the figures of St. James the Apostle and St. Alphonsus Liguori, and the Lady Chapel, St. Elizabeth, St. Catharine, Martyr, and the Angel Guardian.

These were the first works of this celebrated establishment sent across the Atlantic, and the initiative of the movement for the imitation and reproduction of Gothic art, which has advanced so rapidly, and which has added so much to the business of the Mayers.

Mrs. Farrelly generously donated the Sanctuary lamp, and Miss Ann Hogan the ostensorium, both of which were purchased in Lyons, France.

CHAPTER X.

NO provision had been made in the Cemetery for the reception of bodies when, in cases of emergency, inclement weather, or for other reasons, it was desirable to delay burial. Mr. Thomas Allen very kindly donated the stone from his Waterloo quarry, and the construction of the vault was entrusted to Mr. John D. Collins. It was not completed when an epidemic of pneumonia, which carried off more than a dozen of our parishioners, demonstrated its necessity. The weather at the beginning of 1883, which had been unusually fine, set in severely; the frost penetrated more than two feet into the ground, so that to dig a grave holes had to be drilled into the frozen crust as into a rock, thus causing additional labor and delay. Death came so frequently that many were panic-stricken. Every little cold was magnified into an attack of the dread disease, and the priests were in a constant round of sick-calls. In little more than a month its force was spent, and confidence was restored.

At the beginning of the Lenten season Father Flynn felt that the time had come to use his voice and influence against the unlawful sale and excessive use of intoxicants, especially as he had to deal with some cases of a peculiarly distressing character, where the innocent had much to suffer in life and after death from this besetting sin of the age. Before beginning his crusade, the pastor conferred with the Bishop of the diocese, who authorized him to deal with incorrigible drunkards and with those who sold liquor indiscriminately to children and inebriates on the lines marked out by Bishop Bayley five-and-twenty years before. In his opening remarks Father Flynn used the most vigorous language at his command; his manner was earnest, his denunciation against those implicated severe. Unfortunately a garbled report of his remarks appeared in the local newspapers, which were reproduced by journals in and outside of the State.

The public has its moods. These the press watch and play upon. An incident which at one time would pass unnoticed, at another excites widespread comment. It springs up with the suddenness of a storm, and, with the accretions it sweeps up in its flight, assumes a new countenance, so as to be hardly recognizable. Thus, Father Flynn found himself roundly abused for his intolerance by some of the metropolitan journals, and extolled for his zeal by others. Bishop Wigger and some of his friends in the priesthood kindly defended him, explained the true nature of his remarks, and vindicated him from the charge of intolerance. The excitement quieted down, but his voice was not raised in vain. The citizens of Morristown were aroused, and efforts were made at the Spring election to place in the Common Council a body of men who would deal with the license question judiciously and prudently. The Catholics were asked to name a candidate on the citizens' ticket, which, it was understood, advocated, not prohibition but a high and limited license. A ratification meeting was held in Lyceum Hall, which was largely attended by all classes, and especially by the business men and freeholders. On the platform were seated the pastors of the different denominations, and addresses were made by the leaders in the movement, by some of the candidates, by the Rev. J. M. Buckley, D.D., and Father Flynn. The last two speakers insisted that the movement was towards temperance, not prohibition; but the unwise and intolerant language of the others made it clear that there would be no compromise with the liquor-dealer, and that the policy of the candidates, if elected, was to put a stop to it altogether. The regular political parties had not up to this time nominated a ticket. This was soon changed. An opposition ticket was made up, and the election carried on with great spirit. With the exception of the candidate selected by the Catholics, Mr. Morris E. Condon, who came out of the contest with a bare majority, the citizens' ticket was defeated. Mr. Condon distinguished himself in the Council by his consistency, and won for himself the respect of all by his manly stand throughout his term of office.

The question now came up how to manage the necessary incubus of a church debt in a way that, while it would relieve the Church by enabling the Pastor to make, from time to time, as the condition of the treasury would permit, partial payments, the parishioners, who had to meet this obligation, might also be benefited by it. It was shown that in ten years over twelve thousand dollars had been paid out in interest and discounts, and that all this might have passed into the pockets of the congregation had they, instead of an insurance company, held the debt. Father Flynn proposed to issue a number of one hundred dollar bonds sufficient to cover the mortgage, and secured by a first mortgage to Messrs. H. O. Marsh, President, and D. D. Craig, Cashier of the National Iron Bank, as trustees for the bondholders. The interest offered was five per cent., a sum larger than the savings-banks were paying, and the security was equal in all respects to any they could give.

A circular was issued outlining the principal features of the scheme, and distributed among the parishioners. In less than a week over sixteen thousand dollars were taken up, and the debt of the Church placed in the hands of those who were most deeply interested in it, whose liberality would enable the Pastor to pay it off, and who would, moreover, be personally benefited by it. The plan has worked most satisfactorily; and, while it presented obstacles which, elsewhere, might not have made it feasible, with us, through the kindness of Messrs. Marsh and Craig, it was made highly practicable.

The Rev. J. F. Duffy, Father von Riel, and various Paulist Fathers supplemented the work of the Pastor, pending the appointment of a permanent assistant.

On Sunday, May 6, 1884, the Rev. Fathers McInerny and Bohn, Redemptorists, opened a Mission, devoting one week to the women and another to the men. Their ministry was rich in results. One thousand three hundred and six confessions were heard, and over sixteen hundred received holy Communion.

An effort was made to induce one of the first pastors of the Church, the Right Rev. B. J. McQuaid, D.D., Bishop of Rochester, N. Y., to deliver a lecture.

Some of the Old Guard, who had stood by him in the early days of his career, still survived, and, with their children, longed to see and hear once more the one to whom they owed so much. Bishop McQuaid was forced by the pressure of other business to decline the invitation. His answer contains kernels of great historic interest, and for that reason it is reproduced:

"ROCHESTER, N. Y., May 14, 1883.
"*Rev. Joseph M. Flynn:*

"REV. DEAR SIR: I would with much pleasure

accede to your request to lecture in your Church at the time of the Council, but it is certain that no time will be available for anything but its own work. I have even declined to pay visits to some of my friends in New York City who have asked me to do so during the Council.

"My heart always warmed to Morristown until I read in a newspaper that, at the dinner given on the occasion of the dedication of the new Church, the credit of building the old church was given to another priest who was present; and neither he nor any one present corrected the false statement. I built the church and paid for it.

"I cared very little when they stole the credit of Seton Hall from me, and what I did for the Sisters of Charity in Newark and at Madison; but I frankly confess that I felt hurt at the Morristown theft, as that was my baby-work, and therefore my pet. It cost something to build a church in those days. A dollar was a large contribution and was gladly received. In 1848 the people of the Irish famine times were poor, and had to send every dollar they could to their starving relatives at home.

"How kind is Providence, who conceals from us the secrets of the future and the ingratitude of man, that our zeal and devotion may not be chilled by a knowledge of what is in store for us in this world!

"Except old Mrs. Rogers, there is scarcely one in Morristown to remember its old pastor.

"Wishing you much success in your good work, I remain, Rev. dear sir,

"Yours sincerely in Christ,
"✠ B., BP. OF ROCHESTER.

"P. S.—You can claim that in Morristown you

have the second oldest Catholic school in the State of New Jersey, uninterruptedly kept up. Madison has the first. I established both, in a very humble way, it is true; but they helped to establish the principle that Catholic schools were as necessary as churches."

In midsummer Father Flynn ventured upon an excursion. Nothing of the kind had heretofore been attempted, and while many went to and fro from the pleasure resorts contiguous to New York, very many of the old folks had not seen the great City since they landed a quarter of a century before, and some of their children had never been on a railroad train. Father Sheppard, pastor of St. Mary's, Dover, offered to assist in the enterprise, and suggested the union of both parishes in the excursion. This was agreed to. And, on Tuesday, July 31, 1883, the first excursion of the Catholics of Dover and Morristown left the respective cities. Every precaution against danger was taken. At Hoboken a steamer and a barge awaited the party, which was taken down the New York and Raritan Bays, out to the Ocean, past Coney Island and up the East River, to enable those aboard to see the Brooklyn Bridge and the Navy-Yard. It was curious and amusing to witness the interest of the old and young, some searching out old landmarks, others gazing with eyes full of wonder at the sights revealed to them. Except the passing unpleasantness of a little seasickness, experienced opposite Coney

Island, the day was most pleasantly spent, and all reached home in safety, delighted with their first excursion.

The Catholic Benevolent Legion was this year organized in Brooklyn by a number of Catholic gentlemen to provide for their co-religionists a means of life insurance which had been inaugurated by those not of our faith, and which, by reason of oaths of secrecy and a ritual, contained an element of danger. It met with the approval of Bishop Loughlin, who consented to act as its Spiritual Director. Mr. Paul V. Flynn was invited to come and explain the nature and scope of the organization to the male members of our parish. The meeting was held in the school, thirty-eight names were entered as charter members, and the Council called St. Columbanus. This was the fortieth council organized since the inception of the movement, and one of the earliest in New Jersey.

Its excellent features were manifested when at the death of the youngest charter member, Mr. William Foley, the amount of his policy was paid without delay to his sorrowing family.

Monsignor Capel, an eminent English Catholic prelate, visited the country on a lecture tour, and in the month of October came to Morristown. The lecture was given in the Church of the Assumption, and the prestige and prominence of the right reverend lecturer drew large numbers of Protestants to hear him. After the lecture he held a reception in the parlors of Mrs. Revere, when almost all the clergymen and the leading families of the city were presented to him.

New settees, from the establishment of R. Geissler, the gift of Mr. Patrick Farrelly, were now added to the Sanctuary. The legacy of Mrs. Ann Murphy paid for the new pulpit. This gem of the wood-carver's skill is from the atelier of Lamb & Co., New York.

The accommodations in the school were insufficient. There was no hall for entertainments or fairs but the school, and to prepare it for this purpose the partitions had to be taken down and the furniture removed. This sadly interfered with discipline, and entailed loss of time and great damage to the furniture. To obviate this inconvenience, and to meet exigencies and give increased room to the little ones, permission was obtained to erect a pavilion in the rear of the school at a moderate cost. This was finished in the month of October at an outlay of thirteen hundred and fifty dollars. It was provided with a stage, and lighted from the centre with a large Frink reflector. In the school the partitions were extended to the ceiling, and the noise of each class-room was confined to its own limits, to the great satisfaction of teachers and pupils. An amateur dramatic organization, through Mr. Paul Revere, presented scenery, which was added to by the artist Mr. Thompson; and the stage, thus equipped, gave scope to the talented to display for their friends their histrionic proficiency.

At the close of the year the Right Rev. Bishop Wigger made his official visitation of the parish.

CHAPTER XI.

ON April 20, 1884, the Redemptorist Fathers returned to Morristown for the renewal of the Mission. The spiritual exercises were well attended, the success of the previous year was repeated, and the congregation strengthened by many graces.

The little organ placed in the choir at the time of the dedication of the Church did not meet the requirements; and, as an opportunity presented itself to secure a suitable instrument at a very low cost, the Pastor sought advice from the Bishop. After mature consideration permission was obtained to purchase it. This organ was originally built by E. & G. G. Hook, of Boston, for a Protestant Church in Providence, R. I.

It has two manuals, and the compass is from CC to F3, 54 notes, and the pedals from CCC to GG, 20 notes. The great organ contains thirteen stops, viz.: open diapason, dulciana, stopped diapason, stopped bass, principal, flute, twelfth, fifteenth, tierce, sesquialtera, clarionet, trumpet treble, trumpet bass; and the swell organ has twenty-five stops, bourdon treble, bourdon bass, open diapason, viol di gamba, stopped diapason, stopped bass, principal treble, principal bass, night horn, nazard, flageolet, and oboe. It is of unusually sweet tone; its mellowness, no doubt, is due to the seasoning of the

Rev. Eugene A. Farrell

wood. It was purchased from Hilborne L. Roosevelt, and cost, including its decoration, fifteen hundred dollars. A grand concert, including vocal and instrumental music, under the direction of eminent organists, revealed the beauties of the new instrument, whose tones filled the Church and thrilled the audience with admiration.

In the month of April, Bishop Wigger appointed an efficient assistant priest, the Rev. Eugene A. Farrell.

Sister M. Gaudentia, who had labored with so much fruit with the children, the Young Ladies' Sodality, and among the poor, was forced by continued ill-health to withdraw to the Villa at Convent Station. A cold, contracted during the Forty Hours' Devotion, while engaged in her labor of love around the altar, was neglected, and it developed into consumption. She bore her sufferings with that cheerful resignation which never failed her as novice or Sister, in class or community room. At all times she was radiant with peace, patient under trials, ever ready to deny herself if she could serve others. Her charity, like her zeal, had no limit; and when it was question of the poor, there was no care, however menial or loathsome, she would not gladly undertake. Her heart glowed with sympathy for the poor children; and she was always ready to shield and excuse the idle, mischievous, or truant pupil. The best test of the influence of her beautiful life is the reverence with which her memory is still cherished by all who knew her, and, more than all, by those who were the object of her kindness in school. She passed to her reward, consoled by the Sacraments of Holy Church, June 11, 1884.

Catholics never fail to greet warmly the young priest; they crowd the Church to hear his first Mass, the Sanctuary to receive his blessing.

It was our good fortune at this time to receive the Rev. John J. Hughes, of the Congregation of St. Paul, the Apostle, best known as Paulist Fathers, who, lately ordained, came to Morristown to visit his relatives. On Sunday he celebrated Holy Mass, and gave his blessing after Mass, and after the Vesper services, to all those who flocked to receive it.

The Catholic Church has ever inculcated in her children a tender devotion to the departed souls. They are the object of her constant solicitude. As there is no moment when upon her altars the Spotless Victim of Calvary is not raised to stay the wrath of God, and to render to Him a worthy action of praise and thanksgiving; so, there is no moment when the supplications of priests and people, hallowed by the merits of the Precious Blood, do not rise like a sweet incense in the sight of God, to appease His justice and solicit His mercy for "those who have died in the Lord." The beautiful custom, which sprang up in the Ages of Faith, and which prevails in Catholic countries, of tolling the bell at sundown to admonish and summon Christians to pray for their dead, was introduced here November 2.

The vigilance of a priest is not confined to the present wants of his parish. In this country, where the growth of communities is so rapid and villages develop quickly into large cities, he must look to the future and secure the site which may one day be needed for a new congregation. A mere glance at the localities in which our parishioners were grouped, one-half at the eastern, the other at the western limit of the City, a moment's thought of the strides towards material progress and local expansion Morristown was making, would carry conviction of the wisdom of a little foresight for the welfare of religion. Many of the domestics, many of the aged, found it nigh to impossible to attend church if the weather were inclement. For years the Condit property, a fine mansion with a realty of almost ten acres, situated at the junction of Sussex and Speedwell Avenues, went begging for a purchaser, and was a constant temptation to Father Flynn. The sight was eligible. And, although property in that locality was stagnant, it was not because of its unhealthfulness, but of the desire of the holders to induce the wealthy to erect villas, and thus secure good prices for the land. The industrial class did not dare aspire to a residence in that section; and the few who had houses there were little more than tolerated. Whenever duty called him to the neighborhood the Pastor looked lovingly on the big board with its "For Sale" glaring at him; and a voice whispered to him, "Buy it for a future church." More than once he drove away the phantom; but it again returned. Finally, he invited the Bishop to visit it with him. The day fixed for the inspection was gloomy enough with rain and fog to make a Cockney happy; and together in a close carriage the Bishop and Pastor drove around the premises, and considered the present needs and the future prospects of the faithful in that portion of the City. On returning to the Rectory the Bishop said: "When I came here this morning it was with the resolve not to allow you to purchase this property; but after all I have seen I now give you full permission to buy it." Negotiations to this end were entered into. The price asked was twenty-five thousand dollars.

A change in the dominant political party, which for twenty-five years had ruled the country, was effected by the presidential elections. The result was looked forward to with some anxiety by business men; for, it was possible to enact legislation which would hinder prosperity, and precipitate, perhaps, a panic. His Bishop was in Baltimore in attendance upon the Third Plenary Council, and thus the Pastor was deprived of his valuable counsel. He determined to wait. When Bishop Wigger returned and heard of Father Flynn's decision he approved of it, for, during his absence, he shared the Pastor's fears, and was not a little anxious with regard to the financial success of the enterprise.

In the Winter months of 1885 a series of lectures were given to the members and friends of the Young Men's Catholic Association by Fathers M. A. McManus and Flynn. There was no admission fee, and the exercises were varied by recitations and music. They afforded amusement, and were a source of intellectual improvement to all.

The Bishops of the Third Plenary Council, to secure for all the faithful the nourishment their souls need and the Word of God supplies, made it obligatory on all pastors to explain the Gospel for at least five minutes at every Mass on Sundays and solemn feasts. In compliance with their wise enactment a five-minute sermon was written by either the Pastor or assistant and read at the low Masses.

Circumstances heretofore hindered the faithful from taking the active part in its ritual that the Church desires, and which it has insisted upon from time immemorial. The sacred service of song has always been a potent force in the Church, and her Pontiffs and Doctors in all ages have enshrined the dogmas of faith in poetry and music, which the people sang unto edification and instruction. It is not easy to impress a congregation with its ability to enter into song worship. There is timidity, a mutual shyness, and a distrust of vocal powers to overcome. But with patience and encouragement these obstacles may be dissipated, and assured success awaits both pastor and people. The better to secure this result, Father Flynn published a booklet, with the consent of his Bishop, *Lent, and how to spend it*, in which were embodied hymns to be sung at Benediction, and during the devotions popularly known as the Stations of the Cross. The congregation at almost the first attempt succeeded beyond expectation. All entered into the singing with heartiness and zest, and the crowds which thronged the services during the holy season attested the value of this feature, not indeed new but hitherto disregarded.

A parish is the Lord's vineyard, and the fruits thereof are the sturdy Christians who, in the ranks of the laity, daily fight the battles which will one day win for them the victor's crown.

But that is a sterile field which yields only combatants, which sends not leaders for the hosts of God, or virgins to his cloisters to storm heaven by prayer and purity of life while the conflict rages.

Mr. Eugene P. Carroll, born in Morristown, educated in the parish school, at St. Benedict's College, Newark, N. J., St. Charles's College, Md., and at Seton Hall, had pursued successfully his studies, and he was deemed by his superiors worthy of the high

Rev. Eugene P. Carroll.

office of the priesthood. As the diocese was in great want of priests, Bishop Wigger was compelled by the absence of some of his priests, by the sickness of others, to hasten the ordination. On Sunday, March 8, through the kindness of the Delaware, Lackawanna, and Western Railroad Company, a party of his friends, many of them old schoolmates, chartered a train to enable them to witness Mr. Carroll's ordination in the Seminary Chapel, South Orange. The touching ceremony in this exquisite gem of Gothic architecture was witnessed by all with deep emotion. Although not the first child of the parish to be raised to this great dignity, Father Carroll was the first to be ordained for the Diocese of Newark.*

A substantial testimony of the affection and good-will of his friends was presented to the young priest, when the ceremonies were ended, in the shape of a gold watch. Father Carroll celebrated High Mass, assisted by Fathers Flynn and Farrell as deacon and sub-deacon, in our Church, Sunday, March 15. Father Flynn preached a sermon on the "Dignity of the Priesthood," and, after the Mass, Father Carroll gave his blessing to the congregation, which tested severely the capacity of the Church.

Again the attention of Bishop and Pastor was directed to the Condit property. Mr. Cleveland had

* The Very Rev. J. J. McDonald, Dean and Rector of St. Patrick's, Utica, N. Y., in the Diocese of Syracuse, was born in Morristown, but with his family left here at an early age.

been inaugurated President. The change in administration had come and passed, the gruesome anticipation of calamity vanished, the prosperity of the nation flowed uninterruptedly. Once more negotiations were opened; the insurance company who owned the property adhered to their price; and, with the Bishop's consent, this desirable piece of land and tenement became the property of the Catholics. No little excitement was stirred up on all sides when the news spread. Some of our own flock sharply criticised the priest for adding to the burden of the Church, although when he announced the purchase at all the Masses he laid special stress on the fact that Bishop Wigger, and not the Church of the Assumption, held the title of the property, and was answerable for the success or failure. In either event this parish was not to be benefited or mulcted a penny's worth. Others saw their plans shattered, and their dreams fade away from their fancy. The authority to secure the Condit property came in the following:

"SETON HALL COLLEGE,

"SOUTH ORANGE, March 5, 1885.

"DEAR FATHER FLYNN:

"I hereby consent that you purchase the property on Speedwell Avenue for twenty thousand dollars, or as little above that sum as possible, for the purpose of eventually building a church on the same.

"Yours very sincerely,

✠ "W. M. WIGGER,
"Bishop of Newark."

The Condit Property, purchased 1885. From Foundations of St. Margaret's Chapel.

When the transaction was ended, and the title passed, Bishop Wigger warmly congratulated Father Flynn:

"SETON HALL COLLEGE,
"SOUTH ORANGE, March 10, 1885.
"DEAR FATHER FLYNN:

"I congratulate you on the purchase, although it did cost the full twenty-five thousand. I hereby give you permission to begin at once to alter the stable into a chapel for the people. Of course you will pass a resolution to that effect at a meeting of Trustees. I must try and come up there next week to see the big house.

"With best wishes I remain,
"Very sincerely,
✠ "W. M. WIGGER,
"*Bishop of Newark.*"

The assistance rendered to the Pastor by Messrs. H. O. Marsh and D. D. Craig merits more than a passing mention. When these gentlemen met Father Flynn, they asked him to outline his plans for disposing of the property and paying for it. Without solicitation they offered to discount his note for fifteen thousand dollars, that he might pay the insurance company that amount and thus secure a title, without encumbrance, on the bulk of the property, which he proposed disposing of in building lots, and for the balance of the ten thousand the company should be satisfied with a mortgage on the substantial house and land. This offer met the approval of all concerned. Mr. Howell surveyed the land, laid it off in lots, and printed a number of maps for those who contemplated purchasing. A meeting of the congregation was called to order in the pavilion. The object, it was stated, was to dispose of the lots to Catholics, if possible, and, after a reasonable time, to all comers. Father Flynn acted as auctioneer, and most of the best lots were quickly disposed of at good prices. The Water Company laid their pipes through the streets, and thus the location became more desirable for residences.

The streets were named Columba, in honor of the great Saint of Iona; Grant, in honor of the great General of the Civil War, who was then in his death agony, and Bellevue Terrace, from the charming prospect visible from the elevation.

The lot looking north, directly in front of Columba Street, was reserved for the erection of a chapel. In the beginning of April the requisite permission was obtained:

"SETON HALL COLLEGE,
"SOUTH ORANGE, April 7, 1885.
"DEAR FATHER FLYNN:
"I hereby authorize you to erect, when you consider it proper to do so, a little chapel on the new property, to cost about one thousand dollars.
"With best wishes, I remain,
"Yours very sincerely,
✠ "W. M. WIGGER,
"*Bishop of Newark.*"

Louis Hazeltine prepared the plans, and the contract for grading the street was given to Thomas Holton; for the carpenter and mason work, to Eakely & McEntee; for painting and decorating, to William T. Coghlan. No delay was made in the construction of the modest building which was to rear aloft the cross and be a new sanctuary of the Most High. The great devotion of the Celtic race to St. Margaret, Queen of Scotland, as witnessed by their family names—for after Mary there is scarcely another more frequently bestowed upon their daughters than Margaret—her sweet and beautiful life, so much in its details like that of St. Elizabeth of Hungary and in some respects more attractive, prompted the Pastor to honor, even in an humble way, this great Saint, recognized thus for the first time in the United States. At the close of the month of May everything was in readiness for the laying of the corner-stone. It was determined to invest it with all the pomp and ceremony possible. The members of the parish entered heartily into the Pastor's plan, and the ceremony was so grand and impressive that few who witnessed it will ever forget it. The following accurate report was written by an eye-witness:

"Sunday, May 31, 1885, was a memorable day for the Catholics of Morristown. Surrounded by members of the local and visiting clergy, in the presence of a large number of the laity, the Right Rev. Winand M. Wigger, Bishop of the Diocese of Newark, laid the corner-stone of the chapel to be erected to the honor of God and St. Margaret, with all the pomp and splendor of ritual with which the Roman Catholic Church invests such an important ceremony. But, apart from the interest that such an event naturally arouses, the occasion was one of deep significance. It illustrated and emphasized not only the growth of our city, but it was likewise indicative of the rapidly increasing strength of the Catholic Church in our midst. There are some of the members of the Church of the Assumption who can recall the time, not so very long ago, when the nearest Catholic Church was at Madison, then known as Bottle Hill. Hence it was determined to give the ceremony an expression of the significance it justly claimed, to mark it as an era in the history of the Catholic Church in Morristown. And so, despite the threatening weather, the mother Church gathered together her numerous societies, and, preceded by the cross-bearer and the acolytes with waving banners, followed by the clergy in their sanctuary dress and the Bishop in his purple vesture, they marched, over a thousand in number, through the town to Sussex Avenue, where the new chapel is to be erected. A peculiar feature of this procession was the corner-stone, adorned with flowers and carried by four of the oldest members of the congregation, preceded by six little girls in white, all representing the tribute of three generations to this happy event. Arrived at the grounds, the Bishop, vested in cope and mitre, and bearing his crozier, solemnly blessed and laid the corner-stone, in which was placed an iron box containing, besides various coins and copies of the *Jerseyman*, the *Banner*, and the *Chroni-*

cle, a parchment describing the event in Latin, and of which the following is a translation:

"'D. O. M.

"'On the 31st day of May, in the year of our Redemption 1885—Pope Leo XIII. happily reigning, Right Rev. Winand M. Wigger being the Bishop of Newark, and Rev. Joseph M. Flynn, Rector, with Rev. Eugene A. Farrell, his assistant, of the Church of the Assumption; Grover Cleveland being President of these United States; Leon Abbett Governor of the State of New Jersey; and John Taylor Mayor of Morristown—Right Rev. Winand M. Wigger, D.D., in the presence of the clergy and before a large concourse of people, laid the corner-stone of this Chapel to be erected to the honor of God under the invocation of St. Margaret.'

"After the ceremony the Right Rev. Bishop made a short address to the people, congratulating them on the progress of the Church in Morristown, and in particular commending the zeal they uniformly manifest in the furtherance of every good and praiseworthy work in the interests of morality and religion. He concluded with the hope that the day would not be distant when they and their labors would be so blessed that the humble beginning of to-day would ripen into a new, a large, and a flourishing parish."

Huge masses of black clouds rolled up from the southwest; the wind was momentarily increasing in violence, and great drops of rain admonished all to seek shelter from the impending storm. Banners were taken from their poles and put away; white veils were hurriedly exchanged, and soon all were in shelter from the tempest, which disappeared almost as quickly as it sprang up.

The patriarchs who carried the corner-stone from the mother Church were Thomas F. Burke, Thomas Degan, Martin Murphy, and John McGuire, and they were accompanied as a guard of honor by the little Misses Genevieve Welsh, Lulu Clifford, Rose Corcoran, Agnes Lucas, Marguerite Kenny, and Marguerite Martin. The Rev. William D. Hughes, Paulist, a guest at the Rectory, took part in the ceremony.

The corner-stone laid, an effort was made to raise the money to pay for the Chapel as the work went on, so that, if possible, by the time of dedication it should be absolutely free from debt. To this end a bazaar was held, and in three days one thousand and eighty-nine dollars and five cents were realized. All worked with a will, and the parishioners showed their enthusiasm by their attendance in large numbers and generous liberality.

While advancing the material interests of the parish the schools were not neglected. Sister Mariana succeeded Sister Gaudentia as Sister-servant, and, together with Sister Adele, infused an excellent spirit into the children. Regular attendance, close application, active rivalry among the classes distinguished the children, especially in the higher grades. The examinations for graduation and promotion were held in public, and were attended by the parents and friends of the pupils. The un-

1. ST. MARGARET'S CHURCH, JULY 12, 1885.   2. INTERIOR.
3. ON THE ROAD TO ITS NEW SITE.

GENEROSITY RECOGNIZED. 171

wearying patience of Professor Hurley afforded the congregation a pleasant surprise at the closing exercises of the school by the rendition of the operetta "The Pirates of Penzance," the entire part score sung solely by the children.

The unpleasant memories which cling to the 12th of July were varied this year by the dedication of St. Margaret's Chapel.

Generous friends again came forward to signalize their faith and devotion, and to enrich the Church by the wealth with which God had blessed them.

Mr. Patrick Farrelly donated the bell, furnished by McShane & Co., and weighing four hundred pounds; Miss Ella Carroll presented the Stations of the Cross; Mrs. Maggie Howard, the Sanctuary lamp, statues of St. Joseph and the Blessed Mother, and the holy-water stoup; and other ladies, the carpet. At eleven o'clock Sunday, July 12, the ceremony of blessing the Chapel, performed by Right Rev. Bishop Wigger, was witnessed by a congregation numbering over two hundred which filled and overflowed the little edifice. The high Mass, which followed, was sung by the Rev. Eugene P. Carroll, and the sermon was preached by the Rev. Michael P. Smith, the eloquent Paulist. Fathers McCartie, the Chancellor of the Diocese, and Flynn were present in the Sanctuary.

In the afternoon the Bishop administered Confirmation, and blessed the bell for St. Margaret's.

This congregation has never been lacking in

generosity, whether for its own or diocesan purposes. This year the offering of Peter's Pence was so large, and so much in excess of what other churches in the Diocese had contributed, as to merit special encomiums from the Bishop. The following letter was received and read by the Pastor:

" SETON HALL COLLEGE,
"SOUTH ORANGE, August 18, 1885.
"DEAR FATHER FLYNN:
"Your favor enclosing check for two hundred and twenty-eight dollars, Peter's Pence, has been received and is acknowledged with thanks.

"The Bishop desires me to convey to you and to the generous Catholic people of Morristown his grateful appreciation of the very liberal offering. It is the largest contribution hitherto received this year for the Holy Father from any Church of this Diocese, with the sole exception of the Cathedral collection, which exceeds yours only by the small amount of two dollars.

" With respectful regards,
" I remain faithfully yours,
" D. McCARTIE."

During vacation the Sisters' house was altered, improved, and enlarged to afford better accommodations to these devoted teachers.

When they returned, in September, the old house had been so changed that they hardly recognized it, and the inconveniences which they had borne so long without complaint or murmur had altogether disappeared.

CHAPTER XII.

OWING to a serious throat affection, Father Flynn was ordered by his physician to go South to escape the rigors of the winter. But the unusual severity of frost and cold which desolated this refuge of the afflicted in search of balmy air and sunshine, and transformed the land of flowers and orange-blossoms into a veritable Arctic region, did not prove the desirable exchange he contemplated, so the Pastor hastened from this unfriendly climate to the more promising and favored resorts of California. He returned home in March very little benefited by his trip, and on Sunday evening, March 14, entertained the parishioners with an informal talk on what he had seen during his absence.

On his return Father Flynn was met at the depot by the Young Men's Catholic Association, and to the music of the band, amidst lighted torches, was escorted to the rectory, where he was serenaded.

It pleased the Bishop at this time to testify the good esteem in which he held the parish by raising its Pastor, on March 17, to the dignity of Dean of Morris and Sussex Counties.

For a long time it was apparent that the old Church, transformed into a school, had outgrown its usefulness. Various schemes of altering and enlarging were entertained, but it was wisely concluded to wait, as the contemplated improvements would necessitate an outlay which the inadaptability of the building would not warrant, and which if made would be, at best, only a makeshift. Now, however, the time had come when inaction was no longer wise. The health of the little ones was imperilled. In the Spring session they crowded the pavilion, and added to the cares of their new teacher, Miss Mary Mulhall. March 29 the Pastor announced his intention of erecting a new school in the old Cemetery, and requested their friends to remove from it the ashes of the dead.

Once more the old, old cry of distress in Ireland reached the ears and touched the sympathetic hearts of Americans. Coupled with the want which prevailed, especially among the Galway fishermen, was the noble effort made by the Nationalists for some measure of freedom and independence. To the United States both the victims of hard penury and the patriots looked for aid. The members of the congregation took the matter in hand. The Dramatic Club of the Young Men's Catholic Association prepared the Irish play "Eileen Oge," and on April 26 presented it most creditably to the largest audience the Lyceum ever held. The net proceeds were very near one thousand dollars, which were divided equally between both funds.

Bishop Carr, of Galway, acknowledged in a very graceful letter the generous offering sent to him.

The ambition to embellish the Church was still

alive and active. Miss Bessie Carroll, who on different occasions had presented the holy-water stoups at the porch and the adoring Angels on the Altar, presented a silver ciborium.

The Paulist Fathers, M. P. Smith and A. P. Doyle, were invited to conduct the spiritual exercises of the Jubilee retreat. The sermons and instructions drew large numbers during the week it continued, and over eight hundred approached the Sacraments. Now came a splendid manifestation of the faith of our people. It was determined that the visit to the other Church, a condition required by the Holy Father, should be made by the entire congregation processionally. The different societies assembled in the Church at half-past three in the afternoon of Sunday, June 22. Mr. Cornelius Holly acted as marshal, and headed the procession, which was led by the cross-bearer and acolytes. The school children under the Sisters' charge followed, then the women's and men's societies, and behind them those of the parish not enrolled in any society, and finally the priests of the parish and the missionaries in cassock and surplice. The joyous ringing of the Church bell signalled the procession to start, and through the town streamed like a vari-colored ribbon the children, the young, the old—the girls in white, the boys wearing sashes across their breasts, and all the societies bearing aloft their banners.

Mute and reverential respect was shown to this bold and public manifestation of faith.

Arrived at the Chapel, on the porch of which an altar had been prepared, the faithful ranged themselves in front and on the sides. The Most Blessed Sacrament was exposed amid a dazzling array of lights and fragrant flowers. The Litany of the Saints was recited in English, the hymns *O Salutaris* and *Tantum Ergo* sung, and, at the close, the Papal benediction imparted to the kneeling multitude. The impressive ceremony, the kneeling crowd hushed in deepest reverence, the glowing radiance of the setting sun, the smoke of incense, and melody of hymn framed a picture rarely to be seen and never to be forgotten.

It formed the topic of conversation among our fellow-citizens and furnished a text to the pulpits of the different churches. It was commented upon favorably by almost all, and the example was pointed out as commendable and worthy of imitation.

A start was given June 29, by Mr. Patrick Welsh, to the new school project by the generous gift of one hundred dollars. From this grew the subscriptions, large and small, which aided so practically the desires of the Pastor. On October 25 the fence dividing the Cemetery from the street was torn down; the laborers set to work to excavate for the foundations of the new school. The bodies were carefully and reverently moved to the Cemetery by friends, if any remained; otherwise, under the personal supervision of the Pastor.

THE BAYLEY SCHOOL AND HALL, 1887.

To Augustus Eichorn, of Orange, was entrusted the task of embodying the views of the Pastor and preparing the plans and specifications. The Allen Brothers received the contract to furnish the granite from their Waterloo quarries for the foundation and trimming; the responsibility of erecting it was entrusted to the rising firm of old school-boys, Malley, Dempsey & Cooney, and the carpenter work to Lonergan & Brown. It was determined to push the work that the corner-stone might be laid on Thanksgiving Day, and the foundations so advanced that they might be covered in before the rigors of Winter set in. No one was regarded as more fit to preach at the forthcoming ceremony than the first pastor, now Bishop McQuaid. To the invitation he promptly and willingly acceded:

"ROCHESTER, N. Y., November 6, 1886.
"DEAR FATHER FLYNN:
"Do not trouble yourself about me. I will find my way to Morristown without difficulty, as I ought to know the road. I shall be with you Wednesday evening, and will accept with pleasure the hospitality of your house.

"I have told my secretary to get ready and send you a large photograph of me as Bishop (I would send one as Father McQuaid if I had it), handsomely framed, for your bazaar, which you will please accept.

"It is probable that I shall go to New York on the preceding Monday.
"Yours sincerely in Christ,
✠ " B., BP. OF ROCHESTER."

The chronology of events makes it necessary to notice a remarkable cure which, through prayer, was effected in a young woman of the parish. At the time it excited wide-spread attention, and it now deserves a complete and succinct recital. Miss Jennie Smith, living some miles from the Church, near New Vernon, was at once the object of God's chastening hand and his caresses. As none realized more than herself the keen intensity of her sufferings, none can describe them better or tell more vividly the joy she experienced in this sudden and providential restoration of health:

"Early in the Summer of 1880 the pain and weakness of which I had been complaining for some time began to grow serious, and I was placed under treatment. Our family physician, Dr. Van Wagner, of Madison, pronounced it a case of general weakness and dyspepsia; the pain through my back was caused by 'kidney trouble.' I improved and soon gave up taking medicine. In the Spring of eighty-one I began to fail again. Our family doctor having died the previous winter, I was taken to Dr. Lewis, of Morristown. His opinion was that I had 'stomach trouble' and needed 'tonics.' In July I was taken with violent pains all through my body and limbs, but particularly through my back and left side. Having sold his practice in this place, Dr. Lewis could not come here, but recommended his successor, Dr. Pennington, of Basking Ridge. He said I had spinal trouble and rheumatism round the heart. After three weeks had passed I was able to go around once more, but my body and limbs continued to swell and I suffered a great deal of pain. During the Winter I grew real well apparently, but Spring found me losing strength once more. Dr. Flagler, of Morristown, was then consulted. After making a most painful examination, he said I had 'stomach trouble, slight kidney trouble, and needed tonics.' He ordered me to take plenty of outdoor exercise, *riding* and *driving particularly*. I followed his advice as closely as possible, but each time I went for a drive I suffered terrible pain in my back. I kept on with him till Winter, finding myself worse instead of better. I tried Dr. Uebelacker, of Morristown. He said the medicine I had been taking was entirely too strong for me, and that I must *not* ride or drive, as the jarring only increased my suffering. He said I was suffering from liver and stomach trouble, and that was what caused such distress through my back. In some ways his medicine gave me great relief, but the pains kept increasing until the second of February, when I was prostrated. Dr. Uebelacker was very ill just at this time, and Dr. Voorhis, of Basking Ridge, was called in. When he came I was unable to rise from my bed without assistance, and after an examination he said I had spinal meningitis with other trouble. Although always complaining of my back, and never while under treatment being able to walk across the room to my bed if my clothing was unloosed, only one of the doctors ever said I had spinal trouble. I suffered great pain and sat up only a few times during the first few weeks of my sickness. The effort caused me such distress and seemed to do me no good, so the doctor forbade me rising 'for a little while.' Gradually my limbs lost strength, and the pain, that never ceased altogether, was agonizing at times. My flesh was so sore that I could scarcely be touched, and when my bed was made I had to be lifted on the sheet, and the pains caused by moving cannot be described. On March 17 I was placed on an invalid's chair which had been padded and prepared in such a way that it was perfectly smooth, straight, and solid. On this couch, without even a pillow, I suffered for three years, nine months, and twenty days, and no one, not even my faithful sister, who nursed me through it all, ever knew of the bitter agony I suffered there every day, every hour. No one knew but our Divine Lord, and He gave me strength to bear it all. During the early part of my sickness I was troubled with faintness, unusually severe pain, and great difficulty in breathing. While suffering from an attack of this kind, on Good Friday night, I was prepared for death by our pastor, Father Flynn. I rallied, however, and never during the three years that followed was I troubled with another attack of that kind. Dr. O'Gorman, of Newark, was sent for to hold a consultation with Dr. Voorhis. He said I might live that way for fifteen years, but did not say that I would ever be well. I did not change much from this time until January of eighty-five, when I was suddenly stricken with paralysis of the nerves of the head and brain. My arms and limbs were drawn up, and, when conscious again, I was unable to speak for some time and even then only a word at a time. For three months I could not use my eyes, for raising or lowering them would immediately bring on another attack, usually followed by vomiting, the effect of the sympathetic action of the nerves. After applying blisters and many other remedies the paralysis was checked. Later on abscesses formed on my neck and head, increasing my suffering still more. Different times my chair was raised a very little, but each time it brought on the paralysis so it had to be lowered again. Strong bands were passed from the top of my chair to small pads under each arm; thus I was kept from slipping down, for when the weight of my body drew me down, it was only with great care and with intense pain that I could be drawn up again. In this condition I lingered until November, eighty-six—no better, and certainly weaker in many ways. In all this time I was never moved, nor could I even have my bed made. The way it was padded saved me this suffering, and the sheet had to be slipped from under me inch by inch by the hands of a most careful and tender nurse, my sister. At different times we made novenas. I always felt that if I could go to St. Michael's Monastery I would be cured. My sister Mary was going to New York, and promised me she would go to the Monastery and ask the Fathers to offer the Holy Sacrifice for me. Father Albino instructed my sister to have me make a novena. I began the novena on November 13, and at the same time I gave up taking all medicines. When I stopped the morphia the pain increased and was agonizing. The pain was not ordinary, but a throbbing sensation. On Wednesday the paralysis returned, and although my sufferings were so severe that while I did not seem able to stand it, yet the thought of death never came to my mind. Thursday, Friday, and Saturday the pain was such that the thoughts of it now make me shudder. On Monday morning Father Farrell came by appointment to bring me Holy Communion. I was hardly able to make my Confession; yet I desired to make a general Confession. Father Farrell would not allow me at first, as he thought I was too weak; but as I insisted he finally consented. I made my general Confession and received Holy Communion. When Father Farrell had gone away my sister Mary brought me a glass of water, and a light breakfast. This I took; and when she had taken the dishes away, I said, I am going to try to get up. She did not know how to advise me. Her eyes filled with tears, and as she gave me her hand I raised myself with as much apparent strength as ever. I felt no pain. Neither of us for a moment could speak. She asked me how I felt. I answered I had no pain. She bade me wait until she called my papa and my brother Tom. When they came in I was sitting up and this appeared to frighten them. They knelt down by my bedside and said the Rosary together. Then I felt so well I wanted to try to get up. Tom stood on one side of my bed and Mary the other, and each gave me a hand. I pushed myself down to the foot of the bed. They wrapped me in a blanket. My feet touched the floor. I stood up and walked two or three steps alone, and then I was overcome with emotion and nearly fainted. Joy at standing again, gratitude to God, overpowered me. It seemed all like a dream. As I was fainting my brother caught me and placed me sitting in a chair. They thought I was dying, and picking up the bottle of holy water from the Monastery, which I kept by my bedside in my illness, my sister Mary put the bottle to my lips, saying, 'Jennie, swallow some.' I did without knowing what I was doing. Instantly I recovered my senses, and walked alone to the chair. I was cured. My left leg had curved from the knee-joint, but now there was no difference between them."

On the second Sunday from the day of her recovery Jennie drove with her family, in spite of a raging storm and roads roughened by frost, to Church to make her thanksgiving. Unaided she walked to her pew, and unaided she went to the Altar to tell her gratitude; and into the Sacristy after the Mass to pay her respects to the priests. The sight of her thrilled all hearts with admiration and thanksgiving. It may be said that from that time to the present she has enjoyed perfect health and attends to her numerous duties without the slightest fatigue; and has never experienced a return of her old symptoms.

It is time now to turn to the new School. Bishop McQuaid arrived November 24, and in the evening visited the Young Men's Catholic Association in their rooms. The parlor was crowded, and over the Bishop's chair was a bank of flowers with "Welcome" in buds of brightest hue.

The Bishop was most heartily welcomed by the scions of those he had ministered to more than thirty years before. In a brief speech he expressed the pleasure it gave him to be in Morristown again and to witness the progress the parish had made. He told them of the usefulness of Young Men's Associations, urged them to cultivate a spirit of loyalty to the Church, and portrayed the ideal Christian man. His remarks were frequently interrupted with applause, and at the close he was introduced personally to all the members.

The morning of November 25, Thanksgiving day, broke with dull and heavy skies that gave no hope of clearing away. Bishop McQuaid was occupied all the morning seeing the old parishioners and recalling old memories.

At noon Bishop Wigger arrived, accompanied by a considerable number of priests. When the hour fixed for the ceremony arrived the rain poured down in torrents. Under the shelter of an umbrella, undaunted by the storm, Bishop Wigger laid the corner-stone. On his return to the Church, which was filled with people, the school children, Young Men's Association, Catholic Benevolent Legion, and other societies, Bishop McQuaid ascended the pulpit and spoke as follows:

"I am come here this afternoon to assist in the blessing of the corner-stone of this new, grand school-house for the education of the Catholic children of this place. Thirty-nine years ago they of our faith who dwelt in this place were few in number—their resources not over-abundant, with much to dishearten them, strangers in the land, strangers from a far-off country, not finding many friends in those times. Thirty-nine years ago the cry against our holy religion—against the race to which we belong, was heard on every side; we were not welcome in the country. They bade us go to one side: 'Put your church in an out-of-the-way place where no one can see it; go on a side street, you poor foreigners—go on a side street and build your shanty!' But we were heedless of their cries. No wonder we were not much thought of—much regarded by the people

—no wonder there were so many spoke ill of us. At this time you had no church in Morristown. But why should you have one? The other church is not far off—you were but a handful—you were only a handful of people; then it was that this lot, already bought for the Church, but not paid for except with borrowed money—that this lot in the month of April had ground broken for the building of the Church; the site for the new Church was to one side, so that here on the corner might be left the site for the future larger Church.

"There in April, 1848, were dug the foundations of the building for the basement. Some cried out against the excavations for the walls being seven or eight feet high. We were not to put the people to unnecessary expense—four feet would do very well.

"My answer was: These walls must be higher up to have a school. The walls of that church were built, the floors laid, the windows and doors hung August 15, 1848. And it was because the contract called for their completion on that day I chose to call the Church the Assumption. The Church was built in the following year, 1849; Bishop Hughes blessed it and preached on that occasion. In 1849, the Church of Morristown having been completed and the young pastor having no other Church to build—that year opened school in the basement of the Church at Madison; a school for the children of the people of the parish. The school when spoken of—many thought the pastor had lost his senses, for already they were wedded to the public school. In September, 1849, the school at Madison was taught for six months before a word was spoken to the people about how it should be supported. In the following September, 1850, the basement of the Church at Morristown was fitted up for a school; there was grumbling here—every one had a word to say: 'We cannot afford to pay the teacher.' That kind of talk was freely given. But the school-room was finished, the teacher was engaged and placed there.

"At the opening of that school there were twenty-five children present. In Madison we had twenty-four. Many children then walked two, three, four miles to school; there were children who came from Whippany to the Catholic parochial school. These are bits of history which I give you. I know that you will not blame me when I tell you that I feel prouder to-day—prouder by far, that so many years ago I founded and established and carried along successfully the humble Catholic parochial schools of Madison and Morristown, than I ever felt at having established and founded Seton Hall College and Seminary for the education of the rich or education of Levites for the Sanctuary of God. Your mind cannot go back to the memories of mine in 1848. The storm of the battle that raged against us had scarcely passed away; the smoke in the distance still filled the country. We had gone through a terrible trial from 1834 to 1840, and then from 1835 to 1836 the discussion of the school question began; it was one of the greatest minds that led the people—the great Archbishop Hughes, whose superior America has never known. Among men, no matter where you placed him, in the church, in the rostrum, before statesmen, no matter where he was placed, he was a luminary. And when the Archbishop began his laudable career we were indeed a despised race in the land, despised not because of what others had done against us, but despised because we had not the courage of men. We were indeed a despised class in the whole community, and we needed such a holy man, with such power of eloquence and such courage as Archbishop Hughes, to take the Catholics and give them courage and raise them out of their despondency. The worst enemies the Archbishop had to contend against were not the ministers of the churches of the land, they were not the editors of the newspapers; the worst enemies of this noble advocate were his own Catholic friends. It was his Irish Catholic friends that betrayed him—that stabbed him in the back, and many of those belonging to our faith did their best to hinder the Protestant people from rendering us Catholics any assistance. But in the days when the storm raged in the land I was a young man growing up, taking no part in the affairs of the world; but my ears were wide open to everything that took place; then came to me this great truth: If ever we are to hold our Catholics to the faith in these United States, it must be through the instrumentality of Catholic schools for Catholic children. Just at this time Bishop Hughes was defeated in New York City by the treachery of his own friends. Just at this time the young priest came among you. I used to look around over these cities which I was familiar with, I used to look at those boys in New York, everywhere crowding our streets, but not crowding our churches, and many a time I have had occasion to say to myself: If God had not been kinder to me than to these, might I not be much worse? God in his mercy had given me the opportunity of a Christian education. Could I in common gratitude to Almighty God—could I not, then, try to gain children entrusted to my care, could I not try to teach them to know this same God by a Christian education? So we began the school.

"When the providence of God removed me to New Jersey my first thought was to get these Sisters; so I went to Mount St. Vincent on October 18, 1853, and asked for two Sisters, the first to come to New Jersey. And what a blessing they are! It is those women who are creating a Catholic atmosphere; the prayers of the mother at home are continued in the school-room. Who can take their place? You have this blessing in Morristown.

"May God bless all those here and never forsake them! Bless this congregation with added prosperity year after year, and all those who have gone before us, who are now looking down from Heaven upon the good work we are doing! And when to-day I looked down upon the old graveyard on the bodies I placed there—when I looked upon that place where those remains are gathered up and removed to a more beautiful cemetery, the thought came to my mind: Those souls, now in Heaven, gladly make way for the Christian school that is to stand there; gladly resign their resting place for the foundations of the large, beautiful school-house; the saints in Heaven—for many holy ones I placed there—are now looking down upon us."

The services were closed with Benediction of the Blessed Sacrament, and this ever-memorable day died out in mist and rain, as it had dawned.

On December 19 the male members of the parish were assembled, the new School Society was organized, and three thousand three hundred dollars subscribed before the meeting adjourned. William V. Dunn was elected president; Thomas F. Clifford, vice-president; John A. Carr, secretary, and Dean

Flynn, treasurer. It was resolved to have a certificate handsomely executed, and given to each one on the receipt of the amount subscribed, duly signed by the officers, under the seal of the Church. Meetings were held every Sunday and contributions poured in abundantly.

The success elsewhere of Holy Name Societies prompted Father Farrell to introduce a branch among our men, that they might share its blessings and extend its influence in fostering a deeper reverence for the Holy Name and extirpating profanity and blasphemy. Permission from the Rector obtained, he had soon enrolled over a hundred names, and on December 19 the Society was formally established with the approbation of the Right Rev. Bishop.

CHAPTER XIII.

THE great good effected by the guilds, which the piety of our forefathers established in the Ages of Faith, seems to have inspired the formation of associations for Catholic Young Men. The danger of contamination from contact with those of different or even irreligious beliefs, almost wholly unknown in the Middle Ages, threatens now the spiritual ruin of our youth. To this may be added the new peril of "a little learning," enough to read but not to detect the sophistries which the press spreads out daily, the vaporings of error and unbelief. Then the grog-shop, the street-corner, the dance-hall, offer certain attractions and become a pitfall for the youth of both sexes. Hence the Young Men's Lyceum, or Club, or by whatever other name it may be designated, is to-day a necessary adjunct to the Church and School. Not indeed, as the Christian Association of other denominations, to supply the place of the Church, but to extend its influence, to interweave it in the duties and amusements of daily life, and, by its saving power, to shield our young men from the temptations which beset them on every side. The Association in Morristown had thrived and proved to all its elevating efficacy.

But it was merely a tenant. Every dollar spent was for the benefit of another's property, of which

ST. MARY'S YOUNG MEN'S CATHOLIC ASSOCIATION BUILDING.

our Young Men had the use at the good-will of the owner. A desirable property, in the very centre of the City, in the heart of its business, was put on the market. Dean Flynn invited the original members of the Association to meet him in the rectory January 17, 1887, and there proposed to secure a lot and erect a permanent home. It was thought that twenty-five thousand dollars would be the limit of the outlay for site and building. The gigantic character of the undertaking appalled one and all. How would they ever pay for it? There was not a dollar in the treasury. The members almost to a man were struggling mechanics, who could but little more than meet the ordinary and necessary expenses of board and clothes. Yet they saw that the Pastor's heart was in the project, and they were not inclined to oppose him. The motion was passed to authorize Dean Flynn to purchase the property. Once more the Messrs. Marsh and Craig proved the sincerity of their friendship, and accepted with the one hundred dollars, loaned by the Pastor, a sight-note in payment for the lot. When the news spread it caused no little ripple of excitement and wonder.

A recurrence of throat trouble again necessitated a rest from his pastoral duties. Dean Flynn was advised by his physicians to try an ocean voyage. After an absence of three months he returned in time for the duties of Holy Week and assisted in the services on Palm Sunday.

There is the contagion of good as well as of

evil. Once the rock of generosity is struck the waters of charity flow abundantly. Mrs. Patrick Welsh presented to the Church the Pietà from the atelier of Mayer, Munich. It was solemnly blessed Sunday, July 3.

Meanwhile, with the return of fine weather, the mechanics resumed work on the new School. A showery Spring, the fierce heat of Summer, retarded progress and fretted the Pastor, who was determined that the scholars should not go back to the old school, and that the session should open on time. He gave it his personal, daily attention and spurred on the contractors, who avowed that it was impossible to realize his wishes.

The contract for heating with steam not only the school, but likewise the Church and Rectory, was given to Edward Dunn, of Newark, N. J. The steam-fitters did their work promptly and well.

The beginning of September found the plasterers still at work and portions of the roof not slated. Steam was turned on to hurry the drying of the walls. The furniture was moved from the old building, and new desks were put in the highest grades and in the primary department. On September 19 the children assembled in the Church, the Mass of the Holy Ghost was said, followed by an address from the Pastor, and the children took possession of their new quarters.

The interesting ceremony of the blessing of the new School took place October 9, with all that pomp and display which are characteristic of Catholic ritual, and which appeal so strongly to the children of the Church, and impress alike the believer and the unbeliever. All preparations had been made to carry out the ceremony on the preceding Sunday, but the lengthy ceremonial of the consecration of St. Michael's Church, Newark, prevented Bishop Wigger from arriving here in time, and rather than disappoint the Catholics of Morristown he promised to come again, despite the inconvenience occasioned thereby; and kept his word, arriving at the Church about 2 P.M.

The ringing of the bell indicated to the societies attached to the parish that the ceremony was about to begin. The Church was filled by the members of the various societies, and little room was left for outsiders. The altar ablaze with lights; the little boys dressed in dark clothes, with red sashes crossed from the shoulder; the girls with their white veils and scarfs; the variety of banners; the soft light shedding its rainbow hues through the magnificent muriel windows, all blended like the colors on a canvas and presented a beautiful sight. At a given signal the Bishop, preceded by Father Farrell, dressed in the vestments of a sub-deacon and bearing the cross, acolytes in purple cassocks with lace cottas, came from the Sacristy to the Altar with Father Burke as Deacon. Here Bishop Wigger intoned the hymn "Come, O Creator Spirit, bless," which was taken up and sung by the children. After the singing of prayers which invoked God's blessing on what he was going to do, the procession started from the Church to the School. First came Father Farrell bearing the cross, then followed the societies in order: The Infant Jesus, comprising the little boys; the Angels; the Sacred Heart; the Children of Mary; the Young Ladies' Sodality; the women of the Rosary Society; the Young Men's Catholic Association; the Catholic Benevolent Legion; the Rosary Society; and afterward the acolytes and the Bishop.

Various tuneful hymns were sung on the way to the School, where all the societies were ranged in front of the archway. The Bishop then blessed the outer walls with holy water, and the procession then entered the quadrangle, at the south end of which was an oratory, on which were a crucifix and two lighted tapers. Here other prayers were said, and thence the Bishop went from room to room, sprinkling the walls with blessed water and incensing them with the fragrant fumes which curled from the censer. This ended the ceremony, which many followed in the translation of the beautiful Rite made by Dean Flynn and which was sold for the benefit of the School. In his brief but earnest address the Bishop congratulated the Catholics of Morristown on their magnificent building; alluded to the zeal of their priests, and dwelt on the necessity of Christain education. He paid a glowing tribute to the devotion of the Sisters of Charity, who consecrated their lives to the education of youth, and brought his truly eloquent remarks to a close by giving his blessing to his attentive audience. The procession then re-formed and returned to the Church, where Benediction was given. The event will not soon be forgotten and the ceremony marks an important event in the history of Catholicity in this county.

The School is of brick, with granite trimmings, and has a frontage of 135 x 92 feet in depth. The entrance to the class-rooms is from a courtyard 62 x 35 feet. There are four class-rooms 22 x 25 feet; two 26 x 25, and one 26 x 22. The basement on the south side has been concreted, and affords a pleasant recreation-room in stormy weather. On the northeast side is the Hall with stage, 90 x 35 feet.

In the second story are three rooms, held in reserve for future need, divided by glass partitions, and respectively 35 x 31 feet, 29 x 21, and 29 x 34. The largest, fronting on Madison Street, is used by the Young Ladies' Sodality, the rear room by the St. Columbanus Council C. B. L., and the centre by the Senior grades for Cooking Classes.

The style of the building is mediæval, and reflects the good taste of the architect, and is one of the attractive features of our beautiful City.

The Bishop availed himself of the occasion to make his parochial visitation.

On October 29 Bishop Wigger wrote to **Dean**

Flynn: "I am happy to inform you that, at a meeting of the Diocesan Consultors, held September 22, by the advice of these same Consultors, I appointed you one of the three priests to constitute the Diocesan Examination Board." The Fathers of the Third Plenary Council reiterated the monitions of their predecessors to advance the interests of Catholic schools, and, to that end, advised the creation of Examining Boards for teachers and pupils. Bishop Wigger has never lagged in his efforts to enforce the wise provisions of the Council, and the result is evident in the increased excellence of the schools. Grades have been advanced, uniformity of school books and method established, and both teachers and scholars stimulated to extra efforts.

A very successful bazar, which opened November 14, aided very materially in meeting the expense of the improvements in Church and School. A new feature was the *Bazar Journal*, edited by the children, which contained in its different issues interesting excerpts of local history. A society of women had been established to take care of the poor during the Winter months, by sewing for them, making and cutting garments, and providing the needy with coal and provisions. The Rev. Clarence Woodman, Paulist, gave an interesting illustrated lecture in the Church, which netted a goodly-sized increase in their treasury.

The events of the year closed with Midnight Mass, which was celebrated in this Church for the last time. The disorder which frequently annoyed the faithful and provoked scandal inclined the Bishop to forbid its further celebration in the churches of the Diocese.

The new year 1888 was still young when the last payment on the loan for the purchase of the Condit property was made. On January 7 Dean Flynn paid the balance of the fifteen thousand dollar note to the National Iron Bank. This obligation was met, the house furnished, and the streets graded and improved by the sale of the lots.

A surprise was in store for the School. On Monday, January 23, the Rev. M. A. McManus, the Rev. J. Baxter, and the Rev. G. Funcke, the local Diocesan Examiners, visited the scholars, and put them through a searching examination on the matter outlined by the "Schedule of Studies" for the session just terminated. Allowing for a little nervousness and timidity, the school merited the highest commendations of the visitors.

On March 12 we were visited by the "blizzard," which for several days closed our school, stopped the wheels of commerce, and cut us off from communication with the outside world. Nothing like it in severity had visited this locality in the memory of man.

The Young Men's building, for which ground was broken in the preceding Fall, was advancing towards completion.

In the Spring of this year a spirit of patriotism

seized our fellow-citizens, who resolved to mark the site of the old earthwork raised by the patriot soldiers of the Revolution on the lofty summit which commands our City on the west. The granite boulder, about four feet high and weighing about four tons, was the gift of the Allen Brothers, one of whom was our former parishioner. It is inscribed:

>   THIS STONE MARKS
>   THE SITE OF FORT NONSENSE,
>   AN EARTHWORK BUILT BY THE
>   CONTINENTAL ARMY
>   IN THE WINTER OF 1779 AND '80.
>
>   ERECTED BY THE
>   WASHINGTON ASSOCIATION
>   OF NEW JERSEY,
>   1888.

On April 27 it was unveiled with appropriate ceremonies. The stores were closed and business suspended. The buildings and streets were gay with bunting. Flags and streamers floated from their staffs, or were arranged in festoons in front of many of the houses. Among the handsomest was the display made on the Young Men's Catholic Association building. The young men, headed by their Spiritual Director, Dean Flynn, took part in the procession, thus marking their sympathy with the dead heroes, many of them Irishmen and Catholics, who, in the trying days of 1779, erected this barrier against British tyranny and oppression. It was, indeed, a gala day, an event to strengthen the affection of the old and foster that of the young for the land which has been so rich in blessings for all.

On Tuesday, May 1, took place the formal dedication of the Young Men's Catholic Association building.

A large flag floated from the front of the attractive building, while the interior decorations were superb, a wealth of pictures everywhere gracing the walls, supplemented by banks of palms and flowering plants, sprays of cut flowers and smilax, festoons of bunting, and other decorations pleasing to the eye. The committee on decorations were Messrs. W. V. Dunn, M. F. Lowe, J. T. Murphy, and Thomas Holton, the latter furnishing the floral display that on every floor delighted the beholder.

There were two receptions—one in the morning, to the ladies, and one in the afternoon and evening, to the gentlemen. The reception committee was Very Rev. Dean Flynn, Pastor of the Church of the Assumption; President C. H. Knight, and Messrs P. Farrelly, T. Clifford, M. E. Condon, M. F. Lowe, John Murphy, Thomas Malley, T. J. O'Brien, D. L. Fox, and P. Welsh.

In the morning the committee was assisted by a number of ladies, friends and relatives of the members, and the scores of visitors were lavish in their admiration of the arrangement, finish, and equipment of the building. Voss's orchestra was placed in an alcove of the lobby outside of the parlor, and sweet strains of classic music added to the delight which the inspection of the building gave.

A special train brought a large party of out-of-town visitors in time for the afternoon exercises, among whom were Right Rev. Monsignor Doane; Rev. J. M. Grady, president of the National Union of Y. M. C. A.; Revs. P. Corrigan; Theodosius, O.S.B.; J. Nardiello, F. O'Neill, A. Kammer, J. Hanley, J. Hall, E. P. Carroll, P. Connelly, I. P. Whelan, T. O'Hanlon, M. Kane, Walter Elliott, M. A. McManus, John J. Hughes, J. H. Brady, Joseph C. Dunn, C. P. Gillen, J. J. Brennan, and others.

Among the Morristonians present were Rev. Kinsley Twining, D.D.; Rev. R. N. Merritt, D.D.; Rev. T. H. Hughes, D.D.; Rev. Wynant Vanderpool; Fathers Flynn and Farrell; Mayor Werts; Recorder Chisholm; Aldermen Barker and Farrelly; Councilmen Foote, Dustan, Doty, Schureman, Malley; ex-Mayors Miller and Taylor; Doctors Lewis and Pierson; ex-Assemblyman G. W. Jenkins; Chief Engineer H. A. Freeman; Lieut. Com. Miller, Lieut. Turnbull; Doctors Owen, Douglas, and Bradford; ex-Mayor Seidler, Hon. W. W. Cutler; Messrs. G. G. Kip, H. W. Roberts, H. O. Marsh, Paul Revere, Carman Randolph, D. D. Craig, and many more.

The reporter of the *Morristown Banner* gave an accurate report of the proceedings, which is here reproduced:

"The exercises were opened in the handsome hall, seating some one hundred and fifty guests, by President Knight in a graceful address of welcome, which was to have been followed by a dedicatory address by Bishop Wigger, but owing to ill-health he was unable to attend; and Very Rev. Dean Flynn, after reading the telegram of regret from the Bishop, declared the building, in the name of the loved prelate, dedicated to the purposes for which it was intended.

"Dr. Twining was then called upon, and made a most happy and interesting impromptu address. He was followed by the Rev. J. M. Grady, President of the National Union of the Y. M. C. A.'s, in a speech full of encouragement and good advice.

"Right Rev. Monsignor Doane was then introduced to an audience in which he had a personal acquaintance with almost every individual, and made a witty and eloquent address. Among other things he said: 'Morristown has a reputation second to no city in the States. It has often astonished me how a city of eight thousand inhabitants could become so important. It must be the quality, not the quantity!' He also paid a tribute to Mrs. Miller, the mother of ex-Mayor Miller, at whose home he had spent many happy hours in his youth.

"His allusion to Father Flynn's boyhood days and the noble work of his riper years, although made in a vein of humor, were a high tribute to the zeal and ability of the Rev. Father, the Monsignor modestly taking all the credit for the erection of the handsome building in which he stood, the new school building, and other work done here, because he had appointed Father Flynn to this Parish!

"Mr. Thomas J. O'Brien, an active member of the Association, followed in the recital of a historical sketch of the society. Mr. O'Brien's address was heard with closest attention. It was a concise and interesting history of the birth and growth of the Association, and an accurate description of their building. We are glad to be able to give it in full.

"Mayor George T. Werts followed in an impassioned address, congratulating the town and community as well as the Association upon the accession of an edifice so handsome, well equipped, and perfectly adapted to the purposes for which it is designed. The Mayor always handles English well, and his address was a source of pleasure and gratification to all who heard it.

"The closing address was made by Rev. Walter Elliott, C.S.P., who proved that the subject had by no means been worn out. Taken as a whole the addresses were the most satisfactory it has ever been our pleasure to listen to, not one of them being dull or commonplace. Musical selections were rendered between each oratorical effort, and the whole affair was well devised.

"The party was then invited to the gymnasium, where Day had spread a delightful dinner. During its service the band, stationed in the billiard-room opening above it, discoursed choice selections. All were comfortably seated and abundantly served, and the gathering thoroughly enjoyed itself, nor did it break up until the special train left for the City at 10 P.M.

"Many of the superb and valuable things that grace the various rooms are the gifts of liberal hearts, and particularly is this true of those found in the finely-appointed parlor.

"The centre of all observation is a portrait of Bishop Wigger, drawn in pastel and presented by Mother Xavier, of St. Elizabeth's Convent. It is the work of the talented Sisters of that institution, and is life-like and complete in every detail. Framed in heavy gilt, it rests on an easel. The lace curtains are the gift of Mrs. P. Farrelly. A large table-cover and a tidy, embroidered, were presented by Mrs. Eugene Burke; a series of fine pictures, scenes in Rome, by Rev. Father Farrell; others, copies from the old masters, by H. W. Miller; a handsome easel, by George W. Smith; picture shades, by Thomas Murray; piano stool, by P. M. Kain; hall lamp, by Looney & Carroll; clock, by C. K. Johnson. The flowers were the gift of Thomas Holton, whose taste in their arrangement was as artistic as his gift was liberal.

"Then, to crown the event, another gift of $500 was placed in Father Flynn's hands on the day of the dedication.

"Wnile many heads and hands have contributed to the work of perfecting the scheme and completing the building, to Father Flynn more than all others is due the credit of making it possible and bringing it to a happy consummation. Early and late, through storm as well as sunshine, pressed by other duties that were never neglected, always happy and confident, he has studied and watched and directed the erection of another perfect piece of work that shall be a monument to his good taste, ability, force of character, and untiring energy."

ADDRESS BY MR. O'BRIEN.

"About the middle of August, 1881, twenty-six Catholic young men met, at the suggestion of Thomas Malley, in the basement of the old Church of St. Mary's, lately removed to make room for more modern improvements, and in an informal manner united themselves together for the further 'moral, physical, and intellectual' advancement of each other, and founded the Young Men's Catholic Association of Morristown. These informal meetings were held under the guidance of the Spiritual Director, Rev. Joseph M. Flynn, until November 1, when more suitable quarters were secured in the Bates building.

"On November 10 the first regular meeting was held, at which the Rev. Spiritual Director read for the first time the order of business and the Constitution of the society. An election was then held, resulting in the choice of President, R. F. Dempsey; Vice-President, M. E. Condon; Secretary, H. J. Curley; Treasurer, D. L. Fox. As yet the furniture and surroundings of the rooms were very humble, consisting of a pine table and some old wooden benches. A few games of checkers and dominoes were all that offered amusements for the members, until a valuable acquisition, a billiard-table, was presented by Mrs. General Revere.

"With a will, however, the young men worked together, each meeting bringing new applicants desirous of admission to membership. At the expiration of 1881, although but a few months old, the society counted fifty-two members.

"In January, 1882, at the first annual election, the following officers were elected for the ensuing year: President, C. H. Knight; Vice-President, R. F. Dempsey; Secretary, W. V. Dunn; and Treasurer, D. L. Fox.

"With the proceeds of a bazar held in February they were enabled to furnish their rooms much more comfortably. In this they were very materially aided by valuable presents from Father Flynn, Mrs. Higgins, the late Mr. Nelson Wood, and Charles Knight. On August 15 the Association held its first picnic in Childs's Woods.

"As the year closed the society stood upon a

good financial basis and numbered fifty-nine members. The officers elected for 1883 were : President, C. H. Knight; Vice-President, M. Norris; Secretary, M. E. Condon; Treasurer, T. Malley. On April 2 a successful performance of 'The Ticket-of-Leave Man' was given in Lyceum Hall by the Dramatic Association.

"In May the project of starting a Library for the society was mooted, and substantial encouragement received from Dr. Owen, P. Farrelly, F. A. Carrington, and others, who kindly presented some very excellent and suitable works.

"Athletics were not ignored by the society, as shown by the defeat they suffered at the hands of the Morris Base Ball Club, in the game played July 4. On July 31 the first Annual Steamboat Excursion was made to Roton Point. The Dramatic Club performed the drama of 'Time and the Hour' and 'Funny Bones Fix,' in the old school-hall on Thanksgiving evening. A reunion of the members was held in their rooms, December 12. The annual election was held on January 29, 1884, and C. H. Knight was re-elected President; T. Malley, Vice-President; T. F. Welch, Secretary; and M. E. Condon, Treasurer.

"'Solon Shingle,' and by request 'Funny Bones Fix,' were given February 22. On April 1 the society took quarters in the York building, which they have occupied up to the present time. The first target excursion of the members and their friends was made to Newton, October 19.

"The monotony of the winter months was relieved by a course of lectures delivered in the rooms, one by the Rev. M. A. McManus, Newton, N. J., on 'Love,' the other by Very Rev. J. M. Flynn on 'Money,' both of which were brilliant and witty.

'Don Cæsar de Bazan' was presented by the Dramatic Club in the Lyceum, January 19, and by request was reproduced, February 18. At the election held January 28, 1885, President C. H. Knight, Vice-President Thomas Malley, Treasurer M. E. Condon were re-elected; M. F. Lowe was chosen Secretary. March 21 was the day chosen by the Almighty to remind the members of His inevitable decree by calling from their midst Edward J. Mooney, at the early age of twenty-two years. He was a zealous member, known to all for his good deportment and generous sentiment. Very Rev. Dean Flynn and D. L. Fox, as delegates, represented the society in the National Convention held in Newark, May 20. C. H. Knight resigned the Presidency July 5; T. Malley succeeding for the remainder of the year, and R. F. Dempsey became Vice-President. September 17 found the members and their friends enjoying their second target excursion in Newton.

"The emblems of mourning had scarcely been removed before God called upon the society to part with another of its members, and all bowed in humble submission at the death of William P. Foley, on October 19. He was scarcely twenty-five years old, yet he had endeared himself to all his companions, who felt keenly the loss of an active and exemplary brother. The officers elected on January 5, for 1886, were: President, T. Malley; Vice-President, W. V. Dunn; Secretary, M. F. Lowe, and Treasurer, M. E. Condon. The 'Irish Yankee' was produced in Lyceum Hall, February 22. The appeal of the poor fishermen of Galway for help received a hearty response from the society. The beautiful drama, 'Eileen Oge,' was performed for their benefit, in the Lyceum. Father Farrell assumed the duties of Spiritual Director of the Association, and continued to discharge them during the temporary absence of Dean Flynn.

"The excursion to Roton Point took place July 20. The third annual target excursion went to Easton, September 22. Several musical and literary entertainments given in the rooms during the winter months afforded pleasure and amusement to the members and their friends. The officers elected January 4, for the year 1887, were: President, T. Malley; Vice-President, T. Clifford; Secretary, M. F. Lowe, and Treasurer, M. E. Condon.

"In response to an appeal for help by the Ladies of Good Help and the Charities Aid Association a reproduction of 'Eileen Oge' was given in the Lyceum on Washington's Birthday. An entertainment was also given in the old school-hall on March 17. Oscawanna Grove was the place chosen for the Annual Steamboat Excursion, August 10. The target excursion was taken to Paterson on October 5. At the regular election held January 3, 1888, C. H. Knight was elected President, and Vice-President T. Clifford, Secretary M. F. Lowe, and Treasurer M. E. Condon were re-elected. A successful performance of 'Time Tries All' was given in the Lyceum April 23.

"Retrograding, we find that at a special meeting held January 17, 1887, Very Rev. Dean Flynn stated that he so far approved of the desire of the members to erect a building of their own that he proposed to purchase from Messrs. Marsh and Craig a lot on South Street, containing a frontage of 24 and a depth of 136 feet, for eight thousand four hundred dollars. On this site stands the handsome building just completed. It is a three-story design, in style bordering on Queen Anne, with a front finish of terra-cotta brick.

"The lower front floor is divided into two neat and commodious stores; entering the building from the left and ascending a stairway three feet wide, the visitor finds himself in the bright, cheerful lobby, 22 feet square and 16 feet high. Turning to the right, he enters the large, comfortable parlor, which is 28 feet long and 22 feet wide, with a height of 12 feet.

"Crossing the lobby to the rear, he finds himself in the Association kitchen, and going still further on, enters the refreshing bath and toilet rooms; still continuing on through a side hall four feet wide, he stands at the door leading to the janitor's quarters, and after his admission finds a suite of three large rooms, each 15 feet long and 12 feet wide, with ceilings 12 feet high.

"Returning to the lobby he passes down the spacious stairway to the first floor rear, and enters the billiard-room, which is 28 feet long, 22 feet wide, and 10 feet high. Two Collender tables tempt him to indulge in the pleasant pastime of billiards or pool; but looking through the sliding windows in the rear, he is attracted by the merry laughter of the members, and retracing his steps, he descends to the lower floor and finds himself in the gymnasium, furnished with its odd but serviceable implements for the development of health and muscle. The gymnasium is 70 feet long, 21 feet wide, and 21 feet high. On one side is the bowling-alley, and on the other the shuffle-board. On this floor is the boiler-room containing the steam-plant, and a patent steam generating boiler, built by E. Dunn, of Newark, which heats the whole building. The consequent weariness of climbing two flights of stairs is forgotten as the visitor ascends the wide stairway, lost in admiration of the chaste natural wood finish with its blushing cherry-wood trimmings, which predominates through the whole building. He is also attracted by the light-shaft, 16 feet long and 10 feet wide, which runs from the roof to the basement, lighting the entire centre of the building. Arriving on the third floor he rests for a moment in either of the two large library and reading-rooms in the rear, each 14 feet long and 11 feet wide.

"Across is the handsome meeting-room of the members, 45 feet long and 22 feet wide and 12 feet high. Light and ventilation come from the large dome, the circular window in the centre covered with old cathedral glass. The large front centre window with its elliptic arch, and the two smaller side ones, are of French plate-glass; their transoms are of stained glass containing the monogram of the Association. Augustus Eichorn was the architect of this magnificent building, which cost $16,200. Every room is well ventilated, all the floors are deafened, and Looney & Carroll gave particular attention to the sanitary plumbing. John D. Collins did the mason-work, while Lonergan & Brown looked after the carpentering, as did Barrett & Dempsey the painting.

"Although the society is but seven years old, it has matured very rapidly, and is not surpassed by any in the State. It feels a justifiable pride in showing its roll of 101 names, and pointing to 27 of its members who are representative business men of the town. The little acorn planted in 1881 develops into a stout oak in 1888, to remain as a landmark. It owes its health and strength to the invigorating, generous sap given to its root by the many kind friends and benefactors without whose assistance but little could have been accomplished. The society recognizes its inability to express its gratitude for the very many munificent gifts received. Its members will earnestly strive to show their appreciation by so deporting themselves as to reflect as much credit on the citizens as the new Association Hall does upon the buildings of Morristown.

"THOMAS J. O'BRIEN.
"May 1, 1888."

Not content with the splendid reception given to the public, the Young Men added to their reputation for hospitality by holding a reunion and complimentary reception for the members exclusively, and their friends of the gentler sex, on Wednesday evening, May 2. The rooms were newly decorated with flowers, and crowded with ladies and gentlemen in full dress, the whole scene under the brilliant electric light being one of rare beauty and life. Voss's orchestra furnished the music, and promptly at ten o'clock P.M., President and Mrs. Charles H. Knight led the grand march on the waxen floor of the main hall, in which almost a hundred couples participated. The festivities were of a varied character: dancing in the upper hall, music, singing, and recitation, mirth-provoking games, in the parlor. Patrick Sharkey served a tempting array of substantial viands in the gymnasium. The dawn had awakened the birds to their matin song when the members and their guests brought to a joyous close the crowning event of their history.

CHAPTER XIV.

DIOCESAN Ordinances require that a Mission be given at least once every five years. In compliance with this law the Paulist Fathers Nevins, Doyle, and Wyman opened a two weeks' mission on Sunday evening, May 13, 1888. The usual happy results rewarded the zeal of the missioners, and almost the entire adult portion of the congregation availed themselves of the extraordinary blessings which attend these exercises. The temperance feature of them appealed strongly, and many signed the cards which pledged the bearers to self-denial.

From year to year the hand of Death was steadily reaping the harvest and garnering many of the pioneers. Among these, conspicuous by years of faithful devotion and generous deeds from slender incomes, were Thomas Degan and his wife, Jeremiah Callaghan, and Martin Murphy. The first was one of the oldest Catholic settlers. He had hired a yoke of oxen from a townsman, who bore no love to our Church, but rather bitter prejudice; and this man, to his great chagrin, saw the outfit employed in digging out the foundation for the first Catholic church. As for Jerry Callaghan and Martin Murphy, the mere mention of their names awakens memories of deep-rooted devotion and unselfish toil for the welfare of the parish. No picnic was complete without them. It might rain torrents, the ardors of a fierce July sun might beat down upon them, they remained steadfast at their post. The removal by death of such men creates a void, and their absence suggests a feeling of lonesomeness.

Hitherto much care and attention had been given to the young men; it was now time to show some consideration to the female portion of the parish, who by their free and willing, self-imposed labors had in the past made picnics, fairs, and bazars a financial success. The fine large room over the Hall in the School-building, fronting on Madison Street, was handed over to the Young Ladies' Sodality.

They set to work to make it something more than a meeting-room. They would have it for the young women of the parish what the building on South Street was to the young men. To enable them to realize their ambition a festival was held in the Catholic Association building August 29, 30, and 31, and with the proceeds furniture, rugs, shades, and a piano were bought, which transformed the room into an attractive parlor. The busy fingers of the members deftly plied themselves, and good taste and skill are revealed in the many little marvels of feminine fancy which adorn the tables, chairs, and the shrine of Our Lady.

The need of a church in the western section of the City which St. Margaret's supplied was succeeded now by the kindred necessity of a school.

Catholic families multiplied in the vicinity, and scores of little tots awaited the all-important epoch of each one's life—their first day at school. In the most favorable weather it was a long, weary walk, which in storm could not be undertaken.

It was determined to open a primary school, to continue during the fine weather. Some five-and-twenty little ones were seated in the Chapel on Tuesday, September 8, when Dean Flynn celebrated the Mass of the Holy Ghost for them. Misses Ella Kain and Ella Foley were successively the first teachers. The Chapel, as a matter of course, had to be used; but what more fitting place to teach the little ones to love and lisp His praises than the lap of Him who said "Suffer little children to come unto me"—than the very house of their Father? The good seed was sown early; the future will gather the harvest.

Our Young Men now bestirred themselves to reduce their indebtedness, and with the efficient aid of their friends among the ladies opened a two weeks' fair in their building. The excitement of a presidential election gave spice and spirit to the undertaking. Everybody, irrespective of creed or party, was eager to show practical approval of the great work. *The Fair Journal*, issued every night, was replete with news, skits on the members, wit and wisdom. The net returns were a pleasant surprise, and exceeded by far the most successful fair ever held by the Catholics in Morristown. Twenty-seven hundred dollars were turned over to the Treasurer of the Association, Morris E. Condon.

October 24 brought the tidings that Bishop Wigger had honored the parish by making it one of the seven in the Diocese of Newark which fulfilled all the conditions for a permanent rectorship, and the pastor, by appointing him the first irremovable Rector. Congratulations were not confined to the congregation, but came from other quarters. Among the foremost was the following from Archbishop Corrigan:

"NEW YORK, November 28, 1888.

"MY DEAR DEAN:

"I have noticed with great pleasure your appointment as one of the Missionary Rectors of the Diocese of Newark. The news gives me so much satisfaction that I beg to tender you my congratulations, and to wish you every blessing and happiness in the future.

"I am, my dear sir,

"Very truly yours,

"M. A. CORRIGAN, *Abp*.

"V. REV. DEAN FLYNN,
　"Morristown, N. J."

At his own request and for personal reasons the Rev. Eugene A. Farrell was removed, and the Rev.

J. J. Shannessy appointed assistant priest by the Right Rev. Bishop of the Diocese, in the month of November.

The Church was further enriched by the arrival of the precious relic of St. Virgil, which, through the kind offices of Franz Mayer, of Munich, Bavaria, was so graciously given by the Archbishop of Saltzburg. The document which accompanied this treasure conveys ample information of its character and authenticity:

"Francis Albert,

"By the grace of God and favor of the Apostolic See Prince Archbishop of Saltzburg, Apostolic Legate, Primate of Germany, Doctor of Sacred Theology and Philosophy, etc., etc.,

"To all whom it may concern, by these presents attest and affirm, that, for the greater glory of God and His Saints, have reverently placed a portion* of the head of St. Virgil, Bishop and Confessor, and Patron of the Church of Saltzburg, in a silver case, shielded with glass, fastened with red silk thread, and affixed with our larger seal in wax, granting by the tenor of this document permission to retain it or give it to others.

---

* The case which enclosed the relic has the inscription "Reliquiæ ex cranio capitis S. Virgilii, Conf., Ep'pi. et Patroni Salisburg." It bears the seal of the Archbishop.

"In testimony whereof we append our signature under our official seal.

"Given at Saltzburg, the 24th day of March, 1887.

"FRANCIS ALBERT, O.S.B.,
Archbishop.

"Seen and approved :

✠ "WINAND MICHAEL,
"*Bishop of Newark.*"

We have thus come into possession of, perhaps, the only genuine relic of an Irish Saint on this continent. And thus, after the lapse of twelve centuries, this saintly prelate, a voluntary exile from fatherland for the spread of the Gospel, finds among the children of his exiled race, in a land whose existence he maintained almost at the cost of degradation from his high office, a new home, ardent worshippers, and devout clients. That *God is wonderful in his Saints* is still evidenced by the blessings, both spiritual and corporal, which have been so abundantly shed upon us. Gratitude to God demands more than a passing allusion to this manifestation of His power, as well to enkindle greater love and reverence towards Him as to strengthen the faith of the flock.

Miss M—— for years was a sufferer from a severe disorder, and had tried vainly the skill of the local physicians and specialists of high repute. Hundreds of dollars had been expended in this fruitless search for health.

On the advice of Dr. J. H. O'Reilly, and accompanied by him and her sister, she visited the most celebrated specialist in New York. A patient and searching examination convinced the physician that a perilous operation would be necessary, with the chances of surviving it greatly against her. Womanly modesty more than the fear of death made her shrink from the proposition.

On returning home, she began a novena to St. Virgil, and, as is usual, received Holy Communion on the morning of the ninth day. Dean Flynn read over her the prayers for the sick in the Roman Ritual and blessed her with the holy relic.

Full of faith and joy, she went home and announced to her family that she was cured. The scrutiny of the New York physician, whom they again sought, after another diligent examination, could discover no trace of her disease. She was, indeed, entirely cured. Neither medicine nor physician had any part in her instantaneous restoration to health, but the power of God, through the intercession of St. Virgil. To carry deeper conviction the brief history of the case, written by Dr. O'Reilly, is given in full:

"A Short Clinical History of Miss M——.

"In the Summer of 1889 Miss M—— visited me in relation to certain troubles of which she had a long time complained. She gave the following history:

"Perfectly well until the age of nineteen, when she became very much run down on account of some internal disease. Sought the advice of local physicians without relief. Very reluctantly agreed to seek the advice of an eminent Newark specialist, under whose care for three years she gained in health and strength, but the internal trouble remained unimproved. The great expense and inconvenience of going to Newark induced her to seek my aid. Discovering the serious internal disease, I placed her under the care of Professor Lusk, of New York, having in view the performance of a dangerous and radical operation. Receiving but little encouragement from the latter physician, she was informed that it was absolutely necessary to undergo severe surgical treatment. She was advised to return as soon as convenient with her family physician.

"On October 15, 1889, accompanied by me, she again visited Doctor Lusk, but on examination Doctor Lusk exclaimed, with eyes full of wonder: 'Why, doctor, your operation is spoiled. You can see for yourself.' I knew nothing of what she had done until we had left the doctor's office, when she told me that she knew she was cured. She had made a novena to St. Virgil. 'I am feeling,' said she, 'altogether different.' At the present day I have absolute proof that her cure is permanent. What human aid and skill failed to accomplish was effected by some higher power.

"Signed: J. H. O'REILLY, M.D.

"Morristown, N. J., January 14, 1892."

To enable the Ladies of Good Help to carry on their worthy mission during the approaching Winter,

Dean Flynn gave an illustrated lecture on the Holy Land, Sunday evening, December 16, in the School Hall, which was followed on the succeeding Sunday night by Patrick Farrelly, who described "The First American Pilgrimage to Lourdes and Rome," of which he was a member.

The lantern views added greatly to the interest of both lectures, which netted a snug sum for the deserving charity.

Hardly had the New Year greetings of the Pastor died away than he bade them again farewell. Threatened with a total deprivation of vocal power, he was urged to seek treatment and repose abroad.

When the ocean divided him from his flock he determined to make his trip a pilgrimage, pressed to this course by the physician who treated him in Paris. In February, 1889, accompanied by the Rev. Walter M. Fleming, of St. Aloysius' Church, Newark, he sailed from Marseilles, and after a voyage of four days reached Alexandria, Egypt. Thence he sailed for Palestine, and the dream of his life was realized. It was his high privilege to not only visit, but to say Mass in the Sanctuaries which mark the scenes of Jesus' life, woes, and bitter death.

When he returned again to his flock he brought with him and distributed among them as mementos of his pilgrimage rosaries, medals, flowers, and a large crucifix of olive-wood which was blessed and indulgenced in the Holy Sepulchre, and touched to all the places hallowed by our Lord's Passion.

William Ryan, who as an exemplary Christian and trustee, had won the esteem of the parish and the confidence of two pastors, was called to his reward. Thomas F. Clifford was chosen to fill the vacancy caused by this death.

In November the entire Catholic Church in the United States was celebrating the centennial of the consecration of the first Bishop, Right Rev. John Carroll. Although Baltimore claimed and held the honor of holding the festivities in the primatial city, yet the occasion was of general interest. The main feature of the event was the first American Catholic Congress.

Seldom, if ever, in the United States, and never in any country beyond the seas, nor in any age, has been brought together such an aggregate of brains, money, and influence.

Lawyers whose eloquence and legal lore have made their names a household word; journalists whose pens dash off the able leader, keen sarcasm, or incisive wit to instruct and move thousands; millionaire bankers, miners, and railroad men from the East and distant West; poets and historians; brilliant scholars who add lustre to the names of Carroll, Bonaparte, and Willis; soldiers and sailors whose bravery and skill, under the blue or gray, have enshrined their names in the hearts of their countrymen and won for themselves the titles of colonel, general, commodore, and admiral; the free, high-spirited Caucasian; and the venerable Negro whose black face, framed in snow-white hair and beard, stood out in the Congress with the sharpness of a silhouette, a freeman to-day, a slave only a few years ago. Twenty-six hundred laymen, the cream of intelligent Catholicity; eighty-four Bishops and Archbishops from the different Sees of the Union; a Cardinal, five Archbishops, and six Bishops from Canada; two Bishops from Mexico; representatives from the hierarchy of England; the Pope's delegate, Archbishop Satolli; and priests, secular and religious, without number, helped to fill the vast auditorium of Concordia Hall. Every day brought additions to the assembled throng, until the hotels were, without exception, glutted, the hotel managers dazed, the hackmen and storekeepers happy; and apathetic and courteous Baltimoreans amazed.

The weather was beastly. Rain overhead and mud under foot made walking unpleasant; but the ardor and enthusiasm of the delegates were not chilled by these drawbacks. The brilliant and imposing ceremonies of Sunday, commemorative of the consecration of John Carroll, the first Bishop of the Catholic Church in the United States, in which splendor of ritual was mingled with the thrilling eloquence of the Archbishop of Philadelphia, and the classic melodies of Handel and Gounod, were followed on Monday by a Solemn High Mass sung by Archbishop Corrigan in the Cathedral, at which all the prelates and clergy and the delegates to the Congress assisted. The sermon was preached by the

Archbishop of Oregon, and never did orator stand before a more illustrious audience. The Mass ended, the delegates made the best of their way to Concordia Hall, and rapidly seated themselves in the places set apart for the different States and Territories, and marked on a placard for that purpose.

The first opportunity offered to the Catholic laity in this country to voice their loyalty as a religious body to our republic, their sympathy with Leo XIII. in his afflictions, and their allegiance to their bishops and pastors, drew together men illustrious in every rank of life: The Vicomte de Meaux, Chief Minister of Agriculture and Commerce in France; Premier Mercier, of the Dominion Parliament; the Hon. M. J. Power, Speaker of the Dominion Assembly; Judges Daly and O'Brien, of the New York Supreme Court; Semmes, of New Orleans; Carroll, of Little Rock; Kelly, of St. Paul; Dunn, of Florida; Fallon, of Boston; Generals Rosecrans, Lawler, of Wisconsin; Tracy, of New York; ex-U. S. Senator Kernan, Gov. Carroll, Hon. A. Leo Knott, late Second Assistant Postmaster-General, Col. Don Piatt, J. Boyle O'Reilly, Daniel A. Rudd (colored); Chief Joseph, of the Montana Blackfeet, and White Bird, of the Dakota Sioux; millionaires Francis W. Palms, M. W. O'Brien, of Detroit; Eugene Kelly, Joseph J. O'Donohue, and the Messrs. Hoguet, of New York; Mayor Grant and ex-Mayor Grace, of New York; and hosts of others conspicuous for talents and wealth in every city of the Union. Acting Secretary Onahan, of Chicago, who gave the Congress its initiative and impetus, called the delegates to order, nominated ex-Gov. Carroll, the great-grandson of the illustrious Charles Carroll, of Carrollton, temporary Chairman, and who later on by unanimous consent was made permanent President, and thus opened the great Catholic Congress.

Archbishop Ireland, of St. Paul, the well-known temperance advocate, wittily dubbed by Archbishop Ryan "the consecrated cyclone," opened the proceedings with prayer. On taking the chair ex-Gov. Carroll made a speech which, had it not been followed by the brilliant, fervid effort of the silver-tongued Dougherty, would have gone on record as one worthy of the best days of forensic eloquence. While the usual routine of the formation of committees was going on the President announced the Hon. Daniel Dougherty. His first utterance captivated his audience. From sentence to sentence he passed, rising in loftier heights of impassioned oratory, stirring to their deepest depths the hearts of his hearers; stilling them at one time to death-like silence, at another rousing them to tumultuous enthusiasm which broke forth in repeated cheering, all with one impulse rising to their feet, the ladies shaking their pocket-handkerchiefs, grave and venerable prelates mingling by the clapping of hands in this spontaneous outburst of homage to the sublime genius and power of eloquence.

When he declared "the Roman Catholic laity of the United States, for the first time in Congress assembled, are here to proclaim to all the world that their country is tied to every fibre of their hearts, and no mortal power can shake their loving allegiance to its Constitution and its laws," Mr. Dougherty rose above his best efforts, and as he stood, his forefinger outstretched and his arm uplifted to heaven, the mind instantly recalled the statues of Grattan and also his burning periods. A very tempest of applause burst forth; the scene was simply indescribable. All felt that if the Congress accomplished nothing more, it was worth all the trouble, worriment, and expense of organization, all the wearing, tiresome journeying of hundreds and thousands of miles, to have brought out this splendid tribute of affectionate loyalty and gratitude of Catholics to their country.

Those who were privileged to listen to it will never forget it. The ringing, silvery voice, the well-balanced periods and graceful gestures of the orator, the profound emotion, manifested by the tears, silence, and deafening applause of his audience, made a scene rarely witnessed in the cycle of man's life.

The speech of Judge Dunn, removed from the Supreme Court of Arizona by President Grant, was also a remarkable effort. His theme was the state and education. In conversation at the close of the Congress President Carroll declared he had never heard a speaker who infused more enthusiasm into an audience. Although each speaker was limited to twenty minutes, the delegates would not allow Judge Dunn to stop until he had spoken over an hour Mr. Charles J. Bonaparte, of Baltimore, read a paper—"The Independence of the Papacy." Time cuts queer capers. A descendant of the great Napoleon, who imprisoned Pope Pius VII., in masterly, forcible, and merciless logic demonstrated the absolute impossibility of the Sovereign Pontiff, the spiritual ruler of millions in every country and under every form of government, being the subject of any king or parliament. "We do not ask for him honors or rank, least of all money—but freedom. It is not for a parliament of yesterday to confer a patent of honorary precedence on the successor of the Fisherman."

The papers read by John Gilmary Shea, the historian, on "Catholic Congresses"; by the Hon. Honore Mercier, Premier of the Dominion Parliament, on "The Attitude of Canadian Catholics"; by Mr. T. O'Sullivan, on "Young Men's Catholic Societies," brought forth unstinted and well-merited praise.

The Hon. Morgan J. O'Brien, Judge of the New York Supreme Court, Chairman of the Committee on Resolutions, read the report, which was unanimously adopted. Other papers on temperance, church literature, church music, lay action in the church, etc., were read and printed in the report of the Congress. With a few words of admonition from Archbishop Ireland, and resolutions of thanks to the committee of preliminary arrangement, to Cardinal Gibbons, the people and press of Baltimore, and to the presiding officer, ex-Gov. Carroll, the great Catholic Congress was at an end.

On Monday evening a reception to the prelates was given, attended by the delegates and by the *élite* of Baltimore and Washington. The red robes of Cardinals, the purple cassocks of the Bishops, Generals in their uniforms, the French Admiral in full dress and decorations, the varied and elegant costumes of the ladies, the buckskin dresses and feathers of the Indian chiefs, made a brilliant picture. Between three and four thousand were present to greet the Cardinals, Archbishops, and Bishops. Archbishop Elder, of Cincinnati, replied on behalf of his brethren in the Episcopacy to the address of Wm. F. Morris, of Washington, in a speech replete with historic reminiscences, wit, and feeling allusions to his work when the yellow fever devastated Mississippi, and the generous North sent money, provisions, and aid to their unfortunate brethren in the South.

The cathedral, churches, schools, hospitals, orphanages, and very many private dwellings were brilliantly illuminated. The headquarters of the Catholic Benevolent Legion was conspicuous for the gorgeous array of gas-jets, its badge and other beautiful designs emblazoned in light.

On Tuesday evening the rain and mist, which recalled English weather to those who have experienced it, and were calculated to make everything and everybody miserable, ceased, and a few stars peeped at the gathering hosts with torches and lanterns, through banks of sombre clouds.

From every quarter came the different societies, and as the eye ranged along Baltimore Street, with its undulating surface, it looked like a ribbon of kaleidoscopic hues. Torches, lanterns, lamps; red, white, and blue umbrellas with branches of lights underneath; floats, cavaliers, whose suits of armor and prancing steeds recalled the Crusaders; Negroes, studies in black and white, their chapeaux decked with long white ostrich-plumes, to the number of nearly two thousand; cadet-corps; fife and drum corps of men and boys; the splendid band of the New York Protectory Boys; and the unequalled and unique Marine Corps Band of Washington; and so they passed, lighting up the route with rockets and Greek fire, hundreds and thousands, for almost three hours; until the brain whirled with dizziness, and the eye was wearied with the sight of the thirty thousand who took part in the most gorgeous pageant Baltimore has ever witnessed. The midnight hour tolled from the Cathedral tower, and the throngs of sightseers and participants still filled the streets; and the Catholic Centennial went out in a blaze of glory.

Mr. Patrick Farrelly was the accredited delegate of this State to the Executive Committee, and was appointed on the Committee of future Congresses. Dean Flynn, Messrs. Thomas F. Clifford, John A. Carr, Peter Kain, M. E. Condon, E. T. Condon, Thomas Holton, Michael Norris, D. L. Fox, W. L. Fennell, P. Ryan, James Lawless were admitted as delegates, and at the close of the Congress visited St. Charles's College; Doughoregan Manor, the home of the Carrolls, and the burial-place of the signer; the Catholic University, Washington, the Capitol and principal buildings in the city, no longer of magnificent distances, but of magnificent edifices.

THE NEW RECTORY, 1890.

CHAPTER XV.

THE year 1890 was not only to bring additional improvements, but to demonstrate our loyalty to country and veneration for the land and traditions of our forefathers. On Sunday, March 2, Dean Flynn announced at all the Masses that, with the Bishop's permission, he had sold the Sisters' house for four thousand dollars, and that this was virtually a donation of that sum to the parish, since it came to them from him as a gift. He furthermore stated that a Rectory would be built on the site of the old Church, and when completed the priests would take possession of it, and the Sisters of the old Rectory.

Although the festivals of Irish Saints find no place in our Calendar, the feast of St. Patrick has always been marked by observances of both a civic and religious character. A century ago, when toleration was breaking through the mists and gloom of prejudice, Erin's faithful sons dared rally round their Saint and do him honor on his festal day, in Philadelphia, as early as 1771.

But when the handful of exiles had multiplied to thousands, when not scores but thousands of churches dotted the land, the celebration of St. Patrick's Day became more general. Shorn, perhaps, of its first touching simplicity, it has become more imposing with its added elements of banquets, poems, and orations. Morristown's turn came this year. After the High Mass the different Societies and school children gathered in front of the School to unfurl a flag from a staff, both presents. It will not be out of place to permit the local journals to describe the ceremony:

"The services for the celebration of St. Patrick's Day were imposing and interesting. High Mass was celebrated at 9 A.M., at which the Very Rev. Dean Flynn delivered a graphic and touching sketch of the Saint's life, and especially his mission among the Irish people. His remarks were addressed principally to the children to guard them against the vulgar fault of being ashamed of their Irish names, a fault which can only come from ignorance of the glorious history of Ireland, and of its loyalty and adherence to the faith planted by St. Patrick. After this service all gathered upon the terrace in front of the school building, where a pole, donated by Lonergan & Brown, had been erected. The pole is a very graceful one, some sixty-five or seventy feet high, painted white, and surmounted by a golden eagle. The school sang 'America' and other patriotic songs, and Rev. Father Flynn made a very interesting address. He paid a high tribute to the flag and the country it represents. Its references to local history give it an added interest:

"'We are assembled to unfurl our national flag over our parish School, and it is with singular appropriateness that we do so on St. Patrick's Day. For here in Morristown was first given the public and official recognition of Erin's religious and national feast day by the immortal Washington commanding the almost starved and naked patriot soldiers then encamped among our hills. He realized that among the heroes who were fighting the powerful British nation none exceeded the large Irish contingent in bravery. It was March 16, 1780, that in the orders issued by him General Washington directs 'that all fatigue and working parties cease for to-morrow, the 17th day, held in particular regard by the people of the Irish nation. At the same time that he orders this as a mark of pleasure he feels in the situation, he persuades himself that the celebration of the day will not be attended by the least rioting or disorder.'

"'Let none sneer at your nationality or at the nationality of your fathers. Let none use with contempt the scurrillous epithets which ignorance and bigotry have heaped in the past upon the Irish. We are no more aliens on this soil of America than were the Puritans. Irish blood has been poured out freely on every battle-field of the Revolution, and behind yonder hills mingle with the dust the bones of many of the Pennsylvania Line carried off by fell disease.

"'Do not forget that General Sullivan was the son of an Irish and Catholic father. Do not forget that one of Washington's most trusted officers was General Moylan, brother of the Catholic Bishop of Cork; and that the father of the American Navy was another Celt, Commodore Barry. Let it be remembered that among the signers of the Declaration of Independence, when it was by no means certain that victory and liberty were to crown the efforts, bravery, and sacrifices of the Americans, Charles Carroll of Carrollton signed his name and staked his life and fortune on the result. Likewise Thomas Fitzsimmons, of Philadelphia, who gave largely of his means, and commanded a company of Irishmen right here in Morristown. Furthermore, let me tell you that when Franklin was in Paris striving to enlist the sympathies of the French king in our efforts to be free, when everything looked dark and discouraging, when Washington had written him 'that if France did not send over her army the cause must fail,' it was the Pope's Nuncio, at the urgent request of the Catholic priest, Father Carroll, afterwards first Bishop of Baltimore, who succeeded where Franklin failed, and thus we obtained French aid in money, troops, and fleet, which together with the bravery of our own American soldiers culminated in the victory of Yorktown. What was Franklin's gratitude? 'Convey,' said he to the Nuncio, 'to his Holiness the Pope my thanks, in the name of all the American people. We shall never, no never forget Rome!'

"'Again, let me remind you of the splendid tribute paid to Bishop Carroll by Washington: 'Of all men whose influence was most potent in securing the success of the Revolution Bishop Carroll, of Baltimore, was the man.' That influence would have made Canada our ally and one of the brightest stars in our banner but for the bigotry of John Jay, whose namesake and descendant is as conspicuous as his ancestor for his bigotry and hatred to the Catholic Church, to which this country is under a lasting debt of gratitude.

"'In times of peace our countrymen and co-religionists have contributed largely to the prosperity of our land; and in time of war they have rallied to the stars and stripes, and have borne them high above the smoke of battle into the very ranks of the enemy. Shall we ever forget our Corcorans, our Meaghers, our Sheridans?—Sheridan, the bravest of the brave, who dealt the last blow to Lee and his brave army! Shall the heroism of the Sixty-ninth and Eighty-eighth New York and the Ninth Massachusetts pass from our memory? Was it not the descendant of the Irish Catholic, Meade, who won one of the greatest victories of ancient or modern times, the victory of Gettysburg?

"'Children, love and revere that flag! The cross is the symbol of your faith, borne by Catholic missionaries into every land. Your first duty is to your God. The flag is the symbol of your country, love it with the intense ardor of a patriot. Allied to your duty to God is your duty to your country. When gazing upon the folds of this standard remember the lives it has cost, the liberty it has won. God bless that flag! God bless our country, for fairer or freer there is not under God's sun! God grant that our Republic may last through endless ages, and that the freedom we now enjoy may be extended to countless generations!'

"After the address the flag was raised to the top of the pole by Messrs. Patrick Farrelly and James Lonergan, where it was greeted with three hearty cheers by the audience, and the school sang: 'Our Flag is there.' The audience then dispersed, and the Association marched back to the building. The procession both ways was headed by the Bailey Fife and Drum Corps, an organization of small boys from the school, which surprised and pleased every one with its good playing. Altogether the occasion was a very pleasant one, and may the flag of our Union long wave in front of St. Mary's School, and may the boys educated there prove as patriotic, brave, and self-sacrificing as their ancestors when occasion demands it!

"In the evening an entertainment was given before

a large audience by the children of the school in their school hall. Among the many good things, the song and dance by the 'Old Folks' and the broom-drill by the girls of the school should be particularly mentioned.

"In the afternoon of St. Patrick's Day a few enthusiastic and patriotic sons of Ireland decided that the day so auspiciously opened should be fittingly closed by a banquet. The dining-room in Piper's newly-fitted-up hotel was thrown open for the first time, and about fifty gentlemen, admirers of Ireland's patron Saint, sat down to a well-served repast.

"After the tables were cleared, Mr. P. Farrelly moved that those present organize themselves into a Society of the Friendly Sons of St. Patrick. His remarks were greeted with cheers and the suggestion was enthusiastically endorsed. A temporary chairman was immediately appointed, and the Society will meet shortly to elect officers for the ensuing year.

"Rev. Dean Flynn was made toast-master, and by his well-chosen and happy remarks and with rare tact caused songs, recitations, and impromptu toasts to follow one upon the other until St. Patrick's night, 1890, was a thing of the past.

"The recitation of 'Shamus O'Brien' by ex-Councilman Malley, and 'The Pride of Battery B' by Mr. T. J. O'Brien, were heard with great pleasure and received much applause.

"Toasts were given by the Rev. Fathers Carroll and Shannessy, E. S. Burke, J. E. Fennell, Dr. J. H. O'Reilly, T. F. Clifford, F. Danis, and many others, while the songs by J. Romaine, A. Conway, W. Kenefick, and others were also some of the features of the occasion.

"After three cheers were given to the sentiments of 'Long Live the Stars and Stripes' and 'God Save Ireland,' the first dinner of the Friendly Sons of St. Patrick in Morristown was brought to a close."

The old Church and School, around which clustered so many varied memories of joy and sorrow, pleasure and pain, the first effort of struggling faith, the venerated spot in which so many had been baptized, confirmed, married—yes, and borne by loving hands to receive the blessing of the priest before the grave had shut them for ever from mortal gaze—was now deserted. Its day was done. It was to pass into other hands, to serve other purposes. Cornelius Holly bought it for three hundred dollars, moved it to the corner of Madison Street and McCullogh Avenue, and altered it into a dwelling-house.

The old foundations were used in building a low wall on the Madison Street side of the Church property.

On March 22 the arrangements for the erection of the new Rectory were completed, and the digging of the foundation was begun. The contracts were given to Lonergan & Brown for the carpenter work; Malley, Dempsey & Cooney, the masonry and plastering; Kay Bros., the plumbing; Thatcher, the painting, and Augustus Eichorn, Architect, the planning and supervision. The Rectory has thus been described:

"The building is of brick and Waterloo granite trimmings. It has a frontage of 52 feet, and depth of about 65 feet. It is a beautiful structure, showing an octagon bay-window on the west corner and a tower on the east side, the front highly ornamented yet chaste in design, the roof-line showing a finish in battlemented walls, the entrance and windows vaulted and superbly trimmed with the stone finish, the upper sash of the windows showing a neat tracery and cathedral glass.

"Entering the first floor through ample doors, we find a vestibule and a hall 9 x 6 feet that opens into another that is 50 feet long, and runs right through the building from east to west. There is a parlor 12 x 16 feet, and a study for the Rector, of which the octagon forms a part—a cheerful, commodious room that will delight the heart of the occupant. Back of it, and across the hall, is the Bishop's room, 14 feet and 6 inches by 13 feet and 10 inches. The dining-room is also splendidly proportioned, being 14 x 17 feet. The butler's pantry is 7 x 12 feet, and the kitchen 15 x 18 feet. On this floor there is also a fire and burglar proof vault for the preservation of valuable records.

"The upper floors are also well arranged, and the whole structure is an ornament to that part of the town and a valuable addition to what is a splendid church property.

"The building is heated by steam from the boilers in the school building. The Church is now heated from that plant, thus dispensing with all the inconveniences that sometimes attend a furnace in the basement of a house."

In Lyceum Hall, May 23, the Rev. Walter Elliott, the Paulist, gave a vivid description, illustrated by lantern slides, of the battle of Gettysburg, in which he had participated. At its close the veterans of Torbert Post, who were present in a body, warmly thanked the reverend lecturer for the pleasure he had given them, and alluded to the stirring scenes the story recalled. The Ladies of Good Help were the beneficiaries to a large amount.

The great national commemoration for those whose lives were sacrificed in the battles of the civil war and in the prisons of the South, for the maintenance of the Union, did not appear to attract Catholics to any special observance.

Decoration Day came and passed, with its processions, orations, and crowning the monuments and graves of the departed heroes with flags and flowers.

The Paulist community in New York quickly perceived the opportunity to grace the observance with a religious character, and to set the Stars and Stripes closer to the Altar under the shadow of the Cross. The beautiful services inaugurated by them spread quickly to other churches. In this, as in so many other movements for the recognition of the Catholic Church in the United States, the Paulists deserve the entire credit. An humble effort was made here, if not in full imitation, at least within the spirit of their ceremony. Holy Mass was offered for the repose of the dead soldiers. A catafalque, draped with national colors, was erected in the aisle in front of the main Altar, and, at either end, a stand of arms stacked. After the Mass a procession of the male societies connected with the Church, headed by the drum corps of school boys, was formed, and the line of march taken to the Cemetery. There the Rosary and Litany for the Dead were said, and at the conclusion ranks were broken. It was a touching sight to watch the different groups kneeling in prayer at the grave which held some dear departed, strewing it with flowers, watering it with tears. In time the long roll of the drum gathered the scattered ranks. Homeward the procession turned, and thus, it was agreed, the day had been appropriately observed.

Sunday, September 21, Right Rev. Bishop Wigger, D.D., made his visitation of the parish. On his way from St. Margaret's he visited the Young Men's building, and was greeted in the upper hall by almost the entire society. After some words of sound advice he was personally introduced to all the members by the Very Rev. Rector.

The St. Margaret's primary school had so grown as to require the services of an additional teacher. To conform with the discipline of the Diocese, the Sisters of Charity were entrusted with its care. In September the school opened with an increased attendance, under the charge of Sisters Petronilla and Rose Clare. The Chapel, which had adequately met the requirements of the nascent congregation, was now entirely too small. To accommodate their

1. Exterior of St. Margaret's Church, 1891.   2. Interior of St. Margaret's.   3. Residence—Future Rectory.

elders the children had to be excluded. Moreover, the School required desks, blackboards, and other necessaries which the advancement of the children called for. The lot on which the Chapel stood was sold to Peter Kain, and the Chapel moved nearer the site on which some day, it is to be hoped, a nobler and more enduring edifice will be erected. It was backed up to the barn, the two buildings joined together, changed and fashioned into no mean structure. The downward trend of the land fitted the story under the barn in an admirable manner for class-rooms. For a few days, as the Chapel glided down Columba Street, the school exercises were suspended, and only once was Mass dispensed with.

Satisfactory progress had been made with the new Rectory, and to such an extent that on St. Catherine's day, November 25, the furniture was put in place, and the priests took possession of their new home. The same day the busy hands of the Sisters and scholars enabled the former to be transferred from their temporary house to the more comfortable and commodious quarters of the old rectory. Early in December the congregation was invited to inspect the new building. All day long throngs of ladies passed in and out. In the evening the men imitated their example. Lunch was prepared for all, and served by the willing hands of the Young Ladies' Sodality.

It is difficult to understand the ignorance which exists outside of the Church of all the things which pertain to its worship and dogmas; at the present day this ignorance is inexcusable. From time to time the reappearance of an old recrudescent calumny, long considered dead and buried, pains more than it surprises. But, while in the past it was deemed prudent not to notice, but to cast the veil of charity over, these uncalled-for ebullitions of religious hate, the service due to truth and fraternal correction demands to-day their refutation. The public is a willing listener, and inclined to show fair play. When Error, writhing in its wounds, raises its head, Truth must be ever ready to crush it. This preamble will explain the correspondence which followed a newspaper report in the *Jerseyman:*

"The meeting of the McAll Auxiliary in the chapel of the First Church, on Tuesday afternoon, was well attended, and proved exceedingly interesting. After Dr. Erdman had conducted the opening exercises and made a few remarks of encouragement and sympathy with the work, Mrs. Burnham, in an informal address described a meeting which she attended last summer in 'Salle Philadelphia,' Paris, dwelling upon the great simplicity of the entire service, the tender directness of the brief addresses, and the close, eager attention of the hearers, who evidently hunger for the 'bread that satisfieth.' Mrs. Burnham said that the question 'Why should America, the new world, feel that she has a religious duty to perform to the old world?' finds its answer in the contrast between the old and the new. Continental Europe is trammelled by superstitions to a degree that we, living in a Protestant country, can scarcely imagine. The Mass is the central idea, and although the churches are, as a rule, empty of worshippers, this daily sacrifice for sin is going on all the time, conducted by the great body of the priesthood—in many places with a pomp and ceremony and splendor that reminds one of what we read of the old Jewish priesthood and ritual. Prominent in all is the worship of Mary and the Saints, the inscription on one church being 'To God and to Mary, equal with God.' Contrasted with these superstitions is the worship of God in the Protestant churches scattered here and there through Papal Europe; but thousands upon thousands of the people, in breaking away from old traditions and beliefs in which they have ceased to trust, have no belief at all, and shun the church. To these light and hope have come through the simplicity of the Gospel, carried to them by Mr. McAll from Protestant England; and it is the privilege of America to aid in sustaining the noble work."

"NOTES FROM OUR CORRESPONDENTS.

" In the report of McAll Auxiliary, held in the chapel of the First Church, published in your issue of last week, many utterances of Mrs. Burnham are calculated to provoke and irritate those who profess the faith which, in what this good lady calls ' Papal Europe,' she so terribly arraigns; but her sex shields her. There is, however, one blasphemous utterance, which, as the spiritual head of the two thousand and odd Catholics in this city, I cannot permit to pass. I shall place twenty-five ($25) dollars in the hands of the editors of the *Jerseyman*, to be expended in the purchase of coal for the poor, if Mrs. Burnham, or anybody else, will name the church which bears the blasphemous, un-Catholic inscription, 'To God and to Mary, equal with God,' if she will furnish your readers with the inscription in the language in which it is written.

"JOSEPH M. FLYNN."

"RIDGEWOOD HILL, December 13.
"*Rev. Dr. Flynn.*

"DEAR SIR: I wish to say to you that I had nothing to do with the notice of the McAll meeting as it appeared in the *Jerseyman*. I did not see it until I saw it in the paper, and then was shocked to find that statements which were made to illustrate the work of the society, and which were in no way suitable for the public press, had been selected as the basis of the article. I consider it outrageous and indefensible to attack any form of religious faith in the newspapers, and need not say that I am deeply pained to be drawn into a public religious controversy. It is one thing to express an opinion among those of one's own way of thinking, and another thing to publish it to the world at large. The latter I certainly never intended to do. Begging that you will exonerate me from any such intention, I am,

"Very truly,
"C. L. BURNHAM."

"MORRISTOWN, N. J., December 16, 1890.
"*Mrs. C. L. Burnham.*

"DEAR MADAM: I beg to acknowledge the receipt of your favor, and in reply to state that, while almost everything contained in the printed report of your address before the McAll Auxiliary is controvertible, I had not in writing to the *Jerseyman* the remotest desire to lead you into 'a public religious controversy.' I am not responsible for the published statement of your remarks. Either you have been reported correctly, or you have not. In the latter case a line from you will set you right before the public. In the other alternative either the statement made that a Catholic Church in Paris bears the inscription, 'To God and to Mary, equal with God,' is true or it is not. If it be true, the poor of this city will profit by the $25 I shall place in the hands of Messrs. Vance & Stiles, when you furnish me with the name of the church and the inscription as it appears on the church. If it be not true, I shrink from the very thought that a lady, a professed Christian, is capable of making a wilful misstatement, even in the name of religion, to embitter the minds of co-religionists against a very much misunderstood and slandered Church, one which your illustrious Dr. Schaff calls 'the venerable Church of Rome.' Truth fears not the light. It bears the scrutiny of the few as well as the searching inspection of the multitude. To gainsay the truth is never justifiable. To pass over the strong injunctions of Holy Writ to maintain the truth on all occasions, allow me to quote from the 'Larger Catechism,' with which, I presume, you are familiar, page 310, question 144 : 'What are the duties required in the ninth commandment?'

"'The duties required in the ninth commandment are, the preserving and promoting of truth between man and man, and the good name of our neighbor, as well as our own: appearing and standing for the truth, and from the heart sincerely, freely, clearly, and fully speaking the truth, and only the truth, in matters of judgment and justice, and in all other things whatsoever, etc.'

"I beg of you to bear in mind that I do not charge you with any wilful, intentional violation of the injunctions contained in the above. I know from personal experience that rascally guides are plentiful in Europe; and that they are ever ready to mislead the tourists who engage them, especially if they profess a religion different from the Catholic. But in a matter so serious, where a dogma of faith is attacked, where the faith not only of that particular parish, but of all Catholics, is smirched, then we are in justice bound to undo any mischief which a declaration of ours made in good faith has accomplished. A two-cent Catechism, the youngest Catholic child, would be a safer guide to inform you of what Catholics believe than nine-tenths of the guides and apostate priests, who never stop at a calumny or slander when it pays them. In conclusion I do not think I am asking too much, when I request the production of the inscription and the name of the church which bears it; or, in the event of your inability to do so, the source of your authority; or, if you have been wrongly reported, or misinformed, a denial which will have the same publicity as the report of the McAll Auxiliary which appeared in the *Jerseyman* not quite two weeks ago.

"I am very respectfully yours, etc.,
"JOSEPH M. FLYNN."

"WEDNESDAY.

"*Rev. Dr. Flynn.*

"DEAR SIR: Before I received your letter Mr. Burnham and myself had devoted much time to studying the inscription I had quoted, and had discovered that the translation was not correct, and I had written an article to that effect, to appear in this week's *Jerseyman*. I regret having made the mistake, and have done all in my power to rectify it. The truth is dear to me, and I would not willingly make a misstatement on any subject, more especially on a question connected with religion.

"Very truly,

"C. L. BURNHAM.

"NOTES FROM OUR CORRESPONDENTS.

"In referring to the position to which the Virgin Mary has been elevated, and the estimation in which she is held, in many parts of continental Europe, during an informal talk, by no means intended for publication, an inscription was mentioned, by way of illustration, which had been seen on a church in France.

"On further investigation it is found that this inscription, as quoted, is a mistranslation; and it is desired to correct the error as soon as possible, with regrets that it should have occurred.

"The expression mistranslated is as follows: 'Beatæ Mariæ Virginis Dei Paræ.'

"The word 'Paræ' was supposed to be derived from 'par,' meaning 'equal,' although a difficulty arose in the incorrect termination of the genitive. This difficulty was noted at the time, but it was supposed to be a mediæval form of the Latin.

"During a thorough investigation of the subject in the past week various authorities have been consulted. Several scholarly men gave it as their opinion that 'paræ' came from 'par,' and meant 'equal'; but one, more familiar with patristic lore, has given the information that 'paræ' is used in ecclesiastical Latin to signify 'Mother.'

"The inscription should therefore read, the 'Blessed Virgin Mary, Mother of God.'

"C. L. BURNHAM."

"NOTES FROM OUR CORRESPONDENTS.

"I wish to express my acceptance of Mrs. C. L. Burnham's explanation. I cannot but marvel at the scholarship which twists *par*, an adjective declinable as nouns of the third declension, into *paræ*. That boy is sadly lacking in the very elements of Latinity who could not in a moment declare that the nearest approach to *paræ* is the nominative, accusative, and vocative plural *neuter*. He would also unhesitatingly tell his interrogator that *par*, when it signifies *equal to*, *even with*, is construed with the dative, *never* with the genitive.

"He would also say that Deipara has a kindred word in *puerpera*, used by Terence and other classic writers. It is not easy to say who first used Deipara. It is a coined word, an heirloom to us of the discussion in the Eastern Church of the divinity of Christ, the presence of the two natures and their various operations, begun by Apollinaris, developed by Theodore of Mopsuestia, and perfected by Nestorius.

"Cyril of Alexandria claims that Dorotheus, Bishop of Marcianople, first attacked the use of the word *theotokos*, of which *Deipara*, that is, 'Mother of God,' is the Latin translation. Socrates, the historian, tells us of the consternation which a sermon of the priest Anastasius, whom Nestorius brought to Constantinople, caused when he warned his hearers not to call Mary *theotokos*, 'Mother of God.' This attack, he says, on a hitherto accepted ecclesiastical term and ancient belief, caused great excitement among clergy and laity. On the 22d of June, A.D. 431, the Fathers opened the Council of Ephesus, in the Cathedral of Ephesus, which, strange to say, was dedicated, even as the church in Paris to which Mrs. Burnham refers, 'to God and to Mary, the Mother of God,' *theotoko*. In this assembly of holy bishops, confessors, and doctors Nestorius and his heresy were condemned, the use of the word *theotokos* vindicated, ' for,' as Athanasius, the great Bishop of Alexandria, said repeatedly, 'as the flesh was born of the God-bearer Mary, so we hold that Jesus Christ (*the Logos*) was Himself born of Mary.'

"JOSEPH M. FLYNN."

CHAPTER XVI.

ON March 17, 1891, St. Margaret's Church, enlarged, refurnished, and fitted with pews and steam heat, was formally blessed by the Very Rev. Dean Flynn, to whom the Bishop had delegated this power. The Church was filled with worshippers, and the music was rendered by the children's choir under the direction of Wenzel Raboch, assisted by two sopranos of his widely-known boy choristers. After the ceremony of dedication Solemn High Mass was celebrated, the Rev. James McManus, of Seton Hall, lately ordained, Officiant; Rev. James H. Brady, of Netcong, Deacon; Rev. Eugene P. Carroll, Sub-Deacon; Rev. J. J. Shannessy, Master of Ceremonies. Besides the pastor, Rev. J. J. Brennan, of Morris Plains, and Rev. Joseph C. Dunn, of Chatham, were in the Sanctuary. The sermon preached by Father Brady was a masterly effort, every word, every sentence, so clear and so rich in force and meaning as to hold the closest attention of his audience. He reviewed the significance of the ceremonial, and drew practical lessons from the beautiful life of St. Margaret.

The new Church will comfortably seat about two hundred and fifty. The school has all the appurtenances which the rigor of modern views demands. It is well lighted and ventilated. The children have ample recreation grounds. At the present date there is an average attendance of one hundred.

In the evening the Friendly Sons of St. Patrick held their second annual banquet. The account which appeared in the local journals is appended:

"The society was organized only a year ago, and its vigorous growth and present proportions clearly indicate its popularity.

"Members of the society and invited guests to the number of about a hundred met at the Young Men's Catholic Association rooms at 6:30 o'clock, and a half-hour later were seated at an elaborately decorated table in the commodious and inviting banquet hall of Piper's Hotel. Midway down the hall Voss's orchestra, of Newark, was cosily located, and sweet strains of music swelled above the friendly chatter of the Friendly Sons and 'adopted sons' of the Patron Saint whose memory all were there to honor.

"Rev. Dean Flynn, President of the Society, presided, and upon either side of him at the T head of the table sat Rev. Dr. Hughes, Rev. Fathers Brennan, Carroll, Shannessy, McManus, and Brady; ex-Alderman Farrelly, Colonel McAnerney, of Jersey City, and James M. Ward. Among the invited guests were Postmaster Youngblood, H. O. March, Dr. Stephen Pierson, Edward Pruden, Sheriff Lindsley, Prosecutor Cutler, Chief Freeman, Charles H. Green, J. William Burns, and representatives each of the *Jerseyman*, *Banner*, and *Chronicle*.

"The walls of the banquet hall were festooned with the national colors intertwined with the folds of the green flag of Erin, and in harmony with the general fraternizing features of the occasion. The *menu* was served in excellent style by a corps of competent waiters, and the *cuisine* and general excellence of the banquet as a whole was the subject of favorable comment upon all sides.

"Nearly two hours and a half were occupied in discussing the bill of fare, after which cigars were lighted and Rev. Dean Flynn inaugurated the after-dinner exercises by the reading of 'General Orders issued by General Washington, in Camp at Morristown, N. J., March 16, 1780'; and 'Division Orders of Commandant of Pennsylvania Line, Morristown, N. J., March 16, 1780.'

"The first order related to the issuing of extra rations and special holiday cheer to the troops, and the second was similar in character. It was also brought out in this connection that General Washington was an 'adopted' member of the Society of Friendly Sons of St. Patrick, and it was humorously described how this was brought about through the ever-ready wit and versatility of the Irishman. This was followed by music by the orchestra—'St. Patrick's Day.'

"Rev. Dean Flynn read letters of regret from Mayor Werts, detained by accident at Elizabeth, and Messrs Paul Revere, Thomas W. Burke, and C. S. Conkling, detained by illness.

"The President then announced the first toast, 'The Day We Celebrate,' responded to by himself. He gave a brief and interesting account of the life and works of St. Patrick, and its subsequent bearing upon the Church. The address evinced a thorough and complete knowledge of the subject, and was listened to with rapt attention. Music—'Let Erin remember the Days of Old.'

"'The Old Sod' was the next toast on the list, and Mr. Thomas W. Burke was assigned to respond.

In his absence, however, Rev. Father Brennan filled the gap to the entire satisfaction of all present. He gave a brief but comprehensive review of Ireland's history from before the Christian era down to the present time, and wound up with an eloquent tribute to the land of his birth, and gave encouraging promise of brighter things in the near future. Music—'The Harp that once through Tara's Halls.'

"'America—The Land of our Birth and Adoption' was set down in connection with the name of Mr. Paul Revere, but in his absence Colonel John W. McAnerney, of Jersey City, did the subject ample justice and kept his audience in perennial good humor by his happy hits, not forgetting to finish off with an eloquent tribute to the subject of the toast. Music—' My Country, 'tis of Thee.'

"'The Irish Soldier' was responded to by Mr. James M. Ward. He paid an impassioned tribute to the subject of his text, and displayed considerable oratorical ability. His theme was an eloquent one, and he handled it with great ability and with unusual satisfaction to the audience. Music—'Tramp, Tramp, the Boys are Marching.'

"'The Rising Generation' was responded to by the Rev. Father Carroll, the youngest and tallest clergyman present, and he humorously noted these points as the probable reasons why he was assigned to speak to this particular toast. He did the subject full justice, however, and gave unmistakable evidence that he was one of the rising. Music—'Killarney.'

"'The Irish Bar—At Home and Abroad' was wrestled with by John E. Fennell, Esq. He gave an entertaining and instructive history of the more eminent of Irish jurists, and paid eloquent tribute to many such whose memories are dear to the Irish heart. O'Connell and Emmett were the special subjects of his enthusiasm and admiration, and to them he paid the devout homage of a possible candidate for a like illustrious record. Music—'The Sprig of Shillalah.'

"'Soggarth Aroon—Priest Dear,' was responded to by Rev. Father Brady, of Netcong. It was an exhaustive subject, interesting and edifying. Music—'Savourneen Deelish.'

"'The Irish Muse' was remarkably well handled by Mr. Thomas J. O'Brien, who fairly merited and won the laurels of the evening. His eighteen minutes' dissertation on the theme at once so familiar and dear to him was indeed a pleasing revelation to his friends. He was eloquent, poetic, even classic, in his eulogy of favorite Irish bards, and that he was complete master of his subject was evidenced by the graceful ease with which he quoted from memory choice selections from the particular author under discussion. His masterly effort was received with unbounded enthusiasm. Music — 'The Minstrel Boy.'

"'Our Guests.' This toast was assigned to Rev. Dr. Hughes, and the result showed that the committee made no mistake in the assignment. He was most happy in his remarks, said just enough, said it in the best possible manner, and then stopped. Rev. Dr. Hughes is master of the art of knowing what to say and how to say it. Music—'The Valley lay smiling before Me.'

"'The Irish Statesman.' Mr. Eugene S. Burke responded to this sentiment, and very cleverly imitated his immediate predecessor in the matter of brevity and pertinency. Not a little of his thunder had been appropriated by speakers preceding him, yet he discharged his obligation in the premises with admirable grace and tact. Music—'The Wearing of the Green.'

"'The Ladies.' Dr. Stephen Pierson was most happily assigned to the delicate task implied in this toast. He showed himself easily familiar with the subject in hand, and his response as a whole was a gem rich and rare. He proved conclusively that though woman is, ever was, and probably ever will be a more or less perplexing conundrum, man will never give her up. Music—'Rich and rare were the Gems she wore.'

"'The Green Flag at Spottsylvania.' This was a recitation by ex-Councilman Thomas Malley, and was most excellently rendered. Mr. Malley has committed to memory quite a number of popular pieces fitted to his rare oratorical powers, and the eloquent story of how the Irish color-bearer, after having his colors shot away, produced the green flag of his native land and, waving it aloft, led the gallant Sixty-ninth through the thickest of the fight, is among the best and most entertaining of his selections. Music—'Cruiskeen Laun.'

"When the 'feast of reason and flow of soul' ceased with the last number on the programme, it was no longer St. Patrick's Day. Midnight had just passed, and the second annual banquet of the Friendly Sons of St. Patrick was recorded in history, and the sons and 'adopted sons' of Ireland's loved Apostle and patron Saint dispersed and wended their way homeward feeling that it was good to have been there."

"The officers of the Society of Friendly Sons of St. Patrick of Morristown are as follows:

PRESIDENT:
Very Rev. Joseph M. Flynn.
VICE-PRESIDENT:
Mr. Patrick Farrelly.
SECRETARY:
Mr. John A. Carr.
TREASURER:
Mr. Eugene S. Burke.
BOARD OF DIRECTORS:
Rev. J. J. Shannessy,
Mr. Thomas Malley,   Mr. C. H. Knight,
Mr. T. F. Clifford,   Mr. E. J. Looney."

Morristown had hitherto known nothing of the feuds between labor and capital. The kindliest feelings existed between the employers and the employed. Hard times might elsewhere result from strikes, but our mechanics continued their work in full contentment, blessed with prosperity. This utopian ideal terminated in the Spring of 1891. Long-whispered threatenings and rumors gave place to reality. On May 1 the strike was here. Both sides were determined not to yield. Day succeeded day until the first week of the strike ended, and the antagonists were wider apart. No effort was made to reconcile the conflicting interests. Bad feeling was brewing, and the innocent began to suffer. The *Chronicle* correctly outlined the situation. In its issue of May 8 is the following account:

"The backbone of the strike is not only broken,

but the strike itself is virtually ended—unless it breaks out in a new place.

"Notwithstanding there were some indications that the strike might end with last week, it didn't. On the contrary, the fore part and middle of the present week a settlement seemed as far off as on the first day they went out. Some of our clergymen took a hand in, led by Father Flynn. He circulated pretty freely among the men on Tuesday, and that evening there was an informal meeting held in the Young Men's Catholic Association rooms, with Father Flynn and Drs. Merritt and Hughes. They started out in the good work as mediators between men and bosses with the best intentions, and notwithstanding many thought they would accomplish but little if anything, the present situation—the strike virtually ended—is without doubt largely owing to their efforts in the premises. They brought about meetings between committees representing both the strikers and the master-builders, and despite the fact that these conferences between committees at first promised but little in the way of favorable results, persistent effort finally brought about the present happy state of affairs.

"The fact that a large proportion of the strikers went to work yesterday upon terms which they supposed were practically unanimously agreed upon, is a great step toward the early and final adjustment of the difficulty. The lack of unanimity of demand on the part of each side has been one great barrier to the settlement of the case. Where there are two contending sides, each side should first of all agree as to just what they want, and then the case is clear for consideration. Thanks to the good offices of Father Flynn, Rev. Dr. Merritt, and Rev. Dr. Hughes, and the good judgment and mutual forbearance of the contestants on both sides of this controversy, it may generally be understood that the strike is virtually ended, as we confidently trust and believe that not more than another day or two will be required to reach a final settlement of any question or questions which may yet be pending. So mote it be!

"As we go to press the glad tiding reaches us that the masons have come to terms and will go to work at once. The strike *is* over."

On Sunday, May 31, the Rev. William O'Gorman, who in his childhood had been prepared for his first Communion, taught to serve Mass, and the rudiments of Latin by Dean Flynn, celebrated High Mass in our Church, and gave his blessing to great numbers both after the Mass and the afternoon services.

The life and labor of a Sister of Charity combine to shorten the term of exile and to hasten the reward which must crown a career of unselfish devotion to work, unheeded by mortals, but measured and rewarded by the Master alone. Sister Mariana was compelled by continued ill-health to withdraw from her duties, and her place in the senior grade was supplied by Miss McIntyre and Sister Celeste.

The closing exercises of the School, if possible, surpassed those of previous years. The primary grades of the Bayley School and St. Margaret's monopolized one night, the senior grades and graduating exercises another. Both entertainments filled the hall with the relatives and friends of the children.

The capital error of the age is lack of faith. The protagonists who in the sixteenth century led men away from the fold of the Church, by making them believe they had hitherto lived in thraldom and under the tyranny of priestcraft, held out to them the attraction of intellectual and civil freedom. It is as easy to master the forces of nature as to control the human mind when cut adrift from the secure moorings of faith. Every day in the denominations outside of the Catholic Church religion is relaxing its hold on their members, faith is weakening more and more, and Christ merging into the unreality of a myth. The ills of life multiply and become unbearable; the world is restive and uneasy; the rich fear and oppress the poor, and these in turn hold the former in contempt and hatred. Under the guidance of the Divine Spirit the Church seeks to lead men back to happiness and contentment, virtue and justice, by bidding them contemplate the love of the Sacred Heart of Jesus. As men are leagued against Him, so will the Divine Teacher enroll His hosts and followers in a League for the furthering of His honor and glory.

On Sunday, July 12, the Rev. J. Kelly, S.J., explained the nature of the league of the Sacred Heart, and established it in our parish. More than eight hundred members are now enrolled in this society.

In August Sister Marie Agnes was appointed to take charge of the School.

It had long been apparent that the growth of this section called for some provision for the sick, injured, and infirm. For a long time the matter occupied the attention of Bishop and Pastor. The distance to the city hospitals was considerable; the demands made upon them by the exigencies of their surroundings sometimes rendered it difficult to accommodate patients from afar. In the month of November, within the octave of All Souls, the ever-recurring thought returned; but, while the building was attainable, it was a rather more difficult task to obtain Sisters trained and devoted to this kind of work.

While pondering over the perplexing situation a visit from the Rev. James H. Brady helped to find a way out of the difficulties. The Grey Nuns were thought of. This was their special work. Would they come? Dean Flynn and Father Brady quickly made up their minds to go and see.

When they laid the proposal before the good Mother in Montreal she smiled, shook her head doubtingly, and said that while everything contemplated in the Morristown institution was within their scope, she had not subjects to undertake a new foundation. Argument and appeal were alike useless.

Arnold Tavern, 1778—All Souls Hospital, 1891.

Finally Dean Flynn summed up the whole matter. "Mother," said he, "I place the whole responsibility of this project in the hands of the Souls in Purgatory and in yours. If you consent to take charge, I shall consider it as the expression of God's will. If not, I shall drop the matter entirely."

All Mother Filiatrault would promise was to visit Morristown, or send some other in her place to see the property. On the following Saturday Mother Deschamps and Sister Painchaud reached Morristown. In company with Dean Flynn and Father Brady they visited the old Arnold Tavern on Mount Kemble Avenue. Before returning to the Sisters' house on Madison Street they expressed their willingness to undertake the work.

The consent of Bishop Wigger was obtained in the following letter:

"SETON HALL COLLEGE, SOUTH ORANGE, N. J.,
"November 19, 1891.
"VERY REV. AND DEAR DEAN:
"I have read the agreement made by the Grey Sisters of Canada with the Right Rev. Bishop of Springfield, and the By-laws of St. Ann's French-Canadian Orphanage. I am pleased with them, and am willing to receive the Grey Sisters into the Diocese to conduct the Orphanage, Hospital, etc., near Morristown, on the same conditions.
"With best wishes I remain,
"Yours very sincerely,
"✠ W. M. WIGGER,
"*Bishop of Newark.*"

On November 21 the following was received:

"GENERAL HOSPITAL, MONTREAL,
"November 20, 1891.

"*Very Rev. Father Flynn, Morristown.*

"REVEREND FATHER: With pleasure we accept the proposition to go to Morristown, under your direction, to undertake the work of charity you wish to entrust to us.

"As you know, Reverend Father, we must first of all obtain the approbation of the Right Reverend Bishop of the diocese in which we are to labor; and I may add that it will be some time before we have subjects for this new enterprise.

"In the hope that everything will lead to the greater glory of God, I recommend myself to your prayers, and remain most respectfully, Reverend Father,

"Your very humble servant,
"SISTER FILIATRAULT,
"*Superioress-General.*"

The announcement was made to the congregation on Sunday, November 22, and was received with unbounded enthusiasm. It will not be out of place to permit the insertion of the sketch of the work written by the Rev. James H. Brady, of Netcong, for the journals of Morris and Sussex Counties:

"A HOSPITAL IN MORRISTOWN.

"*Eds. Banner:*

"In the course of the ensuing year, when our own people will be making ready to celebrate the four-hundredth anniversary of the discovery of America, our neighbors on Canadian soil will be rejoicing in the two-hundred-and-fiftieth anniversary of the founding of their greatest city, Montreal, the old Ville Marie of the French colonies.

"To the stranger visiting Montreal to-day the most astounding thing, after the number of well-built, well-kept, and well-attended churches, is the number of charitable institutions devoted to the care of the sick and helpless, and the alleviation of every form of human misery. Foremost among these institutions stands the General Hospital, occupying an entire square on Guy Street.

"During the past fifteen years Montreal has seemed to vie with our own great cities in putting on the habiliments of modern growth and progress. The General Hospital has kept pace with her, and to-day the home of the Grey Nuns, the Mother-House of the Sisters of Charity, is without doubt the largest charitable institution upon the American Continent.

"One hundred and fifty-three years ago the Superior of the Sulpicians, the Rev. Mr. Normant, sought in the city of Montreal means to resuscitate the institution founded in 1694, under the royal sanction of King Louis XIV. On the 30th of October, 1738, Madame d'Youville, with three pious companions, rented a small house, laid the first foundation of a new religious order, raised aloft the sign of man's redemption, the holy Cross, and adopted as their motto the historic phrase, ' In this sign shalt thou conquer.'

"As usual in such matters, Madame d'Youville met with great opposition. She and hers were publicly hooted and pelted with stones. In derision they were called, from the color of their habit, the

'Grey Nuns.' Later on this title of derision became a badge of honor and glory. No need to follow them through the century and a half of work for God. History tells of the devoted deeds of the Grey Nuns during the French and Indian and the French and English wars. Madame d'Youville lived to see Canada pass under the dominion of England, and died full of years and good works in the year 1771.

"The work of Madame d'Youville has been bravely carried on. Her order has been approved by the Holy See, and, a few years ago, judgment was pronounced upon the heroic sanctity of her life. The special work of the Grey Nuns is the conducting of hospitals, orphanages, and homes for the aged and afflicted. They are not a cloistered order. Indeed, one of their dearest tasks is visiting and care of the sick in private houses.

"A bright epoch in their history was the era of the Irish famine in 1847 and 1848. The traveller, after crossing the great bridge leading into Montreal, may notice a great bowlder resting on a pedestal in a small enclosure near the water's edge. The inscription on the stone tells the story:

"'To preserve from desecration the remains of six thousand immigrants who died of ship-fever, A.D. 1847-48, this stone is erected by the workmen employed in the construction of the Victoria Bridge, A.D. 1859.' But it says nothing of the heroism of the 'Grey Nuns.' The chronicles of the Grey Nunnery tell us that 'One day the Superioress, who had been to the hospital tents at the Point Saint Charles, summoned her Sisters to the community-room. She told them of the terrible scenes she had witnessed, of the poor strangers dying alone amid the most awful sufferings. "Sisters," she said, "the plague is contagious. In sending you there I sign your death-warrants. But you are free to accept or refuse." In a moment the Sisters arose and as with one voice exclaimed: "I am ready." Their sacrifice was accepted. Numbers of them laid down their lives. But theirs was the victory, theirs the crown of martyrdom, and the fruit of their labors the comfort and solace of the sick and dying.'

"To-day the Grey Nunnery stands a monument to the energy of the Sisters of Charity. Under its roof we find a miniature city. All sorts of industries are carried on. Hundreds of aged and infirm, of foundlings and orphans, there find shelter and protection. No less than ten branches of the parent-house exist in Montreal, and their work is spreading throughout Canada and the United States.

"'But,' you say, 'of what interest is this to the people of this section?' I answer that it is of the greatest possible interest.

"In the course of a few months a colony of these devoted women, the Grey Nuns, will come to take up their abode in Morristown. Poor as their Master, they will come empty-handed. But if it be God's will that they ever abandon the field, they will return to the Mother-House no richer than they came. On Mount Kemble Avenue there stands a building rich in historic reminiscences. The old Arnold Tavern, removed some years ago from the square in Morristown, has long awaited a purchaser. This building sheltered General Washington in 1777. It was his first headquarters. There he spent several months with his chiefs of staff. This is to be the Morristown home of the Grey Nuns. The ball-room of General Washington will be turned into a chapel. The dining-room will become a hospital ward. The broad corridors that a century ago resounded with noise of spur and clank of sabre will take on new life, and be filled with the soft-falling footsteps and rustling garments of the gentle Sisters, there to nurse the sick and afflicted of all races, colors, and creeds. In the building at the rear of the main structure a home will be provided for the aged and the orphans.

"This institution will be the crowning effort of the life of Very Rev. Dean Flynn, Rector of St. Mary's parish. It is his intention to confine the work to the care of the sick and poor living in Morris and Sussex Counties. Humble in its beginnings, it is his hope that the institution will grow and prosper with the growth and prosperity of Morristown, and be a source of glory to God and of peace and comfort to the members of our Lord Jesus Christ, the poor, the suffering, and the afflicted."

The movement to create a fund for the new Hospital was inaugurated November 29; in the afternoon the male pew-holders were invited to meet in Bayley Hall. Paul Revere was chosen Chairman; John A. Carr and Richard F. Dempsey, Secretaries, and Eugene S. Burke, Treasurer.

In the evening the women rivalled the generosity of the men. On the following Sunday all without exception were called upon, and the sight of laboring men and servants handing in donations of money—ten, twenty, and even a hundred dollars—recalled the fervor which impelled the early Christians to sell all they had and cast it at the feet of the Apostles.

The parish was divided into districts, and a collector appointed for each district to receive the contributions of those who had been unable to attend the public meetings.

Steps were at once taken to organize a permanent association, the object of which would be to carry out the good work.

The following semi-official reports, printed in the local press, tell the story:

"THE NEW HOSPITAL.

"On Friday, December 18, the Right Rev. Bishop Wigger, the Rev. Rectors of the Catholic churches of Morris and Sussex Counties, and several prominent laymen of Morristown met in Bayley Hall to discuss matters pertaining to the new Hospital. The Right Rev. Bishop occupied the chair, and the Rev. James H. Brady, of Netcong, was chosen Secretary.

"It was decided to establish a society to be called 'All Souls' Hospital Association,' with headquarters at Morristown and branches throughout the various parishes. Every parish will be represented on the Board of Management. A Constitution and a set of By-Laws were discussed and approved for presentation at a general meeting to be held in Bayley Hall, Morristown, on Monday, January 4, 1892, at 2 P.M.

"The Right Rev. Bishop appointed as Committee on Organization, the Very Rev. Dean Flynn, Rev. Joseph Rolando, and Messrs. Paul Revere, P. Farrelly, and R. F. Hayes, with power to select a list of candidates for the various offices of the Association."

"ALL SOULS' HOSPITAL.

"A well-attended meeting was held in Bayley Hall, Morristown, on Monday, January 4, at 2 P.M., to further the interests of the new Hospital. Representatives, lay and clerical, were present from the various parishes in Morris and Sussex Counties. Right Rev. Bishop Wigger was called to the chair, and the Rev. James H. Brady was chosen temporary Secretary. The Constitution and By-Laws were discussed and adopted, the 'All Souls' Hospital Association' organized, and the following officers unanimously elected: President, Paul Revere, of Morristown; Vice-President, Francis Kluxen, of Madison; Recording Secretary, Rev. James H. Brady, of Netcong; Corresponding Secretary, R. F. Hayes, of Morristown; Treasurer, Eugene S. Burke, of Morristown.

"The object of the Association is, to quote the Constitution, 'to assist the Sisters of Charity, known as the "Grey Nuns," to establish and maintain in Morristown, N. J., institutions for the care of the diseased, disabled, and infirm, and for such other charitable work as may be approved by the Board of Managers.'

"Membership, active or associate, is open to all who contribute each year at least one dollar to the support of the hospital. The payment of fifty dollars at one time makes the donor a life-member.

"The Board of Managers chosen at the meeting include the above-named officers and the following gentlemen: Very Rev. J. M. Flynn, and Messrs. P. Farrelly, A. H. Tiers, Thomas Clifford, P. Welsh, C. H. Knight, M. E. Condon, John E. Fennell, Thomas Malley, of Morristown; T. J. Allen, Netcong; M. Devaney, Newton; J. P. Dolan, Mendham; T. F. Johnson, Dover; M. J. Hyde, Franklin Furnace; John Finnegan, Mt. Hope; Henry Houston, Chatham; P. O'Reilly, Stirling; Walter Cross, Morris Plains; R. Dixon, Madison; R. Coghlan, Whippany; J. McGurk, Hurdtown; D. Madden, Ogdensburg; John J. Stanton, Deckertown. Three parishes are as yet unrepresented.

"After the general meeting a conference of the managers was held, and the following Executive Board was elected: Very Rev. J. M. Flynn, Rev. J. H. Brady, and Messrs. Kluxen, Dixon, Revere, Farrelly, and Hayes. Dean Flynn is Chairman and Rev. J. H. Brady is Secretary to the Executive Board and to the Board of Managers.

"During the course of the meeting several speeches were made.

"Very Rev. Dean Flynn spoke of the general objects of the Association, and gave a history of the buildings to be used for the Hospital, a part of which were formerly known as the 'Arnold Tavern,' on the Morristown Green, which are rich in Revolutionary memories.

"Rev. Father Hall, of Mt. Hope, made some pertinent remarks concerning ways and means, and a general discussion then followed on the best methods of securing sufficient funds annually to meet the expenses of the institution.

"Father Brady made a speech in his usual happy vein, full of humor and good sense, in which he congratulated the meeting on the successful beginning of the enterprise, and prophesied for it a most successful future.

"Mr. Revere stated that the object of the Constitution adopted was to make a permanent Association, which ought to number from fifteen hundred to two thousand active members. This, even at the small dues of one dollar a year, would make a substantial sum annually, and from the liberality already shown and the well-known interest of the people of this vicinity in all charitable work, would doubtless be largely increased beyond this amount. There was no doubt of the successful operation of the institution, and that it would be heartily sustained by persons of all denominations. The institution is for the benefit of all in the community interested, who may need it. All who pay dues, either as active or associate members, should look upon it as a kind of insurance against accident or disease, inasmuch as every one may have need of it, and would feel more at liberty to make use of the benefits of the institution if they had contributed even small amounts to its support.

"Mr. Dixon, on behalf of those outside of Morristown, extended cordial thanks to the people of Morristown, who had already so generously contributed.

"The Right Rev. Bishop congratulated the Association on the excellent beginning of the work, and bespoke earnest effort in the future.

"Mr. Revere moved that the thanks of this meeting be heartily extended to Dean Flynn for his efforts in instituting this important work, for which we should be the more grateful as it is no part of his parish duties, but done out of the sole desire to benefit the people of Morris and Sussex Counties. Also we owe a debt of gratitude to Bishop Wigger and the clergy, who have approved and earnestly sustained the suggestions and plans of Dean Flynn.

"The motion was carried with an enthusiasm which showed that the meeting fully appreciated and sustained the sentiment expressed.

"All those who contribute before the 1st of

March will be enrolled among the 'Original Members' of the Association.

"Donations may be handed to any of the Rev. Rectors or to any member of the Board of Managers, who will transmit names and money to the Treasurer. Mr. Burke reports over $6,500 already subscribed. At least as much more will be needed to place the institution in the hands of the Sisters free from all encumbrance."

So, as we write the closing chapters of our History, the day is almost at hand that will witness the opening of All Souls' Hospital. The name has not been chosen at random. On the way to Montreal the subject had been discussed by Dean Flynn and Father Brady. Dean Flynn proposed the name of "All Souls." It was within the octave of the "Day of the Dead." Standing in the porch of the Grey Nunnery the two priests promised a number of Masses for the Suffering Souls in case their mission should succeed. Their offering was accepted.

The historian of the future may write the chronicles of the new institution. Here you have the narrative of its foundation. The seed has been planted, the showers of Christian charity will water the tender nurseling, and God in His infinite goodness will give the increase.

CHAPTER XVII.

IN the great national conflict which divided the North and South, in 1861, members of our parish were found under both flags. The roll is an illustrious one. On the battle-field, in the prison, in rank and file, the children of St. Mary's gave ample proof of courage and patriotism.

Among all names there is one conspicuous above the rest—General Joseph Warren Revere. Descended from a French Huguenot family, his grandfather was Colonel Paul Revere, of Revolutionary fame.

At the age of fourteen young Revere entered the United States Naval School at New York, and began a long career of service on sea and land in almost every portion of the globe. In his sixteenth year he sailed for the Pacific, and was attached to the squadron employed in suppressing the African slave-trade. After narrow escapes from disease, wreck, and mutiny he was detailed to the European squadron, and visited every country of Europe, and the Mediterranean shores of Asia and Africa. His knowledge of many languages secured him a favorable position through which he met the most distinguished personages of the day. He was an eye-witness of the Carlist War, and served with the Mosquito fleet on the coast of Florida during the Seminole War. In 1838 he sailed in the first American squadron which circumnavigated the globe.

GENERAL. JOSEPH WARREN REVERE.

When in India he saved the British man-of-war *Ganges* from shipwreck, and was presented for his service with a sword of honor by the Governor-General.

Throughout the Mexican War he was on the coast of California. At Sonoma he raised the first American flag north of San Francisco. Soon after this he resigned, and was employed by the Mexican government in reorganizing the artillery services. At the outbreak of the Civil War he offered his services to the general government and received a commission as colonel of the Seventh New Jersey Volunteers. The brilliant record of this gallant regiment, second to none in the service, has been largely attributed to the severe discipline it received under General Revere, whom General Hooker pronounced the best disciplinarian in the service. He was in all the battles of the Peninsular Campaign; was promoted to the rank of brigadier-general, and commanded the Second New Jersey Brigade until after Fredericksburg. He was assigned to the command of the New York Excelsior Brigade; and at Chancellorsville Revere's Brigade led the van in the desperate struggle after the rout of the Eleventh Corps, when Howard's men retreated before the impetuous onslaught of Stonewall Jackson. Censured by General Sickles for his conduct in this battle, Revere was for a time deprived of his rank; the opinion of his troops, and of Generals Meade, Sedgwick, and other high officers, held him innocent of any offence. President Lincoln declared that he had been unjustly treated and restored to him his rank, and he was subsequently named brevet major-general. It was after the Peninsular Campaign that one day, in Washington, brooding over the severe losses his regiment suffered from the terrific struggle, he was led almost unconsciously to a Catholic church. On the moment he felt the impulse, or rather inspiration, to become a Catholic. For years he had carefully studied religious matters, and consequently, when he presented himself to the priest and asked to be baptized, he was found thoroughly instructed in the principles of the Catholic Church. He received holy Baptism October 19, and his first Holy Communion October 26, 1862. Some years later he was confirmed by Archbishop Bayley, in our own Church. During the period of well-merited repose in his delightful home he published in 1873 *Keel and Saddle*, a retrospect of his stirring life, and various magazine articles. The picture of the " Espousals of the Blessed Virgin and St. Joseph," which hangs in the Church in our Lady's aisle, attests his artistic ability. He died April 20, 1880. One of his sons, our respected townsman, Mr. Paul Revere, was received into the Church some years after his father.

Patrick Cavanagh, enlisted August 30, 1861, re-enlisted 1864, in Company C, Eighth New Jersey, was engaged in all the battles of the Peninsular Campaign, Seven Days' fight in the Wilderness, Antietam, Gettysburg—in a word, all the battles of the

Army of the Potomac until the close of the War. He was wounded in the hip at Salem Heights, and was also severely injured in the back while assisting in the building of a bridge. He served throughout as a private, and died of apoplexy in Morristown.

Edward Cavanagh, son of the above, enlisted, when considerably under sixteen years of age, in the spring of 1863, in Company B, Second New Jersey Cavalry. He took part in no regular engagement, and died of typhoid fever in the hospital at Columbus, O., January 24, 1864.

Peter Carroll, enlisted in Company A, New Jersey Volunteers.

John Cody, enlisted September 1, 1862, in Company I, Twenty-seventh New Jersey. This was a regiment of nine months' men, and one of the largest mustered into the United States service. It did good work at Fredericksburg, in Kentucky, and also in the Gettysburg Campaign, although its term of service had already expired. He died September 21, 1881.

Patrick Coughlan, enlisted in the Fourth New York Cavalry, and died in Morristown, New Jersey.

John Darcy, enlisted February 24, 186-, and after serving five months was discharged. He died of consumption in Orange.

Bartholomew W. Dempsey, enlisted in Company K, Seventh New Jersey Volunteer Infantry, October 2, 1861, and re-enlisted December 26, 1863. The obituary notice in the *Banner* says of him:

"Tall in stature, fair of face, slight in form, scarcely sixteen years of age, was that manly, quiet, unobtrusive boy when he signed the muster-roll of Company K. How often and how well he fought the twenty-six battles in which his regiment and brigade were engaged! And yet the brave boy never received a scratch or wound."

Captured June 22, 1864, in front of Petersburg, Corporal Dempsey was immured in the death-pen at Andersonville, Ga. Here he lingered ten months. During this frightful period he was thoughtful enough to keep an exact record of the name, company, regiment, date and cause of death, and number of the grave, of all the New Jersey soldiers who, during that time, succumbed to the horrors of the place and the brutality of its custodians. One hundred and forty-eight names appear in his diary, with the sad details of their death. Although he survived long enough to be released, April 21, 1865, and to return to his native city, he carried with him the germs of the disease which eventually brought him to an early grave. He died of consumption in Morristown, N. J., March 20, 1879, aged thirty-four years.

John Edwards, enlisted in the Fourth New York Cavalry and was killed in battle.

Timothy Fitzgerald, enlisted February 26, 1865, took part in the battles around Petersburg, and was discharged July 22.

Cornelius Hally, enlisted in Company A, Thirty-fifth New Jersey, February 24, 1865, and was discharged August 1.

Peter M. Kain, enlisted October 6, 1862, in Company K, Seventh New Jersey, and served throughout the War. He took part in all the battles of the Army of the Potomac; he was wounded at Gettysburg, and was with Grant when Lee surrendered.

Patrick Kating, enlisted February 24, 1865, was discharged in August, and died in Morristown.

Edward Kenny, enlisted June 11, 1862, in a New Jersey regiment.

John J. Kenny, enlisted August, 1862, in Company K, 176th Regiment, New York Volunteers, and served as a private eighteen months. He was engaged in the battles of the Army of the Southwest, and was wounded in the chin at Brazier City. He died November 19, 1891, of consumption, in Morristown, N. J.

Bernard Lynch, enlisted in the Navy, was one of the crew of the U. S. Ship *Oneida*, sunk by a British ship, and was drowned.

Thomas Lynch, enlisted in the Fall of 1861, in Company K, Seventh New Jersey, was engaged at Yorktown and Williamsburg, where he was wounded. After a long illness was discharged from the Army; but he enlisted in the Navy, and in the frigate *Niagara* saw service with the European squadron. After the sinking of the Confederate privateer *Alabama* he returned home. He served less than a year in the Army, and about two years in the Navy. He died in Dover, New Jersey, 1886.

Thomas H. Murray, enlisted March 10, 1865, in Company D, Thirty-fifth New Jersey. He was with General Sherman in his march through North and South Carolina.

William Murphy, Fourth New York Cavalry, was killed in battle; also John W. O'Donnell; and of John Lonergan, enlisted in 1862, and Thomas Finney, Company C, Seventh New Jersey, and Patrick Finney, enlisted January 17, 1864, there are no records.

Michael McLaughlin, Patrick McShane, Patrick Morrissey, and Charles McLaughlin enlisted in Captain Revere's Company, Fourth New York Cavalry.

George Rooth served seventeen months in the same company and regiment, and died in Morristown, January 12, 1867.

James Shadwell, enlisted in the Seventy-ninth New York Regiment, and died in Morristown.

James Sweeny, enlisted in 1862, in Company H, Eleventh New Jersey, was wounded at Malvern Hill, and was discharged from hospital.

In the Confederate service David W. Smith, born in Morristown and the first boy to serve Mass in the old Church, enlisted in the Fifth Company of the Washington Artillery of New Orleans. He rose to the rank of sergeant and served until captured towards the close of the War.

William Condon went South before the War and

settled in North Carolina. When hostilities broke out he enlisted in an infantry regiment of the Tarheel State and was captured at Gettysburg. Efforts were made to have him take the oath of allegiance and return to his family in Morristown. This proposal he indignantly rejected, saying he preferred to stick to the Stars and Bars, and even die in its defence. He died South after the close of the War.

CHAPTER XVIII.

THE sands of my "Story" have run out. Little remains to record, except the generosity of those who have contributed so much to the beautifying of our Church.

An oversight to mention in its proper place a signal example of exceptional liberality is now noted. When Father Sheeran made known his intention to build a Church, the first to come forward with a donation was a little Italian boy, rescued from the cruelty of a padrone, John Roman. His gift was five dollars, made up of pennies and nickels! Larger amounts were given, but they did not cost the sacrifice of this offering.

The windows in the Lady Chapel have already been mentioned.

The Father Sheeran Memorial bears above the symbol of the pelican, and beneath the inscription:

"To the memory of Rev. James Sheeran, who crowned a life of zeal, energy, and labor by the erection of this Church. Rich in good works, he slept in the Lord April 3, 1881. Merciful Jesu, grant him eternal rest. Amen."

To the left are the beautiful cherubs to the memory of

"John Carr, died November 27, 1876.

"James Carr, died June 16, 1878."

These are the gift of John A. Carr.

On the right of Father Sheeran's window is that of St. Henry and St. Agnes, with the emblem, an anchor. This is the gift of Mrs. Agnes Kelly, and bears the inscription:

"To the glory of God, and in loving memory of the deceased husband of Agnes Kelly. A.D. 1886."

Next is the window of St. Monica and St. Augustine, the gift of Mrs. L. Robeson. A bunch of lilies is in the little rose window, and the inscription reads:

"Daniel Augustine Robeson, died September 20, 1869.

"Sweet Jesu, grant him and us everlasting life."

The window of St. Ann and the infant Virgin and St. Bernard, with the crown as an emblem, is the gift of Mrs. M. Howard, and is inscribed:

"In memory of Ann Martin, died March 4, 1878.

"Loving Jesu, grant her eternal rest."

The window of St. Joseph and St. Patrick was placed by Patrick Farrelly and wife to the memory of their son. At the base is:

"In loving memory of Joseph Patrick Farrelly, died April 21, 1887.

"In thy mercy, Jesu, spare him and all Christian souls."

The emblem is the Sun of Justice.

The executors of the late William Nelson Wood promptly carried out the trust reposed in them by putting in the window containing the figures of St. Paul of the Cross and St. Francis de Sales with the emblem of a chalice and host. The deceased is commemorated in the following:

"Merciful Jesu, spare thy servant, William Nelson Wood, who died full of peace and hope, April 17, 1880."

The gem, perhaps, of all is the St. Cecilia in the porch, whose donor is recalled by the following:

"May God have mercy on Margaret Whelan, died May 6, 1888."

Her mother is remembered in the little window of St. Margaret, Queen of Scotland, with the words:

"In thy mercy, Jesu, grant rest and peace to Margaret Whelan."

In St. Joseph's aisle, the west side of the Church, and over the confessional, are St. John and St. Vincent de Paul, with the emblem of a dove bearing an olive-branch in its beak. It is the gift of Patrick Welsh and wife, in memory of their son:

"To the memory of John V. Welsh, died January 11, 1883, aged ten years."

With the passion-flower above is the window of St. Virgil, Bishop and Abbot of Saltzburg, and St. Brigid, of Ireland, bearing in hand the lighted lamp. This was erected by the Young Ladies' Sodality to the memory of Sister Gaudentia:

"Eternal rest grant, O Lord, to Sister Gaudentia. June 11, 1884."

The other to Father Henry

"Eternal rest, O Lord, grant to Rev. Arthur J. Henry. September 6, 1880."

The Purgatory window is the gift of Bessie Carroll and Bridget Quinn. The Sacred Heart of Jesus is emblazoned above the figures of St. Michael and Our Lady, Comfortress of the Afflicted. The inscription reads:

"May the souls of the faithful departed, through the mercy of God, rest in peace. Amen."

The School Children, in 1887, raised the money to put in the window which represents Jesus blessing the little ones whom the mother brings to Him. The Gospel text recalls it: "Suffer little children to come unto me. By the School Children, 1887." The symbol is a seraph.

The Rosary Society contributed the money for the beautiful window which represents Our Lady and the Divine Infant presenting the Rosary to St. Dominic.

The symbol is the dog, bearing the torch and a globe. The motive which inspired the Rosarians is embodied in the following:

"To the Queen of the Most Holy Rosary. A loving tribute from the Rosary Society, 1887. Pray for us."

Mrs. Ellen Eakely and her daughters perpetuate the memory of their relatives in the window which contains figures of St. Thomas, the Apostle, and St. Helena, with a cluster of grapes and wheat as emblems.

"In loving memory of Thomas Degan, died November 4, 1887. Ellen Degan, died January 16, 1887. May they rest in peace."

James Lonergan, in affectionate remembrance of his

parents, donated the window in which St. Leo the Great and St. Rose of Lima are represented. The emblem is the Lamb and Book of seven seals. The inscription is:

"Jesu, have mercy on James Lonergan, died January 1, 1876. Bridget Lonergan, died July 19, 1873."

The statues of St. Joseph and the Blessed Mother were given by the children.

To worthily commemorate the twenty-first birthday of his son, J. Charles Farrelly, his father enriched the Church with the exquisite Stations of the Cross. They are painted on copper by one of the first artists in Paris, and afterwards enamelled. They are from the art-rooms of Cabane, Paris.

Miss Lizzie Daly presented the crystal candelabra on either side of the Sacred Heart Statue.

The last expression of generosity to note are the holy-water stoups, in spotless marble, the gift of Mrs. P. Farrelly for her little daughter Mary Kate.

Although the opportunity has not been given to all to mark their liberality in a conspicuous way, yet the monuments which the Catholics in Morristown have raised to the glory of God tell in no uncertain tones of a Faith and a Charity without limit. The bounty of God has attended this generosity. He has blessed the soil in which our fathers sowed the seed of faith.

Strange as it may appear, there was not in the Diocese of Newark a single monument to perpetuate the memory of its first Bishop. This, coupled with the fact that the early efforts of Bishop Bayley were devoted to the establishment of parish schools, and that Morristown was the first fruits of his zeal in this direction, impelled Dean Flynn to request Bishop Wigger's permission to call the School after this venerated prelate. This was unhesitatingly granted; and thus the name of Bayley School and Hall, attached to the group of buildings on Madison Street, will keep fresh and alive in the present and future generations the memory of the good and great Archbishop Bayley.

It may not be amiss to call attention to the fruits of the Catholic School here, and to note the names of those who have devoted themselves to the service of God as Sisters in different religious Communities, or the Levites who hope one day to share the priesthood of Christ: Sister Mary John Roache upwards of thirty years ago abandoned home and friends to consecrate her life as a Sister of Mercy, in the sterile field of Bishop Byrne's Diocese of Little Rock, Arkansas; Sister Mary Louise Burke, Sister Sarah Burke, Sister Severina Burke, the daughters of our venerable pioneer Thomas Burke; Sister Eusebia Baxter; Sister Rose Roache; Sister Murilla Mansfield; Sister Marguerite Ryan; Sister Gaudentia Mulhall; Sister Agnes Madeleine Daly; Sister Jovita Cody, and Sister Paulita Morrissey, all of whom entered the Community of the Sisters of Charity whose Mother-house is at Madison, N. J. Some of them have been called to their reward; and the remainder continue to exercise the duties of their vocation, instructing the little ones of Christ's fold unto justice, or ministering to the sick and afflicted.

Sister Walburga Buckley and Sister Sheridan have consecrated their lives to the Negro and Indian Missions in the Franciscan Sisterhood.

Within less than two years James Mulhall, now in the Diocesan Seminary of the Immaculate Conception, South Orange, N. J., if it please God, will be ordained priest, and will add new joy to our parish and another jewel to our crown.

At St. Charles's College, Ellicott City, Md., two of the pupils of the Bayley School, children of this parish, Masters William Dunn and William Kelly, are pursuing their classical studies, and, it is to be hoped, will persevere in their lofty and laudable desire.

The great works, not strictly within the scope of parish efforts, but important auxiliaries to its influence for good, have been marked with exceptional success.

The St. Mary's Young Men's Catholic Association has at present one hundred members. The average annual receipts during the ten years have been three thousand dollars, or a gross sum of thirty thousand dollars.

St. Columbanus Council, No. 40, Catholic Benevolent Legion, has a membership of one hundred and eleven. Since the date of its organization, October 1, 1883, to December 1, 1891, its members have paid to the Benefit fund $23,909.02, and to the

General fund $1,597.25—a total of $23,687.27. The families of its deceased members have received as benefits $19,000.

When the new Catholic Church was building, one of the parish school-boys began life literally at the foot of the ladder. From mason's helper his ambition has led him higher and higher, until now he is at the head of one of the leading firms of builders, and at present Thomas Malley fills the honorable position of Mayor of Morristown.

It may be well to supply an unintentional omission, when treating of the erection of the Bayley School, to state that the entire cost was $24,820.30, and the steam plant which heats the School, Church, Rectory, and Sisters' House $4,316.27. The outlay for the new Rectory, erected on the site of the old Church, was $20,886.98.

So may the good work go on! May the blessings of the past be continued in the future; may the success which has attended the efforts of the different pastors presage the glory which will redound to God and His Church—the happiness, both in this and the next world, the reward of this generous, edifying Congregation, and for other Rectors the consolation which has filled to overflowing the heart of the present Pastor!

If in the brief span of less than half a century the harvest has been so abundant, who can estimate or foresee what another decade or two of years will bring?

APPENDIX.

APPENDIX.

FROM FATHER FARMER'S MARRIAGE REGISTER.

Oct. 20, 1774. At Charlottenburg, New Jersey, Dominick Robertson to Mary Catharine, daughter of Nicholas and Helena Mentzenbach; witnesses, Humphrey Booth and Peter Welker. The nuptial blessing was given afterwards at Mass.

    The same day and place: Thomas Walsh to Catharine Brown; witnesses, Hugh Quigan and William Graty.

    The same day and place: Mathias Bender to Abigail Parmer; witnesses, the bride's parents.

Oct. 24, 1774. At Mount Hope, New Jersey, after dispensation, John Dirk to Hannah Alleton; witnesses, Anthony Schumers, Peter Welker, and Anna Catharine Zech.

May 12, 1777. At Mount Hope, Peter Joseph Grips to Mary Krauskopf; witnesses, James Welker and James Demuth.

    On the same occasion, William Meighan to Elizabeth Tate; witnesses, Thomas Poor and Edmund Darmothy.

Apl. 30, 1782. At Charlottenburg, New Jersey, Anthony Marian to Anna Mary Mentzenbach; witnesses, Martin Bachman, Francis Zech, and others. The blessing was given at Mass.

Oct. 20, 1783. At Mount Hope, in Morris County, New Jersey, Adam Bischoff to Margaret Krauskopf; witnesses, Simon Honig and Catharine Sig.

Oct. 24, 1783. At Charlottenburg, N. J., Peter Dunnel to Elizabeth Seeholtzer; witnesses, John Schmidt and Catharine Wittiger.

Oct. 24, 1785. Near Mount Hope Furnace, in Morris County, New Jersey, Thomas Flanagan to Ann Grey, widow; witnesses, Henry Hager and Christina Emick.

BAPTISMS ADMINISTERED BY THE REV. FATHER FARMER, S.J.

Oct. 21, 1762. Mary, of Michael and Mary Connor, born August 13, baptized; Susannah Kearnney, sponsor.

Oct. 23, 1768. Mary Darmoty, of Edward and Esther, born July 21, 1765; Alexander McConahy and Mary Elizabeth Halter, sponsors, at Charlottenburg, N. J.

Barnabas Darmoty, of same parents, born May 10, 1767; sponsors, Patrick Burke and Mary Catharine Kramer. Same place.

Matthew Demuth, of James and Ann Catharine Demuth, born September 10; sponsors, Matthew Kramer and Juliana Miriam.

Elizabeth Scholtzer, of Martin and Susan Scholtzer, born January 19; baptized conditionally; had been baptized by Nicholas Scholtzer, an intelligent man, his wife being witness, living at Charlottenburg, N. J., ceremonies being afterwards supplied.

Apl. 15, 1769. Bachman, Mary Barbara, of Martin and Anna Barbara Bachman, born April 16; sponsors, Nicholas Jungfleisch and Barbara Her—, at Charlottenburg, N. J.

Apl. 29, 1770. George Brown, of John and Mary Brown, born November —, 1765; sponsors, William Fitzgerald and Catherine Fowler. Same place.

John Rice, of James and Esther Rice, born November 30, 1769; sponsors, Thomas Rice and Elizabeth Campbel. Same place.

Mary Margaret Sutton, of William and Anna Sutton, born December 26, 1769; sponsors, Margaret Engelhardt and Henry Glas. Same place.

Nov. 21, 1770. Mary Magdalen Schot, of Philip and Mary Schot, born September 30; sponsors, Martin Bachman and Magdalen Welker. Same place.

Anna Barbara Cobole, of Daniel and Mary Ann Cobole, born September 5; sponsors, Bartholomew Cobole and Catherine Welker. Same place.

Nov. 22, 1770. Anna Eva Kean, of William and Eleanor Kean, born June —; sponsors, James Brown and Eva Jungfleisch. Same place.

Nov. 25, 1770. Anthony James Butz, of Christian and Catherine Butz, born November 22; sponsors, Anthony Schumers and Barbara Bachman. Same place.

Apl. 20, 1771. Margaret Brown, of James and Grace Brown, born March 27; sponsors James Brown and Grace McDead. Same place.

Apl. 21, 1771. Elizabeth Harris, of Samuel Harris and —— Joice, born March 31, 1767; sponsors, Philip McDead and Grace Brown. Same place.

Samuel Harris, of same parents, born May 9, 1769; sponsors, Philip McDead and Grace Brown. Same place.

Mary Ann Barr, of George and Catherine Barr, born

December 23, 1770; sponsors, Hugh Dougherty and Margaret Englehardt. Same place.

Oct. 26, 1771. Scholtzer, of Martin and Elizabeth Scholtzer, born October 22; sponsors, Nicholas and Elizabeth Halter. Same place.

Anna Elizabeth Reider, of Francis Joseph and Anna Mary Reider, born May 18; sponsors, Joseph Wingart and Anna Elizabeth Marian. Same place.

May 28, 1772. Francis Anthony Bachman, of Martin and Anna Barbara Bachman, born April 20; sponsors, Francis Anthony and Anna Catherine Zech. Same place.

Martha Burns, of Laughlin and Mary Burns, born November 8, 1771; sponsors, James Marniny and Eleanor Callaghan. Same place.

Nov. 20, 1772. Anthony Schott, of Philip and Catherine Schott, born August 30; sponsors, Anthony Schumers and Catherine Demuth. Same place.

Oct. 13, 1774. John Wingart, of Joseph and Anna Elizabeth Wingart, born August 15; sponsors, James and Anna Catherine Demuth, in Morris County.

Oct. 23, 1774. John Power, of Thomas and Susanna Power, born August 28, 1773; sponsors, Peter Boyle and Sarah Christy, at Mount Hope.

John James Olls, of John and Ann Elizabeth Olls, born August 10; sponsors, John James Walker and Elizabeth Welsch. Same place.

Oct. 24, 1774. Peter Kirk, of John Kirk and Joanna Alleton, born, June 4; sponsors, Peter Joseph and Anna Catherine Grips. Same place.

Joanna Kirk (Alleton), wife of John Kirk, adult; sponsor, Anna Catherine Zech. Same place.

May 20, 1775. Francis Weber, of James and Anna Catherine Weber, born April 8; sponsors, Francis Anthony and Catherine Zech, in Morris County.

APPENDIX.

May 21, 1775. Philip Brown, of James and Grace Brown, born February 17; sponsors, William Halfpeny and Mary Pickets. Same place.

Sig, Frederick, of John George (P.) * and Gertrude Sig, born April 4; sponsor, Peter Grips; Frederic Bohm witness. Same place.

James Wider, of Joseph and Margaret Wider, born February —; sponsors, James and Anna Catherine Demuth. Same place.

Darmoty, Edward, of Edward and Esther Darmoty, born February 11; sponsors, Peter Joseph Grips and Hannah Dirk. Same place.

Peter Keiner, of —— and Christiana (P.) Keiner, born February 2, 1774; sponsors, Peter Joseph Grips and Anna Elizabeth Olls. Same place.

May 23, 1775. Anna Price, of Thomas and Catherine Price, born March 13; sponsor, Sarah Christe; Adam Mailgan, witness; at Charlottenburg.

May 24, 1775. William Par, of Sophornia and Catherine Par, born March 19; sponsor, Anna Mary Merzbach; Edward Magill, witness. Same place.

May 25, 1775. Anna Catherine Schot, of Philip and Mary Catherine Schot, born December 1, 1774; sponsors, Daniel Cobole and Mary Anna Quinx (for Catherine Cobole).

Mary Margaret Marchler, of John and Mary Anna Mercler, born February 12; sponsors, Dominic Andler and Mary Schot. Same place.

May 31, 1775. Margaret Connelly, of James and Margaret Connelly, born May 26; sponsor, Francis Dealy; Margaret Brown, witness; at Mount Hope.

Oct. 18, 1775. Mary Catherine Stecher, of Joseph and Anna Stecher, born August 16; sponsors, William

---

* Protestant. One parent a Catholic.

Grafty and Mrs. Mary Mantzenbach; at Charlottenburg.

Helen Bachman, of Martin and Anna Barbara Bachman, born September 11; sponsors, Nicholas Mentzenbach, Joseph and Helen Wingart. Same place.

Mary Anna Cobole, of Daniel and Mary Anna Cobole, born July 26; sponsors, Peter Wilkes and Elizabeth Welsh (for Mary Ann, wife of Bartholomew Cobole).

Oct. 20, 1775. Anna Robertson, of Dominic and Mary Catharine Robertson, born July —; ceremonies supplied. Same place.

May 5, 1776. Dealy, Mary, of James and Esther Dealy, born August 9, 1772; sponsors, Thomas and Magdalen Price; at Mount Hope.

John William Schaffer, of George and Jeannette Schaffer, born August 9, 1775; sponsors, Richard and Mary Murphy. Same place.

Anna Margaret, of Bernard and Mary Dorothy Reuschmid, born April 9; sponsors, Francis Zech and Margaret Englehard. Same place.

Charles Whetcock, of Richard and Mary (Brown) Whetcock, born February 18; sponsors, Caspar Englehard and Grace Brown. Same place.

Mary Welsh, of Thomas and Catherine Welsh, born December 21, 1775; sponsors, Hugh Quigg and Anna Catherine Demuth. Same place.

Caspar Holtzhaser, of Sebastian and Joanna Holtzhaser, born April 2; sponsors, Caspar and Margaret Englehard. Same place.

Apl. 26, 1776. Henry Kean, of William and Elenor Kean, born December 17, 1775; sponsors, Joseph and Anna Elizabeth Wingart; in Morris County.

Apl. 28, 1776. William Kelly, of Luke and Margaret Kelly, born

June 13, 1770; sponsors, James Maruny and Johannah McDonald; at Charlottenburg.

Oct. 20, 1776. Mary Wattcock, of Richard and Mary Wattcock, born September 12, 1768; sponsors, John Burk and Margaret Kelly; at Mount Hope.

Esther Dealy, of James and Esther Dealy, born August 15; sponsors, Edward D. Dormoty and Catherine Welsh. Same place.

Richard Wattcock, of Richard and Mary Wattcock, born September 20, 1773; sponsors, John and Margaret Viche. Same place.

James Kramer, of William and Patience Kramer, born January 18; sponsors, James and Grace Brown. Same place,

Mary Welsh, of William and Elizabeth Welsh, born April 2; sponsors, Caspar and Margaret Englehard. Same place.

Power, Lucy, of Thomas and Susanna Power, born June 28; sponsors, Francis Dealy and Margaret Englehard. Same place.

Anna Mary Gertrude Hayman and John George, twins, of John and Susanna Hayman, born July 7 and July 8; sponsors, John Antler and Gertrude Sig for the former, John George Sig and Anna Catherine Demuth for the latter.

Oct. 21, 1776. Robert Philipps, of John and Mary Philipps, born August 19; sponsors, Caspar and Margaret Englehard. Same place.

Oct. 22, 1776. Sarah Brawer Stuart, wife of John Stuart; sponsor, Catherine Robertson; at Charlottenburg.

John Stuart, of John and Sarah Stuart, born September 9; sponsors, Joseph Wingart and Anna Mentzenbach. Same place.

Oct. 23, 1776. Julianna Wingart, of Joseph and Elizabeth Wingart, born July 19, ceremony supplied; witnesses

APPENDIX. 295

   Daniel Cobole and Anna Mary Reider. Same place.

   Joseph Marian, of Herbert and Anna Mary Marian, born October 22; sponsors, Joseph Wingart and Catherine Schott. Same place.

Oct. 24, 1776. David Schop, of Philip and Mary Eva Schop, born June 27; sponsors, David Fichter and Mary Looisa Schop. Same place.

May 7, 1777. Joseph Gordon, of Hugh and Margaret Gordon, born December 20, 1776; sponsor, Joseph Stecher; at Charlottenburg.

May 8, 1777. Lawrence Stecher, of Joseph and Anna Stecher, born January 16; sponsor, Martin Bachman. Same place.

   Ferdinand Bachman, of Martin and Anna Barbara Bachman, born May 2; ceremonies supplied; sponsors, John Cobole and Anna Eva Jungfleisch. Same place.

   Mary Anna Zech, of Francis Anthony and Anna Catherine Zech, born November 27; ceremony supplied; sponsors, Joseph Wongart and Mary Anna Cobole. Same place.

Sept. 27, 1778. Helen Sig, of John George and Gertrude Sig, born November 4, 1777; sponsors, Francis Zech and Magdalen Welker (for Helen Menzebach); at Mount Hope.

   Anna Mary Power, of Thomas and Susanna Power, born June 24; sponsors, Edward Darmoty and Mary Grinder. Same place.

   Margaret Weber, of James and Anna Catherine Weber, born July 24; sponsor Margaret Englehard. Same place.

   Philip Fechter, of David and Johanna Fechter, born September 11, 1777; sponsors, Louis Herman (for Philip Schup) and Catherine Zech. Same place.

Peter Joseph Holzheber, of Sebastian and Johanna Holzheber, born May 2; sponsors, Peter Joseph and Mary Grips. Same place.

Sept. 29, 1778. Anna Mary Schup, Philip and Mary Eva Schup, born March 27; sponsors, Jacob Fechter and Anna Mary Mentzenbach; at Charlottenburg.

Sept. 30, 1778. Henry Marian, of Hurbert and Mary Marian, born July 18; sponsors, Martin Bachman and Barbara Welker. Same place.

Catharine Cobole, of Daniel and Mary Anna Cobole, born September 29, 1777; ceremony supplied; sponsors, Francis Zech and Catharine Coblin. Same place.

Mary Barbara Seeholtzer, of Martin and Elizabeth Seeholtzer, born July 28; ceremony supplied; sponsors, Daniel Cobole and Barbara Welker. Same place.

Oct. 6, 1778. Anna Elizabeth Schag, of John George and Jeannetta Schaga, born September 2; sponsors, James Welker and Gertrude Sig; at Mount Hope.

Apl. 22, 1779. Benjamin Sheal, of John and Anna Sheal, born December 19, 1776; sponsors, Francis and Catherine Zech; at Mount Hope.

Sarah Sheal, of same parents, born February 25; sponsors, Caspar and Margaret Engelhard. Same place.

May 2, 1779. Anna Catherine Wider, of Joseph and Margaret Wider, born October 18, 1778; sponsors, Francis and Catharine Zech. Same place.

John James Zech, of Francis and Catharine Zech, born January 13; sponsors, James Welker and Eva Jungfleisch. Same p'ace.

Elizabeth Grips, of Peter Joseph and Mary Grips, born January 17; sponsors, John and Hanora Turk. Same place.

June 4, 1780. Margaret Holtzhafer, of Sebastuan and Johanna Holtzhafer, born April 25; sponsors, Caspar and Margaret Engelhard; at Mount Hope.

Henry Schup, of Philip and Mary Eva Schup, born May 12; sponsors, David and Johanna Fichter; in vicinity of Charlottenburg.

Rosanna Hason, of Felix and Margaret Hason, born May 24, 1778; sponsor, the child's mother (for Mary Mentzenbach). Same place.

May 24, 1781. Anna Mary Marian, of Hurbert and Mary Marian, born April 8; sponsors, John Aussom and Helen Mentzenbach; at Charlottenburg.

John Stephen Aussom, born December 25, 1765; Eva Clarissa, born March 31, 1769; Joseph, born February 28, 1773, children of John and Elizabeth Aussom, baptized conditionally May 24; sponsor, Joseph Wingart; at Pompton.

Catharine Osterhout, of —— and Elizabeth Osterhout, born March 12, 1774; baptized conditionally; sponsor, Joseph Wingart. Same place.

Elizabeth Osterhout, adult; sponsor, Elizabeth Aussom. Same place.

——, Peter, a negro boy, about seven years old; sponsor, Joseph Wingart.

May 27, 1781. James Fichter, of David and Johanna Fichter, born November 15, 1780; sponsors, James Fichter and Eva Brady; at Mount Hope.

Francis Anthony Grips, of Peter Joseph and Mary Grips, born November 27, 1780; sponsors, Francis Anthony Zech and Margaret Engelhart. Same place.

May 26, 1781. Christopher Sig, of George and Gertrude Sig, born

December 5, 1780; sponsors, Francis Anthony Zech (for Christopher Thomer) and Anna Catharine Zech. Same place.

Sept. 28, 1781. Joseph Bachman, of Martin and Anna Barbara Bachman, born June 14; sponsors, the priest and Anna Mary Menzebach; at Mount Hope.

Oct. 14, 1781. John Bernard Zech, of Francis Anthony and Anna Catherine Zech, born September 19; sponsors, John and Anna Mary Grinter; at Mount Hope.

John Sheal, of John and Anna Sheal, born August 20; sponsors, Peter Joseph and Mary Grips. Same place,

Oct. 11, 1781. Amos Haycock, of Daniel and Catherine Haycock, born April 26, 1774; sponsor, Hurbert Marian; at Pompton.

Abigail Haycock, of same parents, born April, 1779; sponsors, John Aussom and Anna Elizabeth Wingart. Same place.

Elizabeth Haycock, same parents, born February, 1781; sponsor, Elizabeth Aussom. Same place.

MARRIAGES

PERFORMED BY THE REV. DR. JOHNES AND OTHER MINISTERS OF THE FIRST PRESBYTERIAN CHURCH. (COPIED FROM THE RECORD.)

Jan. 5, 1763. Solloman Boyle to Sarah Alling.
Sept. 11, 1763. John Cooper to Magdalen Boyle.
Nov. 3, 1763. Jacob Frazee to Elizabeth McFeran.
May 11, 1766. John Leferty to Elizabeth Johnes.
Sept. 19, 1774. John Crane to Mary O'Hara.
Apl. 6, 1776. John Knowland to Mary Curtain.

APPENDIX.

May 26, 1776. Hugh McConnell to Susannah Dalrympel.
Feb.   6, 1777. Will McCormick, soldier, to Dramer Cramer.
April 15, 1777. William Rogan, soldier, to Sarah Greer.
July 10, 1777. James Gardiner, soldier, to Nance Burn.
Oct. 21, 1778. John Kenne to Phebe Arnold.
Dec.   3, 1778. George Thorborn to Nancy Kenny, late Nancy McGovern.
Aug. 29, 1779. Jacob Doran to Mary Dun.
Jan. 31, 1780. Christopher Breackin to Mary Briant.
Mar.   6, 1780. Lawrence Brennan, serg't 7 Mary'd Reg't, to Catharine Clancy, of ye 1 Mor. Brigade.
Mar. 22, 1780. James Right to Jane Woodrough, of Capt. Harmon Stout's 10 Penna. Reg't.
Apl.   5, 1780. Griffith Davis to Sarah Conway, both of the Army.
Apl.   9, 1780. Michael Connor to Sarah Hamilton.
May   11, 1780. Allan McLane to Mary Robins.
       14, 1780. John McCarroll, a soldier of the 10 Penna. Reg't, to Kezia Clark.
       20, 1780. Thomas Brown, a soldier, to Elizabeth Nicholson.
       20, 1780. Patrick Rogers and Peggy Brien, Camp folks.
       21, 1780. Elijah Pollock, a soldier, and Catharine Grear, Camp folks.
       24,   "   Matthew Dorham, a soldier, and Mary Davis, from the Camp.
July 28,   "   William McMullen, a soldier, and Jemima Guirin.
Aug. 12,   "   John Smith, waggoner, and Margaret Wilson, Camp woman.
Jan. 24, 1782. John Bolton, a soldier, 2nd Jersey Reg't, Jonathan Holmes Captain, and Catharine Devins.
July   7,   "   George Kelle and Annie Ward, a widow.
Mar. 24, 1783. William Dennine and Margaret Templeton.
May   9, 1784. Daniel Skelly and Catharine Headley.
Jan. 10, 1790. John Brian and Mary Howell.

BILL OF MORTALITY

Taken from the Records of the First Presbyterian Church, Morristown, N. J.

June 1, 1770. Buried child of James Kearney.
Oct. " " " " Patrick McGill.
Mar. 4, 1782. " " " Thomas Kane, aged 8.
Aug. 24, 1784. " Daniel Brady, aged 40.
Nov. 25, " " child of Hubert Duburk.
June 14, 1785. " son " Michael Conner, aged 2.
July 26, " " " " James Smith.
Aug. 16, " " child of Peter Carn.
15, 1789. " daughter of John Powers, aged 20.
July 1, 1791. " Sophia Burke, aged 23.
Mar. 28, 1793. " Margaret, wife of Thomas Cody, aged 23.
Oct. 18, 1794. " Sarah, daughter of Edward Cerey, aged 21.
Feb. 7, 1796. " James O'Hara, consumption, aged 36.
Dec. 3, " " child of Patrick Caunnel.
June 19, 1798. " Rachel, wife of Francis McCarty.
29, 1799. " George Kelly, aged 60.
April 4, 1800. " John O'Neil, aged 65.
March 7, 1801. " Michael Connor, aged 49.
Jan. 2, 1803. " Antoinette Regnaudot, aged 26.
24, 1805. " Mons. Delisle Dupres, aged 38.
Oct. 9, " " Cæsar Dumaine Gachet, aged 25.
28, " " Louise Dovillard Vanschalkwick.
" Vincent Boisaubin Beauplan, aged 33.
26, 1806. " George O'Hara, aged 53 (keeper of hotel).
Nov. 12, " " Nicholas Comissau.
June 1, 1808. " William Delaplaine, aged 50.
1809. " Miriam Comesau, aged 80.

NUMBER OF MARRIAGES

Administered in St. Vincent's Church, Madison, and in the Church of the Assumption, Morristown, as appears on the Records of both Churches. The Figures indicate those who belonged to the Morristown Parish.

1841.	1 Marriage (at Madison).		1868.	22	Marriages(Morristown).
1842.*	"		1869.	18	"
1843.	1 "	"	1870.	22	"
1844.*	"		1871.	23	"
1845.*	"		1872.	14	"
1846.*	3 "		1873.	7	"
1847.*	6 "		1874.	16	"
1848.*	5 "		1875.	19	"
1849.*	3 "		1876.	10	"
1850.*	6 "		1877.	14	"
1851.*	4 "		1878.	5	"
1852	(No Record for 4 years.)		1879.	15	"
1856.	6 Marriages(Morristown).		1880.	9	"
1857.	27 "	"	1881.	27	"
1858.	9 "	"	1882.	14	"
1859.	12 "	"	1883.	14	"
1860.	12 "	"	1884.	7	"
1861.	15 "	"	1885.	15	"
1862.	11 "	"	1886.	17	"
1863.	6 "	"	1887.	14	"
1864.	9 "	"	1888.	16	"
1865.	12 "	"	1889.	20	"
1866.	8 "	"	1890.	27	"
1867.	12 "	"	1891.	18	"

* These years are not absolutely accurate, as the locality has not been specified on the Register.

NUMBER OF BAPTISMS

Administered in St. Vincent's Church, Madison, and in the Church of the Assumption, Morristown, as appears on the Records of both Churches. The Figures indicate those who belonged to the Morristown Parish.

1841. 10 Baptisms (Madison Ch.) 1847. 14 Baptisms (Madison Ch.)
1842. 5   "   "   1848. 12   "   "
1843. 8   "   "   1849. 5   "   "
1844. 12   "   "   1850. *
1844. 7 by Rev. I. P. Howell.   1851. *14   "   "
1845. 2 Baptisms (Madison Ch.) 1852. * 17   "   "
1846. 15   "   "   1855. No record for 3 years)

All the Baptisms that follow were administered in Morristown Church.

1856. 10 Baptisms.   1874. 72 Baptisms.
1857. 65   "   1875. 76   "
1858. 81   "   1876. 75   "
1859. 47   "   1877. 64   "
1860. 51   "   1878. 62   "
1861. 76   "   1879. 60   "
1862. 55   "   1880. 62   "
1863. 52   "   1881. 51   "
1864. 44   "   1882. 77   "
1865. 41   "   1883. 59   "
1866. 56   "   1884. 58   "
1867. 41   "   1885. 66   "
1868. 78   "   1886. 84   "
1869. 90   "   1887. 61   "
1870. 66   "   1888. 77   "
1871. 80   "   1889. 87   "
1872. 86   "   1890. 87   "
1873. 63   "   1891. 89   "

SUMMARY OF FINANCIAL STATEMENTS.

	Pew Rents.	Offertory.	Picnics and Fairs.		Diocesan Contributions.
1856.	—	$21.95	—		—
1857.	$303.67	37.75	—		—
1867.	319.00	86.61	$1,090.63		—
1868.	801.89	234.44	660.65		$300.00
1869.	800.93	208.79	1,010.65		262.00
1870.	759.56	314.65	1,125.25		261.00
1871.	1,116.54	458.71	930.65		248.00
1872.	813.56	574.38	712.00		—
1873.	3,031.12	1,178.89	1,325.00		83.00
1874.	3,410.75	1,533.22	1,034.00		45.00
1875.	3,295.00	1,458.53	1,100.00		95.00
1876.	3,184.25	1,302.74	779.00		93.12
1877.	2,773.17	1,170.34	730.42		41.00
1878.	2,311.95	1,397.13	467.00	$2,122.00 (Fair)	80.00
1879.	2,279.00	1,449.42	663.02	1,021.00 (Fair)	40.00
1880.	2,143.00	1,379.99	670.00	1,109.00 (Fair)	54.00
1881.	2,361.77	1,789.75	729.39		200.00
1882.	2,571.50	1,843.60	921.34		—
1883.	2,827.45	2,202.79	1,189.63		305.00
1884.	3,507.59	2,703.46	538.92		283.00
1885.	3,462.07	2,768.40	261.92	1,089.05 (Fair)	438.00
1886.	3,532.08	3,327.93	320.65	2,619.10 (Fair)	474.74
1887.	4,388.73	3,206.83	173.21	2,731.51 (Fair)	420.00
1888.	5,035.15	3,172.15	—		440.50
1889.	5,258.40	2,836.57	—		289.78
1890.	6,493.70	2,343.52	—	1,939.10 (Bazar)	693.59
1891.	6,569.88	2,188.39	—	2,174.53 "	418.92

VARIOUS SUBSCRIPTIONS.

NAMES OF SUBSCRIBERS AND AMOUNT OF SUBSCRIPTIONS TO THE NEW CHURCH IN 1872.

The Temperance Society, $557.00 Daniel Coghlan, $500.00
Claude M. Gignoux, $500.00 Gen. Joseph Revere, $450.00
Augustus Louanstein, $200.00

$100.00.

Ballentine, Joseph W. Gallagher, James,
Baxter, Hugh, Holly, Cornelius,
Collins, William, Kenny, Bartholomew,
Cutler, Augustus W. O'Brien, Martin,
Degan, Thomas, Rogers, Mrs. Julia,
Dorney, Dennis, Ryan, William,
Sheeran, Rev. J.

Dempsey, Patrick, $90.00 Callahan, Jeremiah, $60.00
Cassidy, Frank, $55.00.

$50.00.

Burns, Thomas, Hughes, Thomas,
Burke, Thomas W. Lonergan, James,
Callahan, Patrick, Lonergan, James,
Carr, John A. McNeil, James,
Carroll, Walter, McDermott, James,
Carroll, William, McEntee, Patrick,
Castillon, Edward, Meskill, Daniel,
Clifford, Thomas, Mooney, William,
Dacy, Michael, Mulhall, Patrick,
Dergen, David, Murphy, Hugh,
Donahue, Patrick, O'Toole, William,
Downey, Mrs., New York, Smith, John, New Vernon,
Dunn, William, Tobin, John,
Dwyer, William, Willman, Frederick,
Geoghegan, William W. Walsh, William,
Hogan, Mrs. Wall, Edmund.

$40.00.

Beers, William H.
Campbell, Michael,
Martin, Bernard,

O'Keefe, Thomas,
Rourke, James,
York, Joseph.

$30.00.

Bayley, Andrew,
Collins, Dennis,
Cooney, Ellen,
Cummings, D.

McGrath, John,
New York girls,
Tankard, James,
Timmens, James,
Timmens, James.

Collection by K. & W., $26.00

$25.00.

Carroll, E.
Cavanagh, Patrick,
Collins, John D.
Coyle, Henry,
Cummings, Jennie,
Cummings, Martin,
Dowd, John,
Doyle, John,
Doyle, James,
Duffy, John,
Eakley, James,
Elliot, Hugh,
English, William,
English, Dennis,
Feely, James D.
Gaffney, John,
Gallagher, Mary,
Goin, Timothy,
Griffin, D.
Hackett, Michael,
Hackett, Patrick,

Hannon, Patrick,
Hughes, Thomas.
Kain, Peter,
Kane, Michael,
Kenny, John J.
Kenny, John J.
Killkenny, Luke,
McGuire, John,
Malley, Peter,
Manning, Mrs.
Morris, John,
Mulhall, J.
Murphy, Martin,
Naughton, John,
O'Brien, Maggie A.
Reilly, Julia,
Rutledge, James,
Sullivan, Agnes,
Sweeney, Daniel,
Vorholz, Frederick,
Whitehead, Mr.

$20.00.

Alexander, Gordon,
Barry, Lizzie,
Belby, John,
Belby, Matthew,
Burns, Hannah,
Cahill, John,

Holly, Patrick,
Kelly, Bridget,
Kelly, Peter,
Keveling, Kate,
Leech, Mary,
Lane, Dennis,

Cahill, James,
Carlin, Bernard,
Casey, Mary,
Clancy, Margaret,
Cogivan, Winifrid,
Coleman, Patrick,
Condon, Michael,
Condon, Mrs. W., widow,
Connors, Mrs., New York,
Costigan, John,
Cullen, Charles,
Curley, Patrick,
Dalton, Mary,
Diver, Annie,
Dolan, William,
Donlin, Ellen,
Doty, Mrs.
Downey, James,
Dowd, Bridget,
Downey, James,
Doyle, Margaret,
Duggan, Mary,
Ducey, John,
Farrell, Andrew,
Fay, James,
Fennell, Mrs.
Fitzgerald, Timothy,
Fitzgerald, Patrick,
Foley, William,
Foley, Jeremiah,
Gannon, Mrs.
Gibbons, Marcella,
Gowing, Edward,
Griffin, Patrick,
Hackett, Dennis,
Hickey, William,
Hickey, Patrick,
Hifley, Lizzie,
Hillock, Patrick,
Hillock, John,
Holly, William,

Lonergan, John,
Looney, Michael,
Lowe, James,
Lyons, James,
McCabe, Margaret,
McDonald, Mary,
McGoldrick, Edward,
McGrath, John,
McGuire, William,
McLaughlin, Mary,
McNamara, James,
McNulty, James,
Malley, Mary,
Mansfield, Kate,
Markey, Laurence,
Martin, James,
Meskill, Julia,
Minogue, John,
Mitchell, John,
Moran, John,
Morrissey, John,
Morrisson, Bridget,
Morrisson, Rebecca,
Murray, John,
Murray, Thomas H.
Murphy, Dennis,
Murphy, James,
Murphy, Mary,
O'Neil, Julia,
Owens, John,
Prendergast, James,
Quilty, Ann,
Riley, Michael,
Rutledge, Mary,
Rutledge, Richard,
Ryan, Patrick,
Smith, Patrick,
Wall, Ellen,
Wall, Patrick,
Walsh, William,
Warner, Mrs.
White, Jeremiah.
Murphy, Kate, $17.00.

APPENDIX.

$15.00.

Barry, Hannah,
Burns, Mary,
Cone, Patrick,
Cummings, Philomena,
Dowd, James,
Gibbons, Ann,
Gibbons, Mary,
Goin, Patrick,
Hackett, Joseph,
Harty, Thomas,
Horan, John,
Kearney, Kate,
Kelly, James,
Kilday, Ellen,
Knight, Mrs.
Mahar, Mary,
Manning, John,
McGrath, Dennis,
Minogue, Martin,
Mitchell, Hannah,
Moran, James J.
Nailor, Roger,
O'Donnell, Catharine,
Quinn, Kate,

School Children.

Holly, James, $12.00.

$10.00.

Beehan, Thomas,
Brady, Alice,
Cahill, Ann,
Cassion, Eliza,
Cleary, Mike,
Cody, John,
Coffey, John,
Coghivan, Michael,
Coleman, Thomas,
Cooney, Laurence,
Cooney, John,
Connell, Mike,
Conners, Patrick,
Conners, William,
Conners, David,
Crane, Thomas,
Dacy, Margaret,
Dempsey, Richard,
Derry, Ellen,
Divine, Annie,
Dolan, Michael,
Donlin, Eliza,
Donlin, Maria,
Donahue, Bridget,
Donahue, Patrick,
Logan, Michael,
Lonergan, Edward,
Lonergan, Thomas,
Lonergan, Edward,
McAvoy, Catharine,
McCarthy, Michael,
McDermott, Bridget,
McDonald, Maggie,
McGrath, Mrs.
Mansfield, Catharine,
Mansfield, Johanna,
Mansfield, Thomas,
Markey, Rose,
Martin, Bernard,
Mason, Thomas,
Meskill, Mary,
Morrissey, Morris,
Morris, James,
Murphy, Mrs.
Murphy, John,
Murphy, Mary,
Murphy, Mrs. Margaret,
Murphy, Joseph,
Nolan, Mrs.
Noonan, Ann,

Dooney, Catharine,
Dooney, Patrick,
Dorney, John,
Downey, Mary,
Doyle, Ellen,
Doyle, Patrick,
Dunn, Kate,
Duffy, Thomas,
Edwards, Mrs.
Fannelly, Elizabeth,
Flanagan, Thomas,
Fogarty, Charles,
Gallagher, James,
Geary, John,
Gerder, Bertha.
Gilrey, Susan,
Gordon, Frank,
Gowing, Nicholas,
Hand, Mary,
Harkins, Edward,
Hogan, Ellen,
Holly, John,
Holton, Thomas,
Johnson, Mary,
Kain, Delia,
Keating, Catharine,
Keating, James,
Keefe, Christopher,
Keefe, Mary,
Keefe, Kate,
Keefe, William,
Kelly, Patrick,
Kelly, Frank,
Kenny, Bernard,
Kilkenny, Patrick,
Leonard, Mary,

Noonan, Frank,
Norris, Michael,
Norris, Julia,
Norris, Mary,
O'Brien, Johanna,
O'Brien, Patrick,
O'Connor, Hannah,
O'Keefe, Daniel,
O'Toole, Jeremiah,
Pentony, Thomas,
Phelan, Edward,
Pillion, Kieran,
Potter, Bernard,
Quirk, John,
Roachford, Mrs. A.
Robeson, Mrs.
Ryan, Kate,
Ryan, Ellen,
Ryan, Bridget,
Ryan, Patrick,
Scally, Ann,
Scanlin, Maurice,
Scully, Mary,
Sergeant, Maria,
Sheehan, Bartholomew,
Sharkey, Mary,
Smith, Francis,
Smith, Bridget,
Stapleton, Ann,
Sullivan, Daniel,
Tallent, Henry,
Wall, Johanna,
Welsh, John Vincent,
Whalen, Laurence,
White, Edward,
Wigger, Dr.
Winn, Mary.

Higgins, Bernard, $8.00   O'Brien, Lizzie, $7.00
McGrath, Mrs., $6.00

$5.00.

Brickley, John,
Buckley, John,

Murray, James,
Murray, Michael,

Cavanagh, William,
Condon, James,
Coyle, Michael,
Cronan, Ellen,
Donahue, Mrs.
Doyle, Owen,
Goodwin, Rore,
Green, Michael,
Griffin, William,
Haffey, John,
Kelly, Dennis,
McDonnell, Jane,
McNerney, Mary,
Mansfield, Johanna,
Martin, Bernard,

Murphy, Catharine,
Naughton, Thomas,
Naughton, David,
O'Neil, Peter,
O'Neil, Margaret,
O'Toole, Frank,
O'Toole, John,
O'Toole, Elizabeth,
Roach, Johanna,
Roman, John,
Ruckert, Hieronymus,
Sweeny, Mrs.
Tailor, A. B.
Walsh, John,
Walsh, Michael.

NAMES OF SUBSCRIBERS AND AMOUNT OF SUBSCRIPTIONS TO THE NEW CHURCH IN 1875.

Mr. Lercher, N. Y., $500.00
Maurice Ahearn, N. Y., $230.00
Mary A. Russell, $150.00
Catharine Denny, $150.00
Martin O'Brien, $110.00

$100.00.

Coghlan, Mr. and Mrs.
Degan, Thomas,
Holly, Cornelius,
Kenny, Bartholomew,
King, Hugh, New York,

Louanstein, Augustus,
Louanstein, Mrs.
Nugent, Mrs.
Ryan, William,
Sheeran, Rev. J.

$50.00.

Baxter, Hugh,
Callahan, Jeremiah,
Carroll, Walter,
Dempsey, Richard,
Donahue, Patrick,
Kelly, Dennis,
McAlpin, Mr.

Meskill, Daniel,
Mulhall, Patrick,
Murphy, Hugh,
O'Shea, Mrs. P., New York,
O'Toole, William,
Sisters of Charity,
Tobin, John,
Wall, Edmund.

Dwyer, William, $40.00
Keefe, Thomas, $40.00
Dacey, Mr., $35.00
Mulhall, Jeremiah, $35.00
Murphy, Martin, $35.00

APPENDIX.

$30.00.

Carr, John A.
Cavanagh, Patrick,
Lonergan, James,

Lowe, James,
Mooney, William,
Walsh, William.

$25.00.

Alexander, Gordon,
Arnold Brothers,
Cassidy, Frank,
Caughlin, Michael,
Coyle, Henry,
Darney, Dennis,
Doyle, James,
Doyle, John,
Dunn, William,
Feeley, James D.
English, William,

Griffin, Dennis,
Hackett, Margaret,
Kain, Peter,
Lane, Dennis,
McDermott, James,
McGuire, John,
Martin, Bernard,
O'Brien, Maggie A.
Sullivan, Agnes,
Sweeney, Daniel,
Willman, Frederick.

$20.00.

Belby, Matthew,
Belby, John,
Burns, James,
Cahill, James,
Carlen, Bernard,
Casey, Mary,
Curley, Patrick,
Dempsey, Ellen,
Donlen, Maurice,
Doyle, Patrick,
Geoghegan, Mrs.
Gibbons, Marcella,
Griffin, Patrick,
Hogan, Mrs.
Kilkenny, Luke,
Levins, Annie,

Looney, Mr.
McGrath, John,
Markey, Laurence,
Martin, James,
Meskill, Julia,
Morrissey, John,
Morrisson, Bridget,
Murphy, James,
O'Melia, Mary,
Quilty, Ann,
Quinlan, Ellen,
Smith, Patrick,
Smith, John,
Sullivan, Dennis,
Tallent, Mrs.
White, Jeremiah.

O'Toole, William, $16.00

$15.00.

Burns, Hannah,
Cahill, John,
Carroll, William,
Condon, James,

McKernan, Bessie,
Martin, Bernard,
Murphy, Andrew,
Nailor, Roger,

APPENDIX.

Cummings, B.
Doyle, Mrs. P.
Geary, John,
Hannon, Patrick,
Kilday, Ellen,
McEntee, William,

Reilly, Mrs., New York,
Rutledge, Richard,
Rutledge, James,
Ryan, Patrick,
Scally, Ellen,
Tallent, Henry.

Burns, Mary, $12.00
McDermott, Susan, $12.00
Parker, Ellen, $12.00

$10.00.

Burke, Delia,
Burke, Ellen,
Burke, William,
Carroll, Edward,
Clancy, Margaret,
Coffey, John,
Cogivan, Mary,
Coleman, Thomas,
Condon, Mrs. W.
Cone, Patrick,
Cooney, Laurence,
Cummings, D.
Donnelly, Elizabeth,
Dowd, Bridget,
Downey, John,
Ducey, John,
Doyle, Ellen,
Doyle, Patrick,
Drake, William,
Duffey, John,
Dugan, Mary,
Dunn, Mary,
Farrell, Bridget,
Foley, William,
Foley, John,
Gallagher, James,
Gilsey, Susan,
Glanville, Julia,
Gordon, Bartholomew,
Hackett, Mary,
Higgins, Kate,
Horan, John,

Johnson, Mrs.
Johnson, Mary,
Lonergan, John,
Lyons, James,
McDermott, Bridget,
McDonnell, Margaret.
McGrane, Thomas,
Mansfield, Johanna,
Markey, Catharine,
Meskill, Mary,
Minogue, John,
Morrisson, Rebecca,
Murphy, Mary,
Murphy, Andrew,
Nolan, Jane,
O'Brien, Johanna,
O'Conner, Hanora,
O'Conner, Hanna,
O'Toole, John,
Roach, Lizzie,
Robeson, Mrs.
Ryan, Ellen,
Ryan, Catharine,
Ryan, Patrick,
Rutledge, Richard,
Sheehan, Michael,
Smith, Bridget,
Smith, Patrick,
Wall, Ellen,
Wall, Johanna,
White, Edward,
A Friend.

$5.00

Dowd, James,
Fitzgerald, Thomas,
Hearty, Thomas,
Johnson, Margaret,
O'Toole, William,
Reilly, Thomas,
Russell, Bridget.

SUBSCRIPTIONS IN 1875.

Gignoux, C., $125.00
Baxter, Hugh, $70.00
Welsh, Patrick, $100.00
Degan, Thomas, $55.00

$50.00

Hally, Cornelius,
Nugent, Thomas,
O'Brien, Martin.

$30.00

Callahan, Patrick,
Callahan, Jeremiah,
Carr, John A.
Collins, William.

$25.00

Burke, Thomas,
Burke, Eugene,
Campbell, Michael,
Eakley, James,
Geoghegan, Mathew,
Griffen, D.
Goin, Stephen,
Kenny, John,
Lowe, James,
Martin, Bernard,
McDermott, James,
O'Brien, Maggie,
O'Toole, William,
Smith, John, New Vernon,
Sweeney, Daniel,
Sullivan, Agnes.

Dacey, Michael, $22.00

$20.00

Carroll, Eliza,
Carroll, William,
Carlin, Barney,
Coleman, Patrick,
Collins, James,
Collins, John D.
Coyle, Henry,
Dolan, William,
Donahue, Patrick,
Doran, Malick,
Lonergan, James,
Looney, Michael,
Lyons, James,
McIntee, William,
McGrath, John,
McLaughlin, Mary,
McNeil, James,
McGoulderic, Edward,
Mahar, Margaret,
Morris, John,

APPENDIX. 313

Dowd, John,
Elliott, James,
Foley, William,
Gaffney, John,
Hally, James,
Hand, Mary,
Johnson, Mary,
Kain, Peter,

Murphy, Mrs. Morris,
O'Melia, Mary,
Smith, Patrick,
Sullivan, Denis,
Tallent, Henry,
Vorholz, Frederick,
Wall, William,
Walsh, William.

Ryan, Mary, $18.00

$17.00.

Garey, John,
Gerdon, B.
Hacket, Margaret,
Mulloy, Elizabeth,
Reily, Jane,

Reily, Eliza,
Reily, Isabella,
Reynolds, Thomas,
Ryan, Patrick,
Smith, Maria.

$15.00.

Alexander, Gordon,
Daily, Mrs. Mary,
Dolen, Maria,
Donahue, Lizzie,
Foran, P. F.
Hearty, Thomas.
Huff, Mary,

Lee, John,
Morris, Daniel,
Murray, Thomas,
O'Brien, Maggie,
Rutledge, Richard,
Smith, Patrick,
Shelley, Ellen,

Wall, Ellen.

Murphy, Mary, $13.00

$12.00.

Murphy, Annie,

McDermott, Mrs. B.

$10.00.

Burns, Hanna,
Cooney, Maria,
Dempsey, Richard,
Donahue, Annie,
Dunn, Edward,
Farrell, Andrew,
Foley, John,
Fitzgerald, Thomas,
Griffen, Patrick,
Hickey, Patrick,
Higgins, Catherine,

Manderville, Julia,
Mansfield, Kate,
Mansfield, Johanna,
Mansfield, Michael,
Markey, Laurence,
Markey, Mrs. Catherine,
Mayhon, Ann,
Morris, Michael,
Morisson, Rebecca,
Nailor, Bridget,
Norris, Mary,

Kain, Delia,
Kearns, Thomas,
Lonergan, Edward,
McAvoy, Catherine,
McCarthy, Catherine,
McGoulderic, Mrs.
McKennic, Sarah,
McShane, Bridget,
Mahar, Catherine,
Norris, Julia,
Norton, Mrs. Julia,
O'Brien, Johanna,
Quinlan, Ellen,
Robeson, Mrs.
Russell, Mary,
Scally, Patrick,
Smith, Fanny,
Stapleton, Ann,
Walsh, Laurence.

O'Donnell, Bridget, $7.00

$5.00.

Ballf, Judith F.,
Bambrick, Richard,
Bermingham, William,
Donahue, Patrick,
Doty, William H.
Doty, Mrs.
Edwards, George,
Kain, Emma,
Lokeman, Delia,
McCann, Margaret,
Moran, George,
O'Toole, Eliza,
Timmons, Annie,
Timmons, Kate,
Timmons, Francis,
Wall, Mary,
White, Maggie.

CONTRIBUTIONS TO THE NEW BAYLEY MEMORIAL SCHOOL IN 1886-1887.

Farrelly, Patrick, $300.00
Foote, John T., $250.00
Lawless, James, $250.00
Kelly, Mrs. Agnes, $200.00
Welsh, Patrick, $200.00
Revere, Paul, $150.00
Burke, Eugene S., $125.00
Lonergan, James, $100.00
Flynn, Very Rev. J. M., $100.00
Looney, E. J., $75.00

$50.00.

Campbell, Miss S. B.
Cody, Morris,
Condon, Morris E.
Farrell, Rev. E. A.
Holton, Thos.
Knight, Charles K.
Looney, W. J.

York, Mrs. J., $40.00
O'Reilly, Dr. J. H., $35.00
Carroll, John, $30.00
Degan, Thomas, $30.00

APPENDIX.

$25.00.

Beston, Maggie,
Burke, Joseph,
Burke, Thomas W.
Carr, John A.
Clifford, Thomas,
Condon, E. T.
Collins, J. D.
Crimmins, Thomas, N. Y.
Cummings, James,
Dacey, Michael,
Daly, Mrs.
Daly, Lizzie,
Dempsey, Mrs. R. F.
Donahue, Patrick,
Donahue, P. W.
Doyle, John,
Dunn, Bridget,
Dunn, Mary Ann,
Kain, Peter M.
Kain, Mrs. P. M.
Kelly, Dennis,
McGoldrick, Edward,
Malley, Thomas,
Martin, Bernard,
Meskill, Thomas,
Mooney, Richard,
Morrissey, Mrs.
Murphy, James,
Murray, Thomas,
O'Brien, Martin J.
O'Rourke, Bridget,
O'Toole, Lizzie,
Robeson, Mrs. J. M.
Ryan, Patrick,
Welsh, Mrs. Patrick.

Rogers, Mrs. J., $24.00

$20.00.

Callahan, Jeremiah,
Conroy, Maggie,
Cooney, John,
Daly, Peter,
Dempsey, Thomas F.
Doyle, John,
Gibson, Robert,
Gibson, Mrs. Robert,
Hand, Mary,
Hally, Cornelius,
Keefe, Thomas,
Keefe, William,
Lane, Dennis,
Lane, Mrs. J. K.
Lowe, John H.
McDermott, Mrs.
McGuire, John,
McKenzie, Kenneth,
Mansfield, John,
Mitchell, Margaret,
Smack, Edward,
Vorholz, Frederick,
White, Edward,
Wilson, Mrs. Robert.

O'Connor, Alice, $16.00

$15.00.

Burke, Frank,
Callahan, John,
Callahan, Mary T.
Clifford, Mrs. T. F.
Condon, Mrs. E. T.
Kenny, Mrs. B. J.
Lowe, Thomas E.
Manning, Mrs.
Mulcahy, Maggie,
Naughton, David,

Costello, Ellen,
Dempsey, Sophie,
Finnessy, Kate,
Hearney, William,
Kenny, John J.
Kenny, B. J.

O'Connors, Bridget,
Ronan, Kate,
Ruckert, Hieronymus,
Welsh, Bridget,
Whelan, Margaret,
White, Jeremiah.

Leary, Norah, $13.00

$12.00.

Ambrose, George,
Belby, John,
Cahill, Mrs. Mary,
Callahan, Jeremiah J.
Curley, Mrs. Hubert,
Dempsey, Richard,
Dempsey, R. F.
Dempsey, William,
Dempsey, Lewis F.
Dolan, William H.
Dowd, John J.
Doyle, James,
Ducey, Thomas F.
Dunn, William V.
English, William A.
Fennell, William P.
Hackett, Michael,

Howard, P. J.
Keefe, Thomas,
Lonergan, John,
Mansfield, William,
Morrissey, Cornelius,
Morrissey, Mamie,
Murphy, Martin,
Murphy, Joseph,
Murphy, James,
Nalley, Joseph,
Norris, Michael,
Riley, Michael,
Rutledge, Richard,
Sheridan, Sylvester,
Smith, Mary,
Welsh, Thomas,
Welsh, Laurence.

$10.00.

Barrett, Robert,
Beston, James,
Beston, Michael,
Brady, James,
Brady, Mrs. M. L.
Cahill, Edward,
Cahill, James,
Camisa, Mrs.
Callahan, Jeremiah,
Callahan, Annie,
Casey, Mary,
Carroll, Bessie,
Carroll, Ellen,
Cavanagh, Annie,
Cavanagh, Mary,

McCarthy, Michael,
McDermott, James,
McDermott, John,
McEntee, Patrick,
McGrath, Mrs. Maggie,
McGrath, John,
McLean, Julia,
McSweeney, Martha,
Manning, Mrs.
Martin, Bernard,
Markey, Laurence,
Meskill, Daniel,
Meskill, Julia,
Mitchell, Mrs.
Mitchell, John,

APPENDIX. 317

Cleary, John,
Cody, Patrick,
Cody; Thomas,
Condon, Michael,
Connors, Patrick,
Connors, Michael,
Costello, Agnes,
Collins, James,
Curley, Mrs. P.
Dacey, Edward,
Dacey, Maggie,
Dacey, Daniel,
Dempsey, E. V.
Dempsey, Mrs. C.
Dolan, Michael,
Donahue, Kate,
Donahue, Maggie,
Donohue, Kate,
Doran, P. F.
Dowd, Bridget B.
Doyle, Nora,
Dunn, Mrs. Ann,
Ducey, P. G.
Dunn, Thomas,
Eakeley, Ellen,
Farrell, Mary A.
Gallagher, James,
Glanville, Julia,
Gougherty, Lizzie,
Gougherty, Minnie,
Griffen, Patrick,
Hall, Kate,
Harris, Charles N.
Hogan, Mrs. Mary,
Hally, C. J.
Holly, William,
Holly, Patrick,
Holly, James,
Holly, Michael,
Howard, Mrs. P. J.
Kain, John,
Keating, John,
Kenny, Elizabeth,

Mitchell, Annie,
Mooney, William,
Mooney, Mrs. Elizabeth,
Mooney, William Jr.
Mooney, Mrs. Richard.
Monahan, Jeremiah,
Moran, Annie A.
Morris, Michael E.
Morrissey, Bridget,
Morrissey, Mary,
Morrissey, Thomas,
Morrissey, Mrs.
Mulhall, Patrick,
Murphy, John,
Murphy, William,
Murphy, Mrs. C.
Murphy, Annie,
Murphy, Benjamin,
Nailor, Mary,
Nailor, Francis,
Naughton, John,
Norris, M. P.
Norton, Mrs. Julia,
O'Brien, Martin,
O'Connell, Mrs.
O'Hara, Annie,
O'Hara, Mr.
Pegden, Alfred,
Perkins, Maud,
Perkins, Mary,
Perkins, Grace,
Quilty, Ann,
Quinn, Bridget,
Reynolds, Mary,
Reynolds, Thomas,
Riley, Owen,
Robeson, Mary,
Robeson, Kittie,
Robeson, Genevieve,
Russell, Bridget,
Rutledge, Mrs. Richard,
Ryan, William,
Shay, Ella,

Kilkenny, John,
Kilkenny, Luke,
Kilkenny, Patrick,
Kirk, John,
Lane, Mrs. D.
Looney, Michael,
Louanstein, William,
Lowe, W. J.
Lyman, Michael,
Lyons, Patrick,
McCann, Julia A.
McCarthy, Nellie,
Sharkey, Mrs.
Sheridan, Catharine,
Spain, Timothy,
Sullivan, Mary,
Sweeney, Mary,
Sweeney, James,
Tierney, John,
Townley, Thomas,
Wall, Catharine,
Wallis, Annie,
Welsh, Pierce,
Whelan, Patrick,
York, Lizzie.

Dowd, Mrs. John, $8.00
Kelly, Thomas, $8.00
Murphy, Mrs. John, $8.00
Riley, Mary, $8.00
Welsh, Thomas F., $8.00.

Mulcahy, Mary, $7.00
Hayden, Mary, $7.50
Welsh, Thomas, $7.50
Welsh, Mrs. T., $7.50

$6.00.

Callahan, Joseph,
Chadwick, Augustus,
Coleman, Patrick,
Condon, John,
Condon, Delia,
Fitzgerald, John,
Holly, John,
Lyons, James,
Mulhall, Mrs. P.
O'Toole, Dennis,
Prendergast, James,
Prendergast, John,
Rutledge, James,
Rutledge, Mrs. James.

$5.00.

Banum, Mary,
Belby, William,
Belby, James,
Belby, Mrs. John,
Boylan, Margaret,
Brennan, Bridget,
Burns, Mrs.
Cahill, James,
Callahan, Mrs.
Campbell, Rosetta,
Campbell, Sarah,
Campbell, Timothy,
Carlin, Bernard,
Carroll, Owen,
Lowe, Annie,
Lowe, Lizzie,
Lowe, James,
Lowe, George,
Lowe, Mary,
Lucas, Edward,
McAvoy, Thomas,
McCarthy, Mrs. E.
McCormick, Patrick,
McCormick, John,
McDermott, Peter,
McDonald, Alexander,
McDonald, Patrick,
McGoldrick, Mrs.

APPENDIX.

Carroll, Jacob,
Cleary, William,
Cleary, Mrs.
Clifford, Lulu,
Clifford, Bart,
Coffey, John,
Collins, Walter,
Collins, James,
Condon, Mrs. James,
Connelly, Kate,
Cooney, Mrs. J.
Cools, Mrs.
Costigan, John,
Coyle, James,
Cullen, Rose Ann,
Cullen, Patrick,
Cunningham, A.
Cunningham, Ellen,
Curley, Lizzie,
Curley, Minnie,
Curtaine, Mary,
Dacey, John,
Dempsey, John,
Dempsey, Willie,
Dempsey, R. H.
Doran, Malachi,
Doran, Annie,
Doran, Mrs. P.
Downey, P.
Doyle, L.
Doyle, Patrick,
Doyle, Lizzie,
Doyle, Mrs. John,
Doyle, Joseph,
Doyle, Mary,
Drake, Edward,
Driscoll, Florence Henry,
Ducey, Adell,
Dunn, Mrs. W. V.
Dunn, Mary,
Farrell, Kate,
Fennell, Kate,
Fitzgerald, Timothy,

McGoldrick, Patrick,
McGrath, Mrs.
McGrath, Mrs. Mary,
McGrath, Ellen,
McGuire, Mary,
McGuire, Sarah.
Machy, Maggie,
Malley, Kate,
Malley, Annie,
Maloney, Mary,
Mannion, Bridget,
Mansfield, Julia,
Markey, Joseph,
Mehan, Bridget,
Mehan, James,
Minogue, Julia,
Minogue, Edward,
Mooney, Annie,
Mooney, John,
Mooney, Marcella,
Monahan, Jerry,
Moran, Mrs. J.
Morrisson, Bridget,
Morrissey, Mrs.
Mulhall, James,
Mulcahy, Bridget,
Murphy, Mrs. C. R.
Murphy, Margaret,
Murphy, Mrs.
Murphy, Mr.
Murray, James,
Myhan, Kate,
Myhan, Annie,
Noonan, John,
Norris, Edward,
O'Brien, Lizzie,
O'Connell, Maggie,
O'Connell, Annie,
O'Connell, Mary,
O'Donnell, Johanna,
O'Donnell, Eliza,
O'Neil, Henry,
O'Rourke, Bridget,

Flaherty, Mrs.
Foley, Thomas,
Foley, Ella,
Fox, Mrs. D. L.
Geary, Patrick,
Geary, Michael,
Glancy, Mrs.
Glanville, Mr.
Gordan, Annie,
Gowen, Edwin,
Gowen, Julia,
Hannon, Patrick,
Hannegan, Margaret,
Hannan, Patrick,
Henry, Bridget,
Heslin, Peter,
Hillock, James,
Holly, Mrs. William,
Holly, Mrs.
Hudson, Mrs.
Hughes, Mrs.
Hughes, Katie,
Jackson, Eugene,
Jordan, Annie,
Jordan, Mary,
Kearney, Mrs.
Kearns, Mrs.
Kearns, Thomas,
Keary, Miss,
Keefe, Margaret,
Kelly, Kate,
Kelly, Margaret,
Kiely, Owen,
Kilday, Annie,
Kilkenny, Kate,
Lane, Mrs.
Lawless, Patrick,
Lenahan, Katie,
Leonard, James,
Lonergan, Mrs. A.
Lonergan, Edward,
Lonergan, Daniel,

Pentony, Kate,
Pentony, Mary,
Pentony, Thomas,
Percy, Mrs.
Percy, Clara,
Petty, Seth,
Pillion, Patrick,
Powers, Michael,
Quinlan, Ellen,
Reilly, Eliza,
Reilly, Mrs. Owen
Reilly, Annie,
Roache, Mrs. Charles,
Rutledge, Mary,
Ryan, Kate,
Ryan, Sarah,
Shea, James,
Sheridan, Hugh,
Sheridan, Sarah,
Sheridan, Ellen,
Shields, Patrick,
Smith, Annie,
Stack, Ellen,
Sweeney, Catharine,
Tankard, James,
Thompson, Margaret,
Tierney, Owen,
Tobin, Katie,
Trainer, John, Sr.
Trainer, John, Jr.,
Tynan, Kate,
Welsh, Laurence,
Welsh, Mary,
White, Maggie,
White, Mary,
White, John,
White, Jeremiah, Jr.,
Williams, Michael,
Woods, Mary,
Wortman, John,
Wyer, Lucy,
York, Joseph,
York, Harry,

APPENDIX.

Condon, Mrs. M., $4.00
Fitzgerald, James, $4.00
Evans, Mrs. Mary, $3.00
McDonald, Mrs., $3.00
Norton, William, $4.00
O'Brien, Bridget, $4.00
O'Donnell, Eliza, $3.00
White, Edward, $3.00
O'Connell, Mary, $3.00

$2.00.

Connors, Mary,
Corbett, Thomas,
Dorsey, Thomas,
Dunn, Willie V., Jr.
Dunn, Lizzie,
Dunn, Thomas,
Dunn, Joseph,
Dunn, Catherine,
Finnessy, Katie, $1.00
Evans, Mary A. J.
Felley, Mary,
Foley, Ella,
Geary, John,
McDonoh, ——,
Murray, Mollie,
Price, Mrs. and family,
Sweeney, Margaret.
Murphy, per E. Murphy, $1.00
Whelan, Nellie, $1.00

CONTRIBUTIONS TO THE NEW RECTORY IN 1890.

Farrelly, Patrick, $500.00
Burke, E. S., $100.00
Lonergan, James, $100.00
Kain, Peter, and wife, $100.00
Hart, J., and family, $100.00
Welsh, P. and wife, $100.00

Condon, E. T., $50.00
Condon, M. E., $50.00
Kelly, Mrs. H., $50.00
Malley, Thomas, $50.00
Revere, Paul, $50.00

$25.00.

Burke, Joseph,
Campbell, Sidney B.
Clifford, T. F.
Collins, John D.
Cooney, John,
Costello, Ellen,
Dempsey, R. F. and wife,
Dempsey, Thomas,
Hayes, R. F.
Hearney, William,
Howard, P. J. and wife,
Kenny, John J.
Kenny, Mrs.
Lawless, James,
Manning, Mrs. J.
Murphy, Moses,
Murray, Thomas,
O'Brien, Martin, Water St.
O'Reilly, Dr. J. H.
Quilty, Ann,
Reilly, Owen,
Robeson, Mrs.
Ryan, Patrick,
Sullivan, Mary,
Willman, Frederick.

APPENDIX.

$20.00.

Fitzgerald, Mr.
Hally, Cornelius,
Lowe, Annie,

Lowe, Lizzie,
Morris, John,
Norris, Mr.
Rogers, Mrs.

$15.00.

Brady, Mrs. and family,
Clifford, Mrs. T. F.
Dacey, Michael,
McGrath, John,

Moran, Annie,
Morrissey, Mr.
Norris, Michael,
Sheridan, Sylvester
York, Mrs.

Hackett, Mr., $12.00

$10.00.

Belby, John,
Boylan, Margaret,
Buckley, Marcella,
Burke, Frank,
Cahill, Edward,
Cahill, Mrs.
Callahan, Jeremiah,
Campbell, Mary,
Campbell, Sarah,
Campbell, Rosetta,
Carr, John A.
Cody, Nellie,
Cody, Patrick,
Coleman, Mary,
Condon, Mrs. Johanna,
Connors, Bridget,
Connors, Michael,
Cottrell, Maggie,
Curley, Mary A.
Cusack, Mary,
Dacey, Maggie,
Dempsey, Sophie,
Donahue, Patrick,
Doran, Malachy,
Doyle, James,
Doyle, John,
Duffy, Annie,

Lane, Dennis,
Larken, Kate,
Lawless, P. J.
Lonergan, Mrs. Julia,
McCann, Mary,
McCarthy, Nellie,
McCarthy, Mary,
McCarthy, Miss and sister,
McDermott, Mrs.
McGoldrick, Edward,
McGoldrick, Patrick,
Mansfield, W.
Markey, Lawrence,
Mason, Thomas,
Meskill, Julia,
Meskill, Daniel,
Meskill, Thomas,
Mooney, Richard,
Moran, Mary,
Morrissey, Rosie,
Morrissey, Thomas,
Mulhall, Patrick,
Murphy, James,
Murray, Gertrude,
Norris, Michael,
O'Brien, Martin,
O'Reilly, Annie,

Duffy, Kate,
Dunn, Wm. V.
Dunn, E. T.
Dunn, Jennie,
Gallagher, James,
Glanville, Frank,
Glanville, Julia,
Glanville, Mary J.
Gogerty, Minnie,
Hand, Mary,
Hillock, Mrs.
Holly, William,
Holly, James
Keefe, Mr. and Mrs.
Kelly, Dennis,
Kelly, Peter,
Kenny, Bernard,
Kilkenny, Lizzie,
O'Reilly, Isabella,
O'Toole, Elizabeth,
Pegden, Alfred,
Percy, Mrs.
Perkins, Miriam,
Perkins, Mary E.
Sheridan, Catharine T.
Sweeney, Mary,
Tighe, Maria,
Tobin, Miss,
Tranor, Miss,
Walsh, T. J.
Welsh, Mary,
Welsh, Thomas F.
White, Edward,
White, Jeremiah,
Wilson, Mrs. R.
York, Elizabeth.

O'Rourke, Bridget, $7.00
Welsh, Nora, $7.00
Rutledge, James, $6.00

$5.00.

Allen, Annie,
Anonymous,
Anonymous,
Baxter, Mr.
Belby, James,
Belby, John,
Boyle, Rose,
Brady, James,
Burns, James,
Burns, Mrs. Sarah,
Cahill, Mary,
Callahan, Mrs.
Callahan, Margaret,
Callahan, Josephine,
Callahan, John,
Carlin, Bernard,
Carroll, Owen,
Cash,
Cashen, William,
Clark, Margaret,
Clifford, Lulu,
Lonergan, M.
Lonergan, Daniel,
Louanstein, A.
Lyman, Michael,
McCarthy, Maria,
McCormick, Maria,
McCrystal, Patrick,
McDermott, Mrs. J.
McDermott, James,
McDonald, Mary,
McDonald, Miss,
McDonnell, Augustine,
McGrath, Mary,
McIntyre, Ellen,
McMahon, Mary,
McManus, Kate,
Macaulay, Mary,
Mahon, Annie,
Maloney, Mary,
Mansfield, Julia,
Masterson, Patrick,

Clifford, Bartie,
Coffey, Mrs.
Coffey, Nellie,
Colligan, Teresa,
Colligan, Maggie,
Costigan, John,
Curley, Mrs. P.
Curley, Mrs.
Curley, Lizzie,
Cullinan, Mary,
Cullen, Rose Ann,
Curran, Sarah,
Dacy, Daniel,
Dalton, Mr.
Davis, Mary,
Dempsey, Richard,
Dempsey, Mrs.
Dempsey, John and Willie,
Donavin, Maggie,
Dowd, John J.
Dowd, Bridget,
Downey, Bessie,
Doyle, Joseph,
Doyle, Maggie,
Doyle, John,
Doyle, Norah,
Doyle, Lizzie,
Doyle, Annie,
Duffy, James,
Dunn, Mrs.
Dunn, William,
Duriss, Annie,
Eakeley, Lucy,
Eakeley, Mary,
Farrell, Andrew,
Farrell, Kate,
Fennell, John E.
Fennell, Maggie,
Finnessy, Mary,
Gahan, Thomas,
Gibson, Mrs.
Gibson, Robert,
Gilligan, Annie,

Mehan, Ellen,
Mehan, Mrs.
Mehigan, Kate,
Minogue, E. J.
Mooney, William,
Mooney, Annie,
Moran, Maggie,
Morrissey, Mrs.
Morrissey, Catharine,
Morrissey, Mary,
Morrissey, Cornelius,
Mowbrey, T. W.
Mulcahy, Maggie,
Mulrooney, Mrs.
Murphy, Mrs. P.
Murphy, Annie,
Murphy, John,
Murphy, Anastatia,
Nalley, Mrs.
Nancarrow, J.
Naughton, John,
Nolan, Ellen,
O'Brien, Mary,
O'Connell, Jane,
O'Connell, Mary,
O'Hara, Mr.
O'Hara, Annie,
O'Melia, Mary,
O'Reilly, Eliza,
O'Toole, Annie,
Perkins, Maude,
Phelan, Annie,
Pillion, Kearn,
Pillion, Patrick,
Price, Mrs.
Purcell, Nellie,
Quigley, Catharine,
Quilty, Maggie,
Quinlan, Ellen,
Raynolds, Thomas,
Rogers, William,
Ryan, Mary,
Ryan, Sarah,

Glancy, Bridget,
Glennon, Mr.
Graham, Nellie,
Griffin, Patrick,
Gogerty, Bernard,
Healey, Ellen,
Hickey, Mary,
Higgens, Mary,
Holly, John,
Hughes, R.
Hyland, Kate,
Kain, Michael,
Keefe, Thomas,
Kelly, Mary,
Kelly, Mrs. P.
Kenny, Jane,
Kettle, Annie,
Kilkenny, Luke,
Lane, Mrs. D.
Langan, Annie,

Russell, Mary,
Rutledge, Mary,
Scully, Julia,
Scully, Mary,
Sharkey, Bessie,
Sheridan, Hugh,
Sheridan, Nellie,
Sheridan, Sarah,
Shields, Mrs. P.
Smith, Ellen,
Tallent, Mrs.
Thompson, Margaret,
Vernon, James,
Vorholz, Frederick,
Walsh, Mary,
Welsh, Lizzie,
Welsh, Thomas and Annie,
Welsh, Pierce,
Whelan, James,
Woods, Margaret.
Wyer, Lucy,

INDEX.

- **A.** Asylum, 90.
- **B.** Bandol, 12, 14.
  Baptisms, 289, 302.
  Bayley, 39, 46, 74, 94.
  Bazars, 196, 213.
  Beeston, 10.
  Bell, 127.
  Boisaubin, 31, 44.
  Bottle Hill, Church at, 4, 29, 44.
  Brockholes, 10.
  Bulger, 30.
- **C.** Catholic Benevolent Legion, 284.
  Celtic Names, 25.
  Cemetery, 91, 146.
  Church, 37, 42, 136, 149.
  Condit Property, 163.
  Congress, 220.
  Corner-stone, 75.
  Corrigan, 84.
- **D.** D'Arcy, 58.
  Dark Ages, 30.
  Decoration Day, 237.
  Donors, 144, 154, 171, 175, 192, 202.
- **E.** Excursions, 152, 207.
- **F.** Farmer, 8, 25, 288.
  Financial Statements, 303.
  Flynn, 92, 116, 173, 196, 214.
  Flag-raising, 230.
  Friendly Sons, 234, 249.
- **G.** Graessl, 11.
  Grey Nuns, 260.
- **H.** Herard, 31, 45.
  Hoey, 50.
  Hospital, 258.
  Howell, 36.
  Hughes, 42.
- **J.** Jubilee, 175.
- **K.** Kearney, 20.
- **L.** League of Sacred Heart, 257.
  Lectures, 205, 218, 237.
  Littell, 27.
  Luzerne, 13.
- **M.** Madden, 49, 59.
  Marriages, 288, 298, 301.
  Mayor, 285.
  McCloskey, 31.
  McGovern, 68.
  McGowan, 48.
  McNulty, 51.
  McQuaid, 37, 86, 150, 177, 183.
  Memorials, 278, *seq.*
  Miralles, 11, 27.
  Missions, 211.
  Moran, 5.
  Morris Plains, 131, 140.
  Mortality Bill, 300.
  Moylan, 11.
- **O.** O'Donahue, 29, 44.
  O'Hara, 26, 29.
- **P.** Picnic, 52.
  Plays, 256.
  Power, 45.

INDEX.

- *R.* Rectory, 235, 239.
  Records, War, 272, *seq.*
  Remarkable Cures, 178, 216.
  Revere, 270.

- *S.* Schneider, 8.
  School, Bayley, 47, 53, 58, 154, 170, 176, 183, 192, 195, 283.
  Senez, 32.
  Shea, 10, 19.
  Sheeran, 70, 81, 88, 91.
  Sisters, 133, 157, 170, 284.
  Societies, 124, 189, 194.
  St. Margaret's, 167, 238, 248.
  St. Patrick's Day, 22, 230.
  St. Virgil, 139, 143, 215.
  Students, Ecclesiastical, 284.
  Strike, 254.
  Steuben, 14.
  Subscriptions, Various, 304, *seq.*

- *T.* Temperance Society, 59, 147.

- *W.* Washington, 11, 13, 14, 18, 22, 55.
  Wigger, 125, 142, 184, 193, 238.

- *Y.* Young, 50.
  Young Men, 134, 285.
  Young Men's Building, 191, 199, 207.

www.ingramcontent.com/pod-product-compliance
Lightning Source LLC
Chambersburg PA
CBHW032016220426
43664CB00006B/262